Standards and Ethics for Counselling in Action

Third Edition

Tim Bond

SAGE Counselling Action
Serias Editor Windy Dryden

Los Angeles | London | New Delhi
Singapore | Washington DC

First edition published 1993
Reprinted 1994, 1995, 1997, 1998, 1999
Second edition published 2000
Reprinted 2007, 2008
This third edition published 2010

SAGE Publications Ltd
1 Oliver's Yard
55 City Road
London EC1Y 1SP

SAGE Publications Inc.
2455 Teller Road
Thousand Oaks, California 91320

SAGE Publications India Pvt Ltd
B 1/I 1 Mohan Cooperative Industrial Area
Mathura Road
New Delhi 110 044

SAGE Publications Asia-Pacific Pte Ltd
33 Pekin Street #02-01
Far East Square
Singapore 048763

Library of Congress Control Number: 2009925987

British Library Cataloguing in Publication data

A catalogue record for this book is available from the British Library

ISBN 978-1-4129-0238-0
ISBN 978-1-4129-0239-7 (pbk)

Typeset by C&M Digitals (P) Ltd., Chennai, India
Printed by CPI Antony Rowe, Chippenham, Wiltshire
Printed on paper from sustainable resources

Mixed Sources
Product group from well-managed
forests and other controlled sources
www.fsc.org Cert no. SGS-COC-2953
© 1996 Forest Stewardship Council
FSC

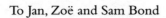
To Jan, Zoë and Sam Bond

Contents

Foreword

All professions are grounded in ethics. What makes counselling virtually unique, however, is that it is the application of ethics. In other words, our respect for our client's autonomy, our trustworthiness, our commitment to maintaining confidentiality are not just corollaries of our work – they are the essence of what we do. As the title of this series might suggest, counselling is ethics-in-action.

And yet, the issue of ethics also raises some complex and challenging questions for counsellors. This may be particularly true for those of us from a humanistic background who have learnt, through our training, to listen to – and trust – our inner, intuitive felt-responses. We have learnt to look inside, but ethics challenges us also to look outside: to collectively agreed codes of appropriate action and intention. More than that, ethics invite us to consider what is 'right': not just what we feel is right or subjectively experience as good, but what is collectively, externally, 'objectively' agreed to be in the best interests of others.

There are no easy answers to tensions such as these, just as there are rarely any simple solutions to the ethical dilemmas that counsellors face. Should we disclose information about a young client who is scarring their wrists? Should we hug a client at the end of a session if they request it? What do we do if a client, halfway through a session, says that they cannot go on with life?

As counsellors, we have learnt that the search for black-and-white answers to such questions can be more hindering than helpful, and that a gentle, reflective, even-handed consideration – holding all the competing tensions – is often the best way forward. Similarly, we have learnt that, at such time, an Other can be of great help. This is not to direct us or tell us what to do, but to offer us a warm and supportive context in which we can acknowledge, and reflect on, the different sides of the dilemma; to help us disentangle some of the key issues; and to help us find a way forward towards our own solutions.

It is, perhaps, in this respect that Tim Bond's work on ethics and standards in counselling over the last twenty years – including the drafting of the BACP's Ethical Guidelines (1996) and its Ethical Framework (2002) – can be considered to have made its greatest contribution. There is no doubt that Tim is a master at providing clear guidance on legal and ethical requirements; yet what may be most valuable about his work is his capacity to reflect back to us a range of competing and sometimes contradictory ethical concerns, and to invite us to determine for ourselves the best course of action. Tim's work is fundamentally about fostering 'ethical mindfulness': an attitude, not of blind obedience to ethical rules and regulation, but of sophisticated, reflective, balanced consideration of complex ethical dilemmas. In this regard, Tim's work has been essential in helping counsellors develop as independent, autonomous professionals: self-reflective agents who can function in situations of incomplete, and possibly contradictory, information and determine, as far as possible, a course of action that is most beneficial to their clients.

It is a great honour for me to be asked to write this foreword to the third edition of Standards and Ethics for Counselling in Action. When I was a counselling trainee in the 1990s, Tim Bond was one of the 'gods', and he remains one of the most respected and influential – albeit approachable – people in the field. This book, the first edition of which was published by Sage in 1993, has become the 'gold standard' of texts on counselling ethics used, not just by people in the counselling field, but by professionals in related disciplines such as psychology. What is more, the book is a key text in Sage's hugely influential Counselling in Action series, which has now passed its 20-year anniversary. In this fully revised third edition, Tim has updated the book with respect to new legislation and ethical sources, and had added several new sections to address contemporary developments in the counselling field. More than that, this new edition of the book – as with previous editions – is informed by Tim's ongoing dialogues with counsellors and therapists from a range of professional bodies. As with all great counselling work, this contribution is not just influential on the field, but profoundly influenced by it.

There is no doubt that, in these first decades of the twenty-first century, counselling is set to go through profound changes and transitions. Yet, at core, our work is always the work it has been: to help people lead more satisfying and fulfilling lives. To function in this capacity, we need texts that can support us through the many contemporary issues and challenges facing our field today and which, more importantly, foster our capacity to function effectively in an increasingly uncertain and complex world. This third edition of *Standards and Ethics for Counselling in Action* does exactly that and, as an enormously wise source of counsel, is an invaluable resource for both trainee and practising counsellors.

Mick Cooper
Professor of Counselling, University of Strathclyde

Acknowledgements

What can I say? Where to begin? So many people have influenced and inspired me over the different editions of this book. Some have shared or debated ideas but foremost are those who have offered love and support throughout the considerable labour of producing a book of this scale and significance to counselling in the UK and further afield.

I am particularly grateful to my close family. Jan, my wife, who has done so much more than discuss ideas but has played a considerable role in these as well. Zoë, our rapidly growing teenager on the threshold of adulthood, has helped format diagrams with more computing skills than I will ever have. She is incredulous as she discovers yet another pool of my ignorance in such matters as she demonstrates how to construct a diagram faster than I can see or take in. Sam, our 12 year old, has never been afraid to ask the big questions with a wicked smile. What is 'ethics'? What is ethics good for? He knows that some of the simplest questions are the hardest to answer. Our dog, Scampi, a not too miniature Schnauzer in size or personality, regularly reminds us of life 'outside the page' and the delights of woodland and coastal walks. Sooty, our black cat, is attracted by the sound of typing and periodically strolls across the keyboard to set new challenges for me and the copy editor as we seek to restore the text. Writing does disrupt family life because it is a largely solitary activity. However, ethics is fundamentally social and informs how we live together in all the diverse forms that human interaction takes with partners, families, friends and strangers. I have never enjoyed ethics more than when discussing them on a good walk in the company of family or friends.

The book would not have been possible without the support of friends and colleagues in the Graduate School of Education at the University of Bristol. Sarah Brownhill, my PA, has successfully protected my time to write from the busy-ness of a large and successful department that I am responsible for leading. My colleagues in counselling, Jane Speedy, Sheila

Trahar, Kim Etherington, and Becky Midwinter have all played significant parts. It is a privilege to work with such talented colleagues.

I am more grateful than I can say to friends and colleagues in the British Association for Counselling and Psychotherapy, especially Grainne Griffin, the Professional Conduct manager and her team who keep me grounded by drawing my attention to ethical issues that they encounter in their work. Amanpreet Sandhu and Barbara Mitchels, co-authors with me in the BACP Legal Resources Series, have been invaluable in offering fresh perspectives and investigating new developments in the law. I particularly want to thank Laurie Clarke, the Chief Executive Officer of BACP and his predecessors who have supported a steady of stream of ethical projects and opportunities for a variety of people in order to enhance ethics for counselling and psychotherapy.

There are a group of people who have raised my awareness of major issues in counselling ethics. I regret that I am not yet sufficiently sure of how to respond to these issues to have incorporated them in any depth in this edition. These are my friends, colleagues and acquaintances from cultures and faiths that differ from the ones in which I am embedded. Embracing cultural diversity in professional ethics is one of our major contemporary challenges and an urgent ethical imperative in order to slow the spread of dangerous social divisions. Progress here will be critical if counselling is to truly contribute to drawing people together in search of individual and collective well-being. The issues raised involve philosophy (in all its forms globally); questions of culture; understanding collective and individual identities; and the adaptation of professional practice to different contexts. These are issues that are much bigger than professional ethics but deserve to find their place within our ethics in a more profound way than mere tolerance of diversity, even if tolerance is an improvement on the alternatives of indifference or outright hostility. I am hoping to turn my attention to these challenges in collaboration with others in future research and writing.

As always, the staff of Sage have been a delight to work with, especially Alice Oven as Health and Social Care Editor and Rachel Burrows as Senior Production Editor. Their professionalism is for all to see. What is less evident is the sense of commitment and fun that they bring to their work.

Finally, I want to thank my clients, supervisees and students from whom I have learnt and continue to learn so much.

Tim Bond

Part I

The Background

1

Introduction

I have been delighted by the positive reception of the earlier editions of this book, which has become the most widely used text on ethics for counsellors and therapists in Britain (McLeod, 1998) and was also well reviewed internationally. My reason for preparing a third edition is not merely to update earlier editions, although this would be reason enough. There have been many changes that impact on ethics and standards for counsellors (see Table 1.1). My interest is also a personal one derived from a longstanding commitment to enhancing the integrity of counselling as a positive contribution to society and to supporting counsellors with ethical dilemmas that arise from their work. However, my most immediate motivation is based on my own experience of receiving and providing counselling and the recognition that therapeutic and ethical issues are not wholly separate categories of interest but have the potential to reinforce or to undermine each other. How I responded as a counsellor to the following ethical dilemmas had profound effects that helped or hindered my clients to achieve what they wanted from counselling:

- What should I do when a client confided in me that she was sexually abused as a child and fears the perpetrator is still abusing other children?
- How should I respond to a colleague who asks for counselling, bearing in mind that we work closely together and attend the same meetings?
- A depressed client talks about being seriously suicidal but refuses any referral for psychiatric help and insists on confidentiality. Should I respect her wishes?
- A client is determined to physically assault someone who has hurt him emotionally. What are my responsibilities to my client and the intended victim?

Each one of these situations and many like them helped me realize the inadequacy of therapeutic competence alone. Each situation could be improved by the application of counselling knowledge and skills but the fundamental dilemma was ethical in its nature. What is the right thing to do? In my experience, issues involving confidentiality and boundaries are some of the most frequent and problematic of counselling dilemmas. However, they are not the only sources of ethical challenges and in the course of the book I will attempt to consider many other issues that have been encountered by a wide range of counsellors.

How to Use this Book

This book is intended to be practical, and I hope that many people will want to read it from cover to cover. I have arranged the contents so that the logical structure of counselling ethics and standards of practice becomes apparent progressively through the book. However, when I am working with clients I do not always have time for extensive reading when I most need information or inspiration, so I tend to dip into books looking for specific topics. I have tried to bear this in mind by grouping related issues together into chapters. The index at the end of the book is designed to help you locate passages on specific topics.

For both the reader who wants to work from cover to cover and those who want to dip in and out, it may be helpful if I explain how I have organized the contents.

I begin by explaining why I think standards and ethics are important, and describe the contribution and role of the British Association for Counselling and Psychotherapy (BACP) and other national organizations in developing standards and ethics for counsellors. The second chapter considers the fundamental question 'What is counselling?' because the answer is so important if we are to decide which matters fall within the scope of counselling and which more properly belong to other roles and are therefore covered by different systems of ethics and practice. The third chapter provides a review of the main sources of material for the production of standards and ethics. An ethical framework for the application of these sources to counselling is proposed in Chapter 4. All the following chapters take a theme or closely related set of issues and explore it in more detail in ways which I hope will be useful to practitioners. It is part of the nature of this subject that, in the last resort, every practitioner has

TABLE 1.1 *Recent changes in counselling with ethical implications*

Ethics
- Greater emphasis on adapting services to meet needs of different client groups and the context in which the service is provided – e.g. surgery, school, community-based, etc.
- Increased expectations that counsellors should be willing to be accountable to their clients, employers and professional bodies for their actions.
- Greater awareness of the need to take cultural differences into account in counselling ethics.
- Greater acceptance of therapeutically beneficial or unavoidable dual relationships, e.g. counsellors living in remote rural communities or as 'embedded' counsellors in particular settings.
- Ethical frameworks and guidelines introduced as alternatives to codes. (BACP, 2007)

Standards
- Statutory regulation of counselling psychology by the Health Professions Council, due in 2009/10, will introduce legally enforceable minimum standards.
- National Institute for Clinical Excellence (NICE) publishing practice guidelines for counselling services, especially in health settings.
- A growing trend towards requiring publicly funded services to take account of research into effectiveness, i.e. evidence-based services which tends to favour cognitive behavioural therapy approaches to counselling although contested by many counsellors and services.
- Introduction of statutory regulation for all counsellors, possibly as early as 2011, will introduce legally enforceable minimum standards yet to be determined.

Legal context
- The law has become increasingly important in how counselling services are funded and delivered.
- Law of confidentiality and concerning adult consent continues to develop.
- The trend towards counsellors giving evidence to courts continues to grow.
- Increasing use of contracts of employment to define expectations of counsellors.
- Ongoing development in child protection, particularly following the tragic death of Victoria Climbié and the subsequent inquiry (2005), creating increased expectations of counsellors in publicly funded services to share information with other services for children and young people.

Developments in practice
- Theory and practice continues to be updated.
- New ways of delivering counselling made possible by digital technologies using the internet, such as counselling by webcam, email or texting, which create new ethical challenges.

---

to assess each situation for themselves and reach a personal decision, so the last chapter proposes a procedure for assessing and resolving dilemmas about standards and ethics.

Concerns about Standards and Ethics

In writing this book, I have drawn heavily on my experience as a member of various ethics and professional conduct committees, but particularly BACP. Over the last twenty years I have been researching and teaching ethics as a major part of my academic work, originally at the University of Durham and more recently at the University of Bristol, and have been involved in a number of ethical and legal projects with BACP. These different aspects of my work have brought me into contact with an enormous variety of counsellors working in very different settings, but often encountering quite similar issues. Some of the issues that are currently causing counsellors most concern are misunderstandings about:

What counselling is, or is not, resulting in

- inappropriate referrals: 'I want you to counsel Brian off this course', 'Would you see Beryl and counsel her to take early retirement because we need to reorganize the distribution of work in her office?';
- inappropriate expectations of the counsellor in relation to confidentiality: 'I wouldn't have asked John to see you if I had realized you wouldn't tell me what he said to you';
- confusion among counsellors about the limitations of confidentiality: 'Am I obliged to report all instances of suspected child abuse?';
- questioning the opportunities and limitations of counselling: 'Wouldn't it be better to intervene to stop people being emotionally traumatized by the bully rather than continuing to patch up the casualties?';
- adapting ethics to different cultural contexts: 'How far should I adapt my counselling ethics to meet the needs of clients from different cultures and social contexts?';
- adapting ethics to new methods of delivering counselling: 'How should I adapt to providing counselling using electronic technologies like webcam, email and texting?'

Counselling-supervision

- confusion between counselling-supervision and accountability to line management: 'As your line manager I am accountable for your work. I don't want someone else confusing matters', or 'No other staff get independent supervision and support so I find it difficult to see why counsellors should be any different';
- the need for ongoing long-term supervision: 'Surely you must be out of your probationary period by now. I can't see why you still need supervision'.

The need for training

- confusion over levels of competence requiring corresponding levels of training: 'We all counsel, don't we? Surely three days' training is more than enough';
- the possibility of creating instant experts in counselling: 'Here are two books on counselling. I want you to read them this weekend and become the counsellor on Monday'.

I have had comments like these reported to me from counsellors in schools, colleges, hospitals, social services, employee assistance programmes, pastoral care, voluntary organizations and private practice.

These and many other issues are the subject matter of this book.

The Importance of Standards and Ethics

Over the past few years I have become acutely aware that the public image of the usefulness, or the dangers, of counselling depends on how effectively counsellors maintain satisfactory standards of practice. Although, so far as I can tell, it is only in a minority of cases that standards are so low that they bring counselling into disrepute, the damage that results is serious both for the client and ultimately for the reputation of counselling as a whole.

Examples of the potential risks to clients of malpractice by counsellors were provided by several clients who wrote to me about their own experiences while I was working on a report on HIV counselling (Bond, 1991b). One person wrote to me about his experience of being offered counselling for himself and his partner to help them with the consequences of a recent diagnosis of HIV infection. From the outset there was potential for difficulties arising from overlapping roles because the counsellor was also the manager of one of the people involved. These difficulties were compounded by the development of a social relationship when the counsellor would go out drinking with him and his partner and eventually would stay with them overnight. Towards the end of the counselling relationship, the counsellor declared that she had always disliked the author of the letter because of his racial origins and that, had the situation been different, she and his partner could have ended up in bed together. His letter concluded with an observation which is not only relevant to HIV counselling as practised then, but can be applied to many other circumstances.

I do not believe for a moment that our experience was typical. Indeed, it was bizarre to the extreme. But this does not mean that such a peculiar and dangerous situation could not develop again.

As the number of people with HIV has increased, so has the number of people coming forward to offer 'counselling'. Whilst many of these people are no doubt extremely competent, caring and professional in their approach to their clients, others may not be so. I refer to the situation that developed between my counsellor, my partner and myself as 'dangerous' because I believe it had the potential to cause far more damage than it actually did. I was fortunate to have a partner and a family that were able to offer support. Others may not have had such support available. I also feel that although many people offering 'counselling' to people with HIV may do so with the best of intentions, this does not mean that what they actually provide is bound to be beneficial. A good intent does not necessarily produce a good result.

It is not difficult to imagine how the counsellor's lack of any standards of practice about the maintenance of boundaries in relationships, particularly when overlapping roles are involved, could have caused much more damage. The tone of the letter suggests that the counsellor set out intending to be helpful but lost her way due to lack of training and insufficient personal awareness of her own needs and prejudices. The author of the letter rightly observed that 'a good intent does not necessarily produce a good result'. Good intentions are insufficient in counselling and are dangerous unless the counsellor is also competent as a practitioner and working to a satisfactory level of standards and ethics.

My interest in ethics has meant that I have been approached by clients and counsellors about unethical practice. One recurrent issue is the treatment of young people. There are many instances when the counsellor appears to have been too closely identified with the difficulties of being a parent to be able to seriously consider the young person's request that they be allowed to manage the situation for themselves. Sometimes this over-identification with the parental role has also clouded assessments of the young person's best interests. I have heard similar versions of events from young people seeking counselling about sexual difficulties, drug use, problematic eating, and HIV infection. In each case the young person has sought confidentiality, which has been resisted by the counsellor. This resistance usually takes the form of urging the young person to inform their parents or insisting that the counsellor will do so if the young person refuses. The common feature of these examples was that the young person had good reasons to expect that the parental reaction would be antagonistic rather then helpful, but the counsellor discounted those fears.

Sometimes the counsellor appeared incredulous that parents could react violently or evict a young person from a family home in circumstances where the young person was so obviously vulnerable and in need of support. In each instance, the young person suffered what they feared would be the consequences of a forced disclosure, usually by being evicted from their home or being ostracized within it. The counsellor may have learnt about how negatively some people can and do respond to their children's difficulties. But it is learning gained at the expense of the young people affected and probably to the detriment of the reputation of counselling in that local area. One young person observed:

> Counsellors are usually very friendly and kind people. They need to remember that not everyone is as understanding of their own children as my counsellor appeared to be. It didn't help me to know that she believed that my parents would come round [i.e. change their minds] and take me back. I wish she had spent more time exploring all the possible courses of action and had involved me in deciding which one to choose.

The rights of young people to confidentiality are complicated and will be considered in Chapter 10.

The potential dangers of counselling, and particularly malpractice by counsellors, have become an increasing source of comment in the media. Probably the best feature of its kind appeared in the *Independent on Sunday*, which published a two-part series on 'Counselling: a solution or a problem?' In the leading article, Linda Grant commented:

> Counselling has helped many thousands of people in Britain. It has rightfully taken its place alongside traditional medicine, and GPs are increasingly referring depressed or troubled patients to counsellors rather than prescribing them drugs. But serious problems about counselling are emerging, as yet relatively unreported.
>
> A rising tide of expectation is creating a demand for counselling which voluntary bodies, in particular, can have no hope of meeting.

The industry is completely unregulated and there is no standard form of qualification, which makes it difficult for the public to know if it is getting a quality service. And complaints are beginning to emerge, as dissatisfied customers struggle to find recognition for their bad experiences at the hands of a profession with no mechanism for dealing with complaints of malpractice. (Grant, 1992)

The series included seven personal accounts from clients of situations in which they felt counselling had damaged them.

Three people described situations in which they questioned the counsellor's basic competence. One stated that an experience of marriage counselling had been

like a boxing match in which the counsellor said very little. He was like a silent referee just occasionally asking a question which seemed designed to spur us on to new revelations. ... I can see the point of getting people to talk and their resentments and anger, if it can be looked at, discussed, dealt with, but it seems to me it is the counsellor's job to facilitate this, to use the information coming up to help people progress. I assumed that this was what marriage guidance training is designed to do. But there was none of that. (Grant, 1992)

One felt deeply distressed by a counsellor who would sit opposite her, often with her hands in fists, and stare. After six months the counsellor suddenly said, 'I don't understand you. I don't know how your mind works. You're not like my other patients', which left her feeling devastated and a fraud.

Another was told by his counsellor that the client had no right to disagree with him and then, after eight months of attending twice a week, he shocked his client. 'Quite out of the blue he announced he didn't want to go on working with me, that I was not working properly and he did not think there was much hope that my mental state would improve. I was shattered. ... It was terrible and with hindsight, I think my therapist treated me in a grossly inappropriate and damaging way.'

Another cause for complaint was the difficulty experienced in getting to see a counsellor and the overall disrespect for the client's needs. Difficulties concerned getting to see a counsellor who was part of a counselling group practice. The initial assessment of one client's suitability for counselling took place over the telephone and was followed by several months' waiting before she saw a counsellor for what seems to have been further assessment and negotiation over the fees. The next session was with a different woman, who was to be the personal counsellor. The client found her to be full of jargon, "'I hear what you're saying", "How does that make you feel?", "You sound a very angry young woman".' It was like a parody of a counselling session. 'I wanted to say: "Don't use those words on me. Don't patronize me."' She cancelled her appointments and found better help by having a fortnightly lunch with a friend whom she had selected as being a bit older, more practical and more sensible than herself.

The fifth complaint resulted from the counsellor kissing a 19-year-old woman on the lips and saying 'I have been wanting to do that for a very long time'. The therapy had been going on three times a week for five years up to that point. This incident resulted in the client breaking off the relationship because she realized that it was a potentially very dangerous situation. She felt devastated and betrayed by someone she had learnt to trust.

The sixth reported case involved a mother and daughter who had been to see an eminent psychotherapist privately and had paid £105 for a 50-minute session. They were shocked when a friend pointed out to them an article written by the therapist which contained a full account of the session. Although the article did not include the clients' names, sufficient details of their background had been included to enable a friend to identify them. The daughter phoned to complain and had a half-hour conversation in which she pointed out 'that at least he could have asked our permission to see if we would mind, but he would not concede that he had done anything wrong. He was adamant that we could not be identified. But the point is not whether or not other people could identify us, but that my mother and I recognised that this was our story, and it has harmed my mother greatly. I feel furious and betrayed.'

The seventh situation was a complaint written not by the client but by someone affected by the outcome of the counselling. A mother wrote of her pain at watching her son distance himself from his family and eventually lose contact for over five years. On the basis of what he had told his friends, she believes 'his counsellor had advised him to give up all contact with his family, who were the root of all his troubles and to start a new life which excluded them'. She would have liked to know the basis for such advice and whether the counsellor is still offering the same advice.

The articles and personal accounts of people dissatisfied with their experience of counsellors and therapists had a considerable impact when the *Independent on Sunday* first published them. My own post bag grew as people wrote to me to draw attention to the articles and ask for my opinions. I think it was the first time for many counsellors that they had seen such a catalogue of potential causes for grievance experienced by clients. As a result, many counsellors who read the article reviewed their own standards of practice. I did this myself. For example, the possibility that clients might identify themselves in an account of a case, from which names had been excluded and background details given in fairly impersonal and abstract terms, seems not to have been considered before publication of this article. Knowledge of the identity of the therapist seen by clients is a crucial factor. It was this knowledge that had helped the friend to identify them, even in an anonymized account. The obvious conclusion is that greater safeguards are needed if any account of counselling could result in clients identifying themselves, or someone else who knows the identity of the counsellor they have seen identifying them. This lesson is still being learnt by some clients and counsellors. Some of the other examples of dissatisfaction appear all too familiar. Poor standards of practice and unethical behaviour do occur from time to time. I hope this book will enable conscientious counsellors to avoid some of the pitfalls mentioned in this salutary and useful series of articles.

It is not easy to obtain an accurate overview of the current pattern of complaints actually made against counsellors. The fact that the agencies to whom complaints can be made range from national professional organizations to local counselling agencies is a significant complication. Some of these agencies are reluctant to release information about complaints received because of a desire to protect the agency's reputation or funding in combination with a concern for protecting confidentiality about client work. It is also possible that many complaints are directed towards Citizens' Advice Bureaux or solicitors, especially when these concern independent practitioners working in private practice. National organizations probably only see the tip of the iceberg, which means that the pattern of complaints dealt with probably tell us more about patterns of concern than about quantity of complaints. Emotional and sexual abuse remains one of the most significant issues across all the caring professions.

Few people can be better placed than Fiona Palmer Barnes, who has been prominent in developing and running complaints procedures in BACP and the United Kingdom Council for Psychotherapy (UKCP) to have a sense of the pattern of complaints received by the national professional counselling organizations. She identified several categories of complaint. These related to the counsellor's lack of competence, conflicting expectations of client and counsellor due to inadequate contracting, poor management of confidentiality, mistakes and malpractice (Palmer Barnes, 1998). Even this overview may not be comprehensive. It is probable that most grievances go generally unreported and that some issues may be less likely to be reported than others. For example, the decision about when to terminate counselling may be experienced differently by client and counsellor. Significant numbers of clients may feel that their counselling has been extended unnecessarily to the benefit of the counsellor's income. However, I doubt that this would be reported to a complaints procedure unless the continuation of counselling was both lengthy and manifestly exploitative. In most other circumstances, the client would be more likely to cut their losses by simply ending the counselling rather than compounding them by putting time and resources into making a complaint. If complaints procedures are envisaged as a net, it is a net with a large mesh, through which an unknown but possibly large number of smaller but possibly significant grievances escape.

Complaints procedures cannot by themselves protect the ethical standards of counselling. It is not simply that many complaints do not reach them. Many clients may be deterred because they do not expect to be taken seriously. Alternatively, they may fear that a professional organization will be primarily concerned with protecting its own members rather than considering a grievance from a member of the public. Some complaints may simply fall outside their scope. Even when serious malpractice is proven, there are limitations in the sanctions that can be imposed. The most serious sanction is expulsion from membership of that organization. However, it is extremely difficult to stop someone from continuing to practise. It usually comes as a shock to realize that someone can leave prison after serving a sentence for fraud or serious assault and immediately set up as a counsellor or psychotherapist. It is sometimes suggested that this situation would be significantly altered if we achieved statutory registration, like medicine and many professions allied to medicine. It is probable that statutory registration would make a limited improvement, but not to the point of excluding a minority of determinedly ill-intentioned people from practice. They can often create employment opportunities for themselves in the less well regulated sectors of their profession. It is not unknown for doctors or lawyers who have been expelled from statutory registration for gross professional misconduct to continue working in very closely related roles. This is likely to be a more frequent occurrence in counselling and closely related roles because of the difficulty of defining exactly where counselling stops and other kinds of activity begin. Statutory regulation increases control but does not give total control to the profession or provide guaranteed protection to the public.

This raises the question, why should counsellors be concerned to act ethically and maintain standards of practice? After all, a counsellor could argue, 'If I act unethically, the worst that can happen to me as a counsellor will be my expulsion from any counselling organizations I belong to. They cannot stop me from continuing to take clients.' I believe this kind of response misunderstands the nature of counselling and also the interdependence of personal and professional ethical integrity. It is useful to ask the fundamental question: why be ethical?

Why be Ethical?

Unless counselling is provided on an ethical basis, it ceases to serve any useful purpose. Clients usually seek counselling because they are troubled or vulnerable; they wish to be sure that the primary concern of the counselling is to help them to achieve a greater sense of autonomy and well-being and that counselling is not being used in order to serve some other purpose. This means that counselling, by its very nature, needs to be an ethical relationship.

However, clients are not usually well informed about the ethical standards of counselling, so they are more likely to judge the ethical basis of their counselling by assessing of the personal integrity of the counsellor. This is much more familiar ground. Every day, all of us are engaged in assessing the trustworthiness of the people we meet. One of the first concerns of a client at the start of counselling is 'How far can I trust this person to be my counsellor?' Typically, it is assumed that if the counsellor appears to have personal integrity, then the ethical standards that she applies to her counselling will be of a similar level. By definition, trust always involves a leap of faith, which overrides lack of information and ignorance in order to place confidence in a person or system. This is a major step for many clients. Some manage the risk by testing out the counsellor on less serious issues before disclosing the real concern.

Others are so driven by the urgency of the situation or their distress that the problem comes tumbling out before they are sitting down. In either situation, the act of trust is at a time of considerable vulnerability for the client and gives the counsellor considerable power over them for good or harm. This is why the counsellor's personal commitment to being ethical is so important. One person's vulnerability creates a corresponding obligation on the other in their exercise of power and professional expertise.

Without the act of trust, counselling is impossible. Sufficient trust needs to be present to enable the client to participate with appropriate frankness and active commitment. Counselling is not like a medical procedure that can take place on a passive or anaesthetized patient. Establishing a high level of trust in the counselling is considered to be so fundamental that it is the primary principle in some constructions of counselling ethics (Bond, 2006; 2007). It is also the basis of the legal protection of confidences imparted in counselling in many jurisdictions, including English law. Even when trust is not regarded as the primary ethical requirement for counselling, it is always high on the list of ethical priorities. Different approaches to the construction of counselling ethics are considered in Chapters 3 and 4. The one thing that unites the people who developed these approaches is the conviction that a commitment to being ethical is the best way of protecting the interests of the client and enhancing the reputation of counselling in general.

2

What is Counselling?

Creating a definition of counselling is surprisingly difficult. The major challenge is to distinguish a specific use of counselling for human development and therapy from the more general use of the term in everyday life where 'counselling' is widely used, sometimes in ill-defined and contradictory ways. Counselling is a fashionable feature of contemporary life and as a consequence there is an ever-growing list of examples of how the label has been co-opted for many purposes. In its everyday usage 'counselling' is non-specific. The meaning can range from simply listening to someone in the spirit of a 'problem shared is a problem halved' to giving authoritative advice: 'I counselled him to return to work as the longer he puts it off, the harder it will be.' Sometimes 'counselling' can be a thinly veiled method of selling products, as in 'fashion counselling' or 'double glazing counsellor'. 'Debt counselling' ranges from almost fraudulent selling of unsuitable financial products to desperate people to highly professional and impartial help in managing financial difficulties. In these examples, the meaning has to be inferred from the context in which the term is being used. There are also examples of the use of 'counselling' where the term has taken on a very narrow and technically specific meaning. 'Counselling', in some disciplinary proceedings, represents 'a serious talking to about the need to change behaviour' as a form of oral warning which is the precursor of a written warning or dismissal. In this context, the interpersonal dynamics are both judgemental and authoritative. Counselling can also mean imparting expert advice in an authoritative manner, such as 'I counselled him to watch for problems with ... but did he pay any attention?' Counselling is not a fixed term with an established meaning. There is always the potential for two people using the term to misunderstand each other because they are using it in different ways. The existence of such a variety of meanings in everyday use makes it a problematic term to apply to a significant and rapidly developing professional role.

In this chapter I intend to examine a range of approaches to defining counselling. Identifying these approaches sets the context considered by this book. Establishing an agreed meaning is important to establishing the boundaries of what activities are included within, and what activities are excluded from, the ethics and standards of counselling.

For example, when a pupil approaches a tutor for help with a personal problem, or when a nurse listens to a patient's worries about being away from home, is counselling taking place? When a social worker assists parents preparing for the return of their children from residential care, or when a priest helps someone who has been recently bereaved, is counselling taking place? Or is it some other activity, perhaps subject to different standards of practice and ethics?

Even within the field of counselling covered by this book, there are wider and narrower definitions.

The Meaning of 'Counselling' Internationally

At the international level there is a definite tendency to make the term 'counselling' all-encompassing, in order to accommodate a diversity of cultures and practice. In languages where there is no equivalent to 'counselling', often the terms 'guidance' or 'advice' act as an equivalent. Alternatively, the term 'counselling' is simply imported into the vocabulary of the language. The International Association for Counselling (IAC) (incorporating the Round Table for the Advancement of Counselling (IRTAC)), which is recognized by the United Nations as a non-governmental organization, uses an all-encompassing definition that can be adapted to different national and social contexts. The determination to encompass diversity in order to encourage contextually appropriate practice is counterbalanced by identifying the purpose of counselling. The tensions between being internationally inclusive and establishing a shared professional identity appears to be carefully balanced in this definition:

The term 'counselling' has many meanings according to its cultural and professional context. Nonetheless it is possible to identify a definition that encompasses this diversity.

Counselling may be described as a profession of relating and responding to others with the aim of providing them with opportunities to explore, clarify and work towards living in a more personally satisfying and resourceful way. Counselling may be applied to individuals, couples, families or groups and may be used in widely differing contexts and settings. (IAC, 2003)

The close relationship between counselling and guidance in many countries is acknowledged:

Whereas the counselling is primarily non-directive and non-advisory, some situations require positive guidance by means of information and advice. (Hoxter, 1998)

This wording, by the late founder of IAC, simultaneously suggests a distinction between counselling and guidance while seemingly validating advice and guidance in a way which suggests that they might be incorporated within some approaches of counselling. This ambiguity reflects the practical realities of counselling world-wide, where it can take a considerable variety of forms according to the cultural context and purpose for which counselling is being used.

In the modern world, cultural diversity does not simply exist between nations but also within countries as people migrate or relocate following conflict in their place of origin or are taken over by a different nationality or ethnic group.

The most recent statement about the criterion for membership of the American Counseling Association (formerly the American Association of Counseling and Development – note spelling of 'Counseling' with one 'l' in American usage) is as broad as that of any international association, but has a strong multicultural focus:

Association members are dedicated to the enhancement of human development throughout the lifespan. Association members recognize diversity and embrace a cross-cultural approach in support of the worth, dignity, potential, and uniqueness of people within their social and cultural contexts. (ACA, 2005)

The first part of this definition probably constitutes one of the widest definitions of counselling in current use. An earlier statement acknowledged the difficulty posed by using such a wide definition in setting standards.

> The Association recognizes that the role definitions and work settings of its members include a wide variety of academic disciplines, levels of academic preparation, and agency services. This diversity reflects the breadth of the Association's interest and influence. It poses challenging complexities in efforts to set standards for the performance of members, desired requisite preparation or practice, and supporting social, legal and ethical controls. (AACD, 1988)

The counselling movement in the USA is probably further ahead in providing multicultural counselling than is currently the case in the British Isles. It may be that the current approach to the definition of counselling is more of an obstacle than an asset in developing a stronger multicultural base for counselling. The use of all-encompassing definitions by international and more multiculturally developed counselling organizations seems to point to this conclusion. However, there may be other more significant factors that explain the slow development of a multicultural dimension to counselling on this side of the Atlantic. It is probably fair to say that the development of definitions of counselling in Britain has been more concerned about role differentiation and highlighting distinctive aspects of counselling that could well be overwhelmed unless entrenched within a definition.

'Counselling' in Britain

Within Britain there is a long-established use of the term 'counselling' in its wider meaning. Stephen Murgatroyd (1985) regards the professionalization of counselling by training and certification as the prerequisite of a select few working in specialist roles. However, in his view, the strategies used in counselling should not be confined to these select few. He argues in favour of deprofessionalizing counselling in order to make its methods available to as many different people as possible. Counselling and helping are therefore synonymous. Philip Burnard (2006) reaches a similar view about the meaning of the term 'counselling', but offers a different explanation for doing so which arises from his experience of working in the health service. As a nurse tutor, he was concerned to discover that nurses are reluctant to use facilitative skills with patients. This is not merely a matter of skills but of an attitude and a belief that the nurse knows best, or at least better than the patient. This is contrary to the growing practice of involving patients in decisions about their own care. Burnard is interested in extending the nurses' skills to include more facilitative interventions that involve the patient in making decisions for himself about his treatment. He draws on John Heron's six categories of therapeutic intervention as the underpinning model. Heron (2001) divides the possible interventions into authoritative and facilitative. Authoritative interventions include: prescriptive (offering advice), informative (offering information) and confronting (challenging). Facilitative interventions include: cathartic (enabling expression of pent-up emotions), catalytic (drawing out) and supportive (confirming or encouraging). Burnard concluded that it is desirable for nurses to use the full range of interventions and therefore defines counselling as the effective use of verbal interventions involving 'both client-centred *and* more prescriptive counselling' (his emphasis). He is therefore taking an all-encompassing view of counselling. These debates about whether counselling should develop into a separate profession or is better understood as part of another professional role, such as nursing or teaching, are ongoing. Perhaps the biggest divide is between those who support counselling developing into a regulated profession with its identity entrenched in law and those who see it more as an inclusive social movement committed to maximizing human potential and therefore distinct from the scientific and medical culture of related professions. The debate between a perceived narrowing of counselling to meet a professional agenda and a wider vision of the potential contribution of counselling to society is ongoing on both sides of the Atlantic (Bates and House, 2003).

In contrast to the wider definitions of counselling, there are two narrower definitions in popular use that are mutually exclusive.

The first of these regards counselling as the same as giving advice. This view has a long tradition that reaches back to at least the seventeenth century. In 1625, Francis Bacon, the essayist, wrote 'The greatest Trust, betweene Man and Man is the Trust of Giving Counsell'. It is a reasonable inference that he is thinking of advice because as he develops his argument he identifies the 'Inconveniences of Counsell'. These include 'the Danger of being unfaithfully counselled, and more for the good of them that counsell than of him that is counselled'. He also states that only people with expertise are suitable to provide 'counsell'. This use of counsel to mean expert advice is the only definition given in the 1982 edition of the *Concise Oxford English Dictionary*. Counsel is defined as 'advise (person to do); give advice to (person) professionally on social problems etc.; recommend (thing, that)' (Sykes, 1982). This meaning is still actively used in legal and medical circles. When I was working on a report about HIV counselling, a doctor who was committed to this usage wrote to me to express exasperation at all the fuss being made about counselling, which he regarded as merely a 'popular term for giving advice to people' (Bond, 1991b). This narrow definition of counselling is valid, but is incompatible with an increasingly prevalent use of the term 'counselling' which has a history stretching back at least seventy years. A more recent edition of the *Shorter Oxford English Dictionary* recognizes that a distinction in meaning has developed between 'counsel' and 'counselling'. As a noun, 'counsel' retains its historical association with advice-giving and communication of opinion. In contrast, it defines 'counselling' as 'a therapeutic procedure in which a usually trained person adopts a supportive non-judgemental role in enabling a client to deal more effectively with psychological or emotional problems or gives advice on practical problems' (Trumble and Stevenson, 2002).

This more modern use of the term has emerged from, and in a reaction against, the traditions of psychoanalysis and psychotherapy. It has its origins in the 1920s in the USA. When Carl Rogers started working as a psychologist in America, he was not permitted to practise psychotherapy, which was restricted to medical practitioners. Therefore he called his work 'counseling' (Thorne, 1984). However, Carl Rogers was not the inventor of the term. It is widely believed in North America that the originator of 'counseling' was a radical social activist. Frank Parsons (1854–1908) was energetic in his condemnation of American capitalism and competition. He advocated the replacement of capitalism with a system of mutualism, a combination of co-operation and concern for humanity. A political activist proposing public ownership of utilities and transportation, the vote for women and a managed currency, he has been called 'a one man American Fabian Society' (Gummere, 1988). In 1908, he invented the 'counseling centre' when he founded the Vocation Bureau in the North End of Boston, a part of town crowded with immigrants. The centre offered interviews, testing, information and outreach work. It seems that Parsons placed more emphasis on social action and the importance of the social culture than most modern counsellors. In North America, attention is periodically drawn to the origins of counselling and Frank Parsons, especially when it appears that counselling is in danger of becoming 'overly parochial and perhaps irrelevant' (Zytowski, 1985).

In Britain, the association of counselling with political activism has probably been greatest in the women's and gay movements. Elsewhere the link is less obvious, but many use counselling to conduct a quiet revolution by drawing attention to the need to humanize education, health care and the essential human qualities of relationships in society. Paul Halmos (1978) pointed out that even tough-minded social scientists might think counsellors are wrong but on the whole they are assessed as having a good influence on society. Insights from counselling and psychotherapy have changed hospital procedures that separated mothers from young children. Counsellors have had a major role in exposing the long-term human suffering caused by the physical, emotional and sexual abuse of children. This quiet revolution is inspired by the counsellor's faith in the need to love and be loved, and one of the characteristics of most models of counselling is the counsellor's emotional warmth towards the client or concern for the client's well-being as the foundation of the counselling relationship. Although counselling has changed since it was first espoused by Frank Parsons, the emphasis has remained on counselling as the principled use of relationship with the aim of enabling the client to achieve his own improved well-being. Two major ethical principles are closely associated with this way of counselling: respect for the client's capacity for self-determination and the importance of confidentiality. This is the use of the term 'counselling' espoused by the British Association for Counselling and Psychotherapy.

> Counselling occurs when a counsellor sees a client in a private and confidential setting to explore a difficulty the client is having, distress they may be experiencing or perhaps their dissatisfaction with life or loss of a sense of direction and purpose. It is always at the request of the client and no one can properly be 'sent' for counselling. (BACP, 2008a)

The concluding sentence suggests an ethic which prioritizes respect for the clients' capacity to make choices for themselves, which has also been variously referred to as 'self-determination', 'autonomy', 'self-reliance' or 'independence'. The choice of word often depends on personal preferences but the essential meaning is the same. The respect showed to the client's autonomy is fundamental to counselling as viewed by BACP and acts as the cornerstone of its values, from which the ethical principles are derived and ultimately standards of practice are set.

The definition adopted by the Division of Counselling Psychology in the British Psychological Society reveals a different set of preoccupations which are less concerned about distinguishing between facilitative and authoritative forms of counselling than asserting the place of counselling within psychology. Undoubtedly, this preoccupation reflects the struggle that this division experienced in establishing itself within a professional discipline that previously had been heavily committed to traditional scientific knowledge, often derived from laboratory experiments.

> Counselling Psychology is a distinctive profession within psychology with a specialist focus, which links most closely to the allied professions of psychotherapy and counselling. It pays particular attention to the meanings, beliefs, context and processes that are constructed both within and between people and which affect the psychological wellbeing of the person. (BPS, 2008a)

It is probably inevitable that scientific knowledge holds the highest status within many professional bodies and in society in general. It is a type of knowledge that has transformed the world we inhabit by creating new technologies, especially in developed countries. However, the primary focus of counselling is on subjective experience and this requires modifications to existing scientific methods or possibly other approaches to acquiring knowledge. This is reflected in the description of counselling psychology as the basis for guidance on professional practice. 'Counselling psychology has developed as a branch of professional psychological practice strongly influenced by human science research as well as the principal psychotherapeutic traditions' (Division of Counselling Psychology, 2007).

Counselling and Other Roles

Identifying overlaps and distinctions between counselling and other roles is no longer a concern simply of practitioners. It has become a matter of social policy as government is becoming more interested in encouraging a systematic approach to the delivery of counselling services in the voluntary and statutory sectors. A major project was sponsored by the Department for Education and Employment to organize a progressive sequence of training for workers offering befriending, advice, guidance and counselling or using counselling skills. This was an ambitious programme involving many people. I was a member of a team concerned with one part of it: role differentiation (Russell et al., 1992). As so often happens, the moment I concentrate on a particular theme, in this case the differences between the roles, the opposite leaps out at me. Despite the well-established arguments that distinguish counselling from advice and other roles, I became conscious of a different perspective on their common roots.

From an historical perspective, the development of befriending, advice, guidance, counselling skills and counselling is strongly associated with movements to enable citizens to become better able to participate in the democratic process and to take control of their own lives. Advice and guidance services have received state funding in response to a series of government reports going back to the 1920s to help people cope with the complex network of benefits and laws that form part of modern society. Befriending has an history in British social welfare which goes back at least as far as 1879 when lay missionaries were appointed by magistrates to advise, befriend and assist offenders, who were often too illiterate to understand court procedures and too poor to afford legal representation in the courts. Befriending has continued to be used to reach out to socially isolated groups of people whose needs are not adequately met within formal social welfare services. Counselling and counselling skills have been adopted not only as methods of problem-solving or therapy, but also to serve other functions. Within education and health services, they are used to help people make informed choices about the options open to them. In this way, the increasing use of counselling and counselling skills in the statutory sector is linked with a shift from viewing the users of services as wholly dependent on the expert providers of services, such as doctors, teachers, social workers, etc., towards enabling the users of those services to participate in decisions about their own future. It seems to me that there is a closer relationship between the roles of advice, guidance, befriending, counselling skills and counselling than I had previously appreciated. More recent additions are advocacy and mediation (Craig, 1998). In different ways, they are all rooted in a movement towards democratizing society and empowering the individual to exercise control for themselves. In this sense, they all share similar origins and can be regarded as belonging to a single family or 'genus' of roles. However, there are also important distinctions to be made between the roles. Metaphorically, if they were to be included in a biological classification, they are separate species within the same genus. Therefore, it is worth considering what is distinctive about each of these roles.

Counselling and Advice

Advice is generally thought of as an opinion given or offered as to future action. It usually entails giving someone information about the choices open to them and then from a position of greater expertise or authority a recommendation as to the best course of action. Rosalind Brooke (1972), writing about Citizens' Advice Bureaux, describes the advisory process as having two aspects: 'The advisor not only may interpret the information in order to sort it to the needs of the enquirer, but may also offer an opinion about the wisdom of obtaining a solution in a particular way.' This description highlights the difficulty 'advice' poses for the counsellor. The aim of counselling is to enable the client to discover their own wisdom rather than have wisdom imparted to them by the counsellor. The counselling process is intended to increase the client's ability to take control rather than depend on another. This difference between counselling and advice does not mean that advice is an inappropriate way of offering help. It is a different method and perhaps more suitable for practical problems than for making decisions about relationships, coping with transitions or other psychosocial issues.

In more recent times advice-giving and counselling have grown closer together in their methods. In an influential discussion paper prepared for the National Association of Young People's Counselling and Advisory Services, Arthur Musgrave (1991) observed: 'Most advice work training focuses on content. All too often workers are left to learn what they can of strategies and tactics as they go along.' He rejected this practice and advocated combining training in advice work with counselling skills. This view is now well established and embedded in how many advisers work, for example in the National Association of Citizens' Advice Bureaux,

[a]dvisers don't tell clients what to do, but explain their options and the possible outcomes of different courses of action. Clients are encouraged to make their own decisions and act on their own behalf. We enable clients to manage their own problems by focusing on their needs as individuals. (NACAB, 2008)

When advice is delivered in this way by respecting the recipients' rights to be actively involved in making choices, it is much closer to the methods and process of counselling than when it is given authoritatively.

Counselling and Guidance

'Guidance' has been used in as many different ways as 'counselling'. During the late 1960s and the 1970s, a time when guidance services were expanding rapidly in social welfare and education, the terms 'guidance' and 'counselling' could be used interchangeably. Aryeh Leissner (1969), defined guisssdance as:

being available for an occasional chat to help a troubled person to gain some insight and better perspective with regard to relatively minor problems. It may take the form of more structured short-term counselling aimed at 'working through' some difficulties or changing certain irrational attitudes. Guidance may also entail the process of enabling a client to understand the need for referral to more intensive, specialised treatment services, and to prepare the client for the referral.

The implication of her definition is that longer-term work of a more intensive kind would be regarded as 'therapy', which is beyond the scope of guidance or counselling. In her thinking, both guidance and counselling are a longer form of contact than advice.

It appears that some time since the 1970s, the use of guidance has developed in two different directions. One trend has emphasized the kinds of values and methods of working associated with counselling. This trend is characterized by a very strong emphasis on working in ways that enable the recipient of guidance to make his own decisions. In this sense, the guide is like a signpost, pointing out different possible routes and helping someone to select their own destination and way of getting there. Information-giving and advising may be more prominent in the worker's interventions than would be the case in counselling, but the emphasis on values based on the client's autonomy mean that this form of guidance is very closely related to counselling, and in some instances they are the same kind of activity. This use of 'guidance' has become well established in educational settings and is encouraged by many writers and commentators on educational advice, guidance and counselling services (Ali and Graham, 1996; Gothard et al., 2001; Evans, 2008).

An alternative use of 'guidance' appears to have developed in reaction against the use of 'counselling' to mean 'non-directive interventions'. In this use, 'guidance' is deliberately used to fill the gap left by non-directive counselling in order to validate information-giving and advising. The provider of guidance is therefore more than a signpost but actively indicates the best route and may guide someone along it. For example, I have been told that there has been a struggle within the Department of Health concerning the choice between 'pre-test counselling' for HIV antibodies (the indicators of HIV infections and the potential development of AIDS) and 'pre-test guidance'. This was to escape any confusion about pre-test counselling being directive or non-directive. The policy-makers who wished to substitute the term 'guidance' were doing so to indicate that they wanted whoever conducted the pre-test sessions to feel free to offer expert opinion and to guide or direct people towards behaviours which reduce the likelihood of HIV infection. In other words, the realities of HIV infection should be borne in mind by the person conducting the session and they should actively seek to prevent further infection. In practice, the use of 'counselling' has prevailed prior to giving someone a medical test for the presence of HIV antibodies because this is considered more appropriate to ensuring that someone has given consent to being tested. The historical associations with counselling as a non-directive intervention have doubtless contributed to this outcome.

Recent developments in services for young people following the Children Act 2004 and the policies known as *Every Child Matters* (Department for Children, Schools and Families, 2009) have been so radical that they may have changed the professional landscape for all people involved in these services. The emphasis on integrating services across old professional divisions has also brought information-giving, advising and guidance closer together within a single service. One of the consequences may be a blurring of boundaries between them as they are brought together under the same umbrella. There are suggestions of this in the following definition of information, advice and guidance:

> 'Information, advice and guidance' is a key element of Local Authority integrated youth support services. It is an umbrella term. It covers a range of activities and interventions that help young people to become more self-reliant and better able to manage their personal and career development, including learning.
>
> It includes:
>
> - the provision of accurate, up-to-date and objective information about personal and lifestyle issues, learning and career opportunities, progression routes, choices, where to find help and advice, and how to access it
> - the provision of advice through activities that help young people to gather, understand and interpret information and apply it to their own situation
> - the provision of impartial guidance and specialist support to help young people understand themselves and their needs, confront barriers, resolve conflicts, develop new perspectives and make progress
> - support for curriculum development [of courses and programmes].
> (Department for Children, Schools and Families, 2007)

The bringing together of information, advice and guidance in this way raise the question of what is the appropriate collective term. Within the official literature it tends to be known by the abbreviation IGA, as a means of creating a new brand for long-established ways of helping. However, I am sure that there is a need for a term that validates advising and giving information. In the English vocabulary, 'guidance' is the obvious candidate. It would reduce some of the confusion over roles if the term 'guidance' was used for this purpose. This would mean that 'non-directive guidance' would be better known as counselling. As with giving advice, the potential directiveness of guidance is reduced by the use of counselling skills to maximize client choice within the parameters offered by the interviewer. So the use of counselling skills helps to make even a directive form of guidance quite different from merely telling someone what they should, or should not, do.

Counselling and Befriending

The best known of the organizations committed to providing a befriending service is the Samaritans. Chad Varah, their founder, had a strong preference for providing a befriending, rather than counselling, service. He believed that befriending is a role which is more readily understood by callers and one which is more attractive to people who may feel socially isolated and unable to approach people already known to them about their problems. A substitute 'friend' has a more powerful appeal in these circumstances than a 'counsellor', a term that might be perceived as emphasizing the difference in emotional vulnerability between helper and helped, thereby increasing the sense of the caller's personal isolation rather than focusing attention on the usefulness of the human relationship.

The use of befriending to counter the social isolation of specific groups of people is a goal shared by all providers of this service. The social isolation may be due to physical circumstances, for example people who are housebound due to illness or disability, or isolated by public attitudes, for example people who are mentally ill or have learning difficulties, the dying, and offenders. National FRIEND is an example of an organization which provides befriending for those who feel set apart by their sexuality and who want the support of people who share similar experiences of being gay, lesbian or bisexual.

As an organization that provides both befriending and counselling services for people affected by HIV or AIDS, the Aled Richards Trust, Bristol (now incorporated in the Terrence Higgins Trust), has had to consider the boundary between these roles. Meg Price, the Co-ordinator of the Buddying Services, wrote to me about how they distinguish between counselling and buddying, the American term for befriending. She observed:

> Counselling occurs within the framework of a specific contract – to look at agreed issues, usually one hour sessions on a regular basis, and in a specific setting (usually the counselling room or the client's home). Whilst Buddies are not trained as counsellors, their role is to listen and to be available at times of particular stress and they may well often be the only person that the client can really talk to and confide in. Buddies, like counsellors, attempt to work in as non-judgmental a way as possible but also have the freedom of a higher level of self-disclosure than have most counsellors. Boundaries are

far wider and more flexible in buddying, buddies usually being expected to perform practical tasks for the client, to engage in social activities (e.g. have meals together, visiting the pub, going to the cinema, etc.) and occasionally the client may become involved in the buddy's personal life (e.g. meeting his/her own family and friends). None of these things would be seen as appropriate for a counsellor to be undertaking. (Bond, 1991b)

Counselling and Psychotherapy

The British Association for Counselling and Psychotherapy has long held that it is not possible to make a generally accepted distinction between counselling and psychotherapy. In this respect, it follows well-founded traditions which use the terms interchangeably, in contrast to others which distinguish them.

When the terms 'counselling' and 'psychotherapy' are used in their widest sense they are the same. On the other hand, these terms are sometimes used to distinguish between two roles. The historical origins of psychotherapy are closely related to attempts to find ways of curing mental illness, especially in the USA (McLeod, 1998). The direct influence of psychoanalytic ideas is more evident in psychotherapy than in counselling. As a consequence, some people have sought to establish clear distinctions between counselling and psychotherapy on the assumption that responding to mental health issues requires working at greater depth (Figure 2.1).

Attempts to distinguish counselling and psychotherapy have proved problematic in the UK. Many people with a psychodynamic background would tend to support the existence of a distinction linked to the history of this approach and a much stronger sense of professional hierarchy through psychodynamic counselling, psychotherapy and psychoanalysis. Entitlement to progress through the hierarchy and to work in greater depth with clients is linked to levels of training and personal therapy or analysis. Some humanistic approaches to therapy have adopted similarly structured professional hierarchies, such as transactional analysis. These hierarchical approaches to different levels of therapy position counselling as dealing with problems that are primarily pressures from the outside environment, rather than deeply embedded difficulties resulting in rigid neurotic patterns. Counselling is restricted to helping people who have the capacity to cope in most circumstances but who are experiencing

	Characteristics of
Counselling	**Psychotherapy**
Educational	Reconstructive
Situational	Issues arising from personality
Problem-solving	Analytic
Conscious awareness	Pre-conscious and unconscious
Emphasis on working with people who do not have severe or persistent emotional problems	Emphasis on 'neurotics' or working with persistent and/or severe emotional problems
Focus on present	Focus on past
Shorter length of contract	Longer length of contract

FIGURE 2.1   *The characteristics of counselling and psychotherapy (adapted from Brammer and Shostrum, 1982)*

temporary difficulties, or making transitions or adjustments in their life. Issues arising from difficult relationships at home, making decisions, coping with serious illness, bereavement, addiction, etc., may all be within the scope of counselling. If issues are merely symptomatic of something deeper, or the client is experiencing more entrenched problems such as persistent phobias, anxiety states, low self-esteem or difficulty in establishing relationships, then psychotherapy may be more appropriate. This would imply the need for a difference in training and expertise between counsellors and psychotherapists. In my experience, the distinction between counselling and psychotherapy is much harder to establish in the UK than appears to be case in the USA. This is partly because clients do not present themselves in such neat categories. A seemingly superficial problem in the present may have deeper origins in the past. Sometimes problems arising in the past can be best resolved by communications between people in the present changing long-terms patterns of behaviour and distress. Several empirical studies of what counsellors and psychotherapists actually do with their clients have also failed to uncover differences. Perhaps one of the reasons why it is hard to establish a general difference across the professional roles is that practitioners of different therapeutic models disagree profoundly about the desirability of any distinction. It is one of the issues that has divided psychodynamic and person-centred therapists for many years.

In a paper delivered to the 16th Annual Training Conference of the British Association for Counselling (BAC), Brian Thorne (1992) suggested that the quest for difference between counselling and psychotherapy is illogical and invalid. He argues that implicit in the kinds of distinctions most frequently made between counselling and psychotherapy is the idea that counselling is concerned with cognitive problems and psychotherapy with affective problems. He debunked this line of argument in the following way:

> I would suggest that it takes only a moment's reflection to reveal the uselessness of such distinctions. Clearly, cognition and affect are both involved in all behaviours. No choice, for example, can ever be simply logical and rational. What is more, a serious personality problem usually brings with it many situational and environmental dilemmas and a situational problem may well have its source in a personality disturbance. It would, of course, be highly convenient if problems could be categorised and circumscribed so neatly but to suggest that they can is to fly in the face of the facts.

In his paper he argues against all the distinctions between counselling and psychotherapy made by Brammer and Shostrum (1982) and many others. I have no doubt this debate will continue unresolved for some considerable time. The debate may have more to do with status and money than with substantive differences. I am frequently told that in private practice the label 'psychotherapy' attracts higher fees from clients than 'counselling'. However, so far as I can tell, there is a great deal of common ground between counselling and psychotherapy. Clients talk about their experience of being on the receiving end of counselling or psychotherapy in very similar terms. Fee differentials notwithstanding, the difference between the two appears to be more important to practitioners than to clients. From an ethical perspective, it is clear to me that counsellors and psychotherapists work within the same ethical framework. It may be that if differences between the two roles can be established, there will be some corresponding differences in standards of practice or training, but even these may simply be details in comparison with the many standards shared in common. (See note at the end of the chapter.)

Counselling, Counselling Skills and Embedded Counselling

The development of a distinction between counselling and counselling skills has played a significant part in enabling the development of counselling as a distinct professional role. However, the notion of counselling skills remains controversial and is much criticized by those who prefer 'embedded counselling'. In this section I will set out how counselling skills emerged as a term for particular types of activity before considering the criticisms of this development. Although I was an early advocate for 'counselling skills' (Bond, 1989), I recognize that there is some validity in the concerns about this development. The issues are slippery so I will start by considering a common misunderstanding.

The most obvious misunderstanding is based on the idea that 'counselling skills' is a label for a set of activities unique to counselling. Although the term is sometimes used in this way, it is quickly discredited because any attempt to list specific 'counselling skills', e.g. active listening, paraphrasing, using open questions, reflective responses, etc., quickly looks indistinguishable from lists labelled social skills, communication skills, interpersonal skills, etc.

In order to understand what is meant by 'counselling skills', it is useful to take the two words separately.

'Counselling' is an indication of the source of the concept historically. It indicates that even though these skills are not unique to counselling, it is the way they have been articulated in counselling that has been useful to other roles. For example, advice-giving has a much longer history than counselling skills, but the tendency has been to concentrate on the content of the advice rather than the way it is delivered. However, the methods advisers use to communicate with clients can be adapted to improve the way advice is given and maximize the client's involvement in the decision-making. 'Counselling' in this context is acknowledging the source of the concept and method of communication. Similarly, nurses, tutors, personnel managers, social workers and many others have all recognized that there are advantages in adapting the methods of communication used in counselling to aspects of their own role. One way in which an outside observer might detect that counselling skills are being used is the pattern of communication. This is illustrated in Table 2.1.

Imparting expertise involves the expert in communicating her knowledge and expertise to the recipient and therefore takes up most of the time available. This contrasts with conversation, where both participants tend to contribute for equal lengths of time and in a pattern which flows backwards and forwards. The use of counselling skills will usually change the pattern of communication in favour of the recipient, who speaks for most of the available time. Part of the expertise in using counselling skills is learning how to communicate briefly in ways which do not interrupt

TABLE 2.1   *Differences in communication*

Style	Pattern of flow	Time ratio
Imparting expertise	Interactor ⇒ Recipient	80:20
Conversation	Interactor ⇔ Recipient	50:50
Counselling skills	Interactor ⇐ Recipient	20:80

the flow of the speaker but at the same time help the speaker more effectively address the issue that is concerning them. When counselling skills
are being used, an outside observer might notice that the recipient is
encouraged to take greater control of the agenda of the dialogue than in the
other styles of communication. The values implicit in the use of counselling
skills are similar to those of counselling which place an emphasis on the
client's capacity for self-determination in how help is sought as well as
for any decisions or actions that may result.

Other things, which might be apparent to an outside observer, would
be the way the recipient is encouraged or enabled to participate in deciding the agenda for the total transaction. So the values implicit in the
interactions are similar to those of counselling, which place an emphasis
on the client's capacity for self-determination.

The term 'skills' in 'counselling skills' is sometimes taken in a very literal
sense to mean 'discrete behaviours' but this is not the way the term 'skills' is
understood in the social sciences. Skills that are used to enhance relationships can be distinguished from 'physical skills' as in sport or work, and
'mental' and 'intellectual' skills not merely on the basis of observable behaviours. They are inextricably linked to the goal of the person using them. For
instance, Michael Argyle (1981) states, 'by socially skilled behaviour I mean
behaviour which is effective in realising the goals of the interactor'. In the
context of counselling skills, those goals are to implement the values of
counselling by assisting the self-expression and autonomy of the recipient.

One of the ways in which an independent observer might be able to
distinguish between 'counselling skills' and counselling is whether the
contracting is explicit between the two people. This is highlighted in one of
the alternative definitions of counselling which is still in popular use: 'People
become engaged in counselling when a person, occupying regularly or
temporarily the role of counsellor, offers or agrees explicitly to offer time,
attention or respect to another person or persons temporarily in the role
of client' (BAC, 1984). This definition was originally devised to distinguish

between spontaneous or *ad hoc* counselling and formal counselling. The overt nature of the latter, involving 'offers' and explicit agreements, was seen as 'the dividing line between the counselling task and the *ad hoc* counselling and is the major safeguard of the rights of the consumer' (BAC, 1985). The definition also provides a useful basis for distinguishing when someone is using counselling skills in a role other than that of counsellor or when they are counselling.

This set of views provides the basis for determining when counselling skills are being used. Counselling skills are being used:

- *when* there is intentional use of specific interpersonal skills which reflect the values of counselling;
- *and* when the practitioner's primary role (e.g. nurse, tutor, line manager, social worker, personnel officer, helper) is enhanced without being changed;
- *and* when the client perceives the practitioner as acting within their primary professional or caring role which is *not* that of being a counsellor.

The values of counselling would focus on respecting the client's values, experience, thoughts, feelings and their capacity for self-determination, and aiming to serve the best interests of the client.

There are three frequent misconceptions that I encounter in discussions about counselling skills. These are as follows:

Using counselling skills is always a lower-order activity than counselling This is not the case. Arguably, the user of counselling skills may be working under more demanding circumstances than the counsellor, who usually has the benefit of more extended periods of time which have already been agreed in advance. In comparison, the user of counselling skills may be working more opportunistically with much less certainty about the duration of the encounter. Users of counselling skills can be more or less skilled, just like counsellors. However, using counselling skills is not a role in itself but something important to enhance the performance of another role. This means that the capacity to use counselling skills effectively depends not only on being skilled in their use but also on someone's competence in their primary role, e.g. nurse, tutor. For all these reasons, some people may require a higher level of competence to use counselling skills than may be required in counselling. It certainly cannot be assumed that using counselling skills is a lower level of activity.

People in occupational roles, other than counsellor, cannot counsel   This would mean that doctors, nurses, youth workers, etc., cannot counsel but can only use counselling skills. This is not the case. With appropriate training, counselling supervision, and clear contracting with the client in ways consistent with counselling, it seems to me that anyone can change to taking on the role of 'counsellor'. There are important issues about keeping the boundaries between different roles clear and managing overlapping roles or dual relationships. But not all dual relationships are undesirable, provided the boundary between the relationships can be clearly identified and is respected by both the counsellor and client. Usually it is easier, whenever possible, to avoid the potential pitfalls of dual relationships by ensuring that the counsellor is independent of the provision of other services and other relationships, whether personal or professional, with the client.

Anyone with the occupational title 'counsellor' is always counselling   This is not the case. As the concept of counselling has narrowed down into a specifically contracted role, there is a need for 'counsellors' to distinguish between when they are counselling and when they are performing other roles, such as training, supervision or managing. In each of these other roles a counsellor is likely to be using counselling skills.

The distinction between counselling skills and counselling may have been helpful in pursuing the professionalization of counselling as a distinct role by distinguishing a more defined approach to counselling from situations where someone uses a more loosely defined approach to using counselling to support some other helping role, such as being a tutor, a health worker or other role that has its own identity and expertise. Professionally, within organizations like BACP, the creation of counselling skills provided the conceptual and political space to give better focused attention to what is entailed ethically to being a counsel-lor. The complications of other professional cultures and constraints could be set aside in order to concentrate on counselling as it was devel-oping, in all its variations, as a specialized service. Such distinctions can lead to unequal attention being given to each part so that one becomes favoured over the other and, in this case, one type of role, namely counselling, becomes more central to professional development than the other. This fragmenting of roles can have undesirable consequences. The process of defining and restricting professional identity, even if it is to advance ethical and professional standards, cannot avoid problems associated with becoming more exclusive and professionally inward-looking. The notion of the 'embedded counsellor' provides a substantial challenge to such exclusivity and may prove to be a useful remedy to any exaggerated sense of professional identity by redirecting attention to the extent to which counselling is used in its wider sense within so many other types of helping role and reaffirming the value of such work. John McLeod has written eloquently in favour of the embedded counsellor. He argues that it is socially and culturally important to explicitly acknowledge all the counselling that takes place in brief episodes embedded within other professional tasks (teaching, nursing, and career advice):

> I believe that it would be a good thing if teachers, nurses and other human service workers allowed themselves to respond to the emotional pain of their clients and listened to their personal stories. We live in a world characterized by an all-consuming drive towards efficiency and a bureaucratic approach to people. In this kind of world, a bit of counselling is humanizing factor. (McLeod, 2007)

The concept of the 'embedded counsellor' is a welcome development if it helps to rebuild links with other professions that may have been broken in the quest for a professional identity for counsellors and revives a shared focus on humanizing values that are so precious in everyday living. Approached in this way, the use of the label 'embedded counsellor' invites us to re-engage with the radical values that prompted the origins of counselling in ways that are relevant to current life.

Conclusion

The creation of a definition of counselling is difficult. 'Counselling' is a word and an activity that has several different meanings. Generally in society, it is used in many diverse and sometimes contradictory ways. It is important to distinguish between whether the term 'counselling' is being used to refer specifically to activities that fall within or outside the scope of the counselling movement and, more specifically, the use of the term 'counselling' by national professional counselling organizations. This distinction determines whether or not the role is subject to published ethical standards and guidelines. Even within these organizations, there are differences of view about whether counselling is a narrowly or more widely defined activity. The wider meaning refers to the groups of activities incorporating any or all of counselling skills, counselling, psychotherapy and psychoanalysis. Narrower definitions tend to differentiate between these activities and may assume a hierarchy in expertise and knowledge. The dual use of the same term in a narrow and wide usage is not unique to counselling. This practice recurs throughout the caring professions. Perhaps the greatest range is encompassed by the term 'social services', which in its narrow usage refers to specific social work agencies but may also be used to encompass social work, housing, education, health care and other provisions of the welfare state (Mays et al., 1975).

The potential for adapting counselling to new social contexts and needs is probably endless. One of the major current challenges for all British professional counselling organizations is the under-representation within their membership of the cultural diversity of the general population. There is also some evidence that the delivery of services is unevenly distributed across different sections of the population. As professional bodies and agencies grapple with these issues and how to make counselling more multicultural, it may be that they will also move towards a wider definition of counselling in order to incorporate greater cultural flexibility. Preliminary evidence from international conferences appears to suggest that some of the defining characteristics of counselling that are significant in Britain are less important or may even be inappropriate to other national contexts. For example, the importance attached to being non-directive, which is probably weakening in the British counselling movement as it is increasingly viewed as a characteristic of specific models of counselling rather than of counselling in general, may not even have been adopted in other cultures and national associations. International associations incorporate potential and actual diversity within counselling by adopting wider definitions of counselling than those generally adopted by national-specific counselling organizations. Where this occurs, the definition is expanded to incorporate activities and roles such as advice, guidance and possibly befriending. It may be that there will be a trend in a similar direction within the counselling movement in Britain. This would reverse a trend towards narrower definitions of the role, which, in comparison to the international counselling movement, have been more preoccupied with the therapeutic aspects of counselling rather than its social and its educational potential.

Definitions of counselling are not permanent or universal. Counselling is a term that is being used in different ways within society in general and within the national and international counselling movement. The only way of communicating clearly about counselling is to clarify the intended meaning from the outset. Not to do so risks confusion about what is considered appropriate to a particular role. Counselling is used in this book to refer to a role and type of activity delivered in accordance with professional standards that emphasize the ethical significance of enabling clients to increase their capacity to act for themselves and to gain an improved sense of personal well-being.

3

Sources of Counselling Ethics

The construction of counselling ethics is fundamentally a social process, which draws upon many different sources of ethical insight. Sometimes these sources are compatible but this is not always the case. Differences between current concerns and contexts may lead to different views. Careful consideration of any divergences in ethical direction is usually the best way forward in developing an ethical position. Such a position is usually most secure when many sources coincide in reaching the same conclusion. Each of the sources can be regarded as a different kind of ethical narrative which counsellors draw upon in their response to very specific situations with their clients as well as in the production of collectively agreed statements about ethical standards.

In my research and at training workshops, I am interested in asking counsellors to identify ethical issues or dilemmas that arise in their work and how they resolve them. It has been my experience that counsellors generally draw upon a selection of six sources. These are: (1) personal ethics, (2) ethics implicit in therapeutic models, (3) agency policy, (4) professional codes, frameworks and guidelines, (5) moral philosophy and (6) law. The urgency of a situation may restrict the choice to one or two sources and greater leisure may expand the choice beyond six. In these circumstances, presenting six sources rather than any other number is somewhat arbitrary. The list could easily have been expanded to include religious and political sources or contracted to exclude moral philosophy. My reason for excluding the former two is the sense that the direct influence of any religious and political source tends to be downplayed by counsellors in the interests of respecting their clients' values. As a consequence, religious and political beliefs tend to be included within the counsellor's personal ethics and values. My reason for including moral philosophy is based on my observation of ethical discussions involving counsellors. It is apparent that when ideas derived from moral philosophy have been mentioned they are valued as a source of language and concepts for articulating ethical issues. It would be difficult to have a credible professional ethic that did not take into account insights derived from moral philosophy. The six ethical sources of counselling ethics are represented in Figure 3.1.

After making some preliminary observations about each of them I will consider the relationship between these sources and the construction of ethical frameworks.

Personal Ethics

Taking on a professional role may create a tension between personal ethics and those that you consider appropriate to your role. This is most evident if you consider how you would respond to a friend or a client in similar circumstances. What may seem ethical in one relationship may seem inappropriate in the other.

One clear example comes to mind. A counsellor who learnt that a friend was considering dating someone with a serious infectious illness considered how he had discovered that information. If he had learnt about the risk of infection from social conversation, he would feel entitled to warn his friend. On the other hand, if he had discovered it from his work, he would feel obliged to remain silent. This dichotomy of ethical responses can be very uncomfortable and can raise fundamental choices between personal and professional integrity. However, the degree of separation between personal and professional ethics is probably an inevitable part of adapting to a specialized role and taking into account the collective ethic of other members of that profession.

Counsellors who seem most at ease with this dichotomy appear to recognize a distinction between their personal and professional ethic but have integrated both ethics in a deeper sense of self. As a consequence, a potentially contradictory dichotomy is more likely to be experienced as complementary aspects of the same person, whether that person is viewing themselves from the inside or is viewed from the outside by others. Where this is the case, the sense of overall integrity will be high

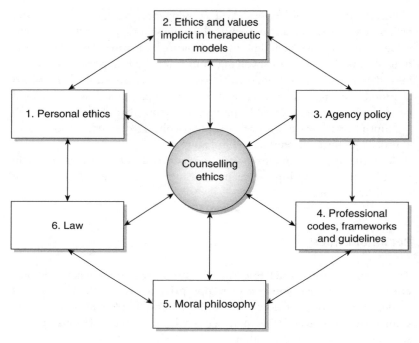

FIGURE 3.1   *Sources of professional ethics*

and will enrich the ethical dimension of counselling. This sense of integration may be a goal to work towards, rather than something to be taken for granted. It may be that for many of us life is too short to resolve these dichotomies totally. Our integrity will then rest on our openness to the possibility of new learning and insights that will help us towards greater personal integration. Ultimately, the ethical responsibility of counsellors is both personal and professional. But the construction of a personal ethic does not take place in a social vacuum: it is influenced and supported by other ethical sources.

Ethics and Values Implicit in Therapeutic Models

Our choice of therapeutic orientation will have ethical implications. Therapeutic models are usually produced to serve therapeutic ends rather than as exercises in secular ethics. Nonetheless, they incorporate ethical orientations and beliefs, usually implicitly. The choice of therapeutic model may be a source of insight into your personal ethical predisposition. A comparison between person–centred and psychodynamic counselling will illustrate this point. Carl Rogers, the founder of person–centred counselling, emphasized the client's capacity for self-determination. Counselling is not viewed as a process of doing something *to* the individual, or inducing him to do something about himself. Rather, it is freeing him for personal growth and development and from obstacles so that he can again move forward. The core conditions of congruence, empathy and unconditional positive regard are simultaneously both an affirmation of client autonomy and a constraint on the counsellor's direct influence on that autonomy. The client is not only assumed to have an innate capacity for growth, but is also the expert on how to achieve this. In contrast, a Freudian psychodynamic model vests the counsellor with a higher level of expertise in the alleviation of distress in the client, partially through a greater awareness of the influence of the unconscious. The therapeutic theory is based on psychological determinism in which a causal link between past experience and present psychology is assumed. The ultimate goal of achieving client autonomy may be shared with the person–centred counsellor but the route to achieving that end is different. The counsellor uses her expertise within an ethic of welfare in which she assumes responsibility for assessing what is in the client's best interests in order to alleviate distress and enhance insight. It is also assumed that the trained psychodynamic counsellor is better placed to detect the links between past and present experience than the untrained client. Other therapies that rely on therapeutic expertise to alleviate distress, such as cognitive, systemic and some humanistic approaches, tend towards an ethic of welfare, i.e. the counsellor knows what is psychotherapeutically best for the client and is required to use that knowledge for the benefit of the client. In contrast, person–centred models and other approaches that are optimistic about accessibility of personal insights, such as transactional analysis, tend towards an ethic of autonomy, i.e. the client is considered to know what is best for them in the context of their life and experience. Once these associations with different ethical approaches are acknowledged, it becomes much easier to question whether inbuilt ethical biases are appropriate. Person–centred counsellors may find themselves working with clients who, for one reason or another, have considerable difficulty in working within an ethic of autonomy and respond better to a transitional phase in which the counsellor works within an ethic of welfare. Conversely, a psychodynamic counsellor may have a client who is more appropriately counselled within the ethic of autonomy.

The recent rise of cognitive-behavioural counselling is driven by a combination of values concerning beliefs about the importance of scientific knowledge and evidence in planning publicly funded services and making scarce resources available to the greatest number of people. Brief and time-limited therapy may be more open to other approaches to therapeutic models but typically shares a concern to make the best use of limited resources. However, it is wise not to take the values behind any therapeutic movement as unquestionable truths, and even if the values appear justifiable they may not match the 'facts' or results of what happens in the implementation of those values. The facts are often more friendly and mutually inclusive of different thera-peutic orientations than any analysis based on differences in values might suggest (Cooper, 2008). Like many other people, I have a sponta-neous attraction to or repulsion from therapeutic models that are not part of my usual repertoire. I have learnt to question these reactions before joining in the tribal warfare that can surround therapeutic differences. Most often I find that my strength of attraction or repul-sion is about protecting my own identity or loyalty to others with whom I strongly identify. Just occasionally it is fear of addressing something in myself that I have been able to leave undisturbed until I encountered a different approach to therapy. In such situations I am confronted with the uncomfortable truth that my values, which I intend for doing good, may also be self-serving mechanisms to defend me against less comfortable personal insights.

I take two things from my reflections about the values implicit in a therapeutic model. First, values ought not to be taken for granted or adopted unquestioningly. Our preferred choice of therapeutic model and its implicit values provides important insights into ourselves as counsel-lors which are well worth periodic reflection and self-examination. Secondly, from a client's point of view, the values inherent in our partic-ular approach to therapy will shape their therapeutic journey for good or bad. An unexamined value may become dangerous or counterpro-ductive as an unacknowledged cause of the client's therapeutic strug-gle. Unexamined values can set counsellors against their clients just as easily as therapist against therapist. Once value differences can be openly acknowledged and discussed, it becomes easier to find points of human contact and mutual understanding even if agreement cannot be reached. Although the implicit ethical bias of a therapeutic model ought not to be accepted unquestioningly, it is one of the ethical compass points to guide us through the complexities of providing counselling and therapy.

Agency Policy

If a counsellor works within an agency, it is commonplace to be required to follow specific protocols and procedures with regard to some ethical and therapeutic dilemmas. For example, many agencies have adopted a policy that child protection takes precedence over individual client confidentiality. It is not unusual to find that observance of these policies is a term in the counsellor's contract of employment or that volunteer counsellors are asked to give a written undertaking to observe certain policies.

A precise evaluation of the appropriateness of individual policies will need to take into account the context in which the agency provides its services, its range of clients and their needs as well as the organizational ethos of the agency. I will concentrate on the last of these, as the other factors are the subject matter of most of the following chapters. The expansion of the availability of counselling means that it is provided by a whole variety of agencies: some dedicated exclusively to providing counselling and others where the counsellor may be a single person working alongside several different professions providing a variety of services (e.g. counselling in primary health care) or a single profession providing a highly regulated service (i.e. in schools). Sarah Banks, in a groundbreaking study of ethics and values in social work, makes a useful distinction between different models of practice (see Table 3.1). The professional model is characterized by a high degree of client and counsellor autonomy. It would be fairly typical of a group of counsellors working in private practice. The committed/radical model is founded on a relationship of equals working together as allies to overcome personal difficulties or social disadvantages. It is typical of counsellors working within community and self-help projects. Both these models probably fit easily with counselling ethics. I have also seen counsellors in health care, education and employment assistance programmes employed on this basis. On the other hand, I have seen counsellors undertaking comparable work in these settings within the bureaucratic model. The characteristic of this model is that both counsellor and client hold relatively little power in comparison to the counsellor's obligation to follow

TABLE 3.1 *Models of practice*

	Committed/radical	**Professional**	**Bureaucratic**
Social work as	vocation/social movement	profession	job
Social worker as	equal/ally	professional	technician/ official
Power from	competence to deal with situation	professional expertise	organizational role
Service user as	equal/ally	client	consumer
Focus on	individual or group empowerment/societal change	individual worker– user relationship	service provision
Guidance from	personal commitment/ ideology	professional code of ethics	agency rules and procedures
Key principles	empathy, genuineness/ raising consciousness, collective action	users' rights to self-determination, acceptance, confidentiality, etc.	agency duties to distribute resources fairly and to promote public good
Organizational setting that would best facilitate this	independent voluntary agency or campaigning group	private practice or large degree of autonomy in agency	bureaucratic agency in voluntary, statutory or private sector

Source: Banks (2006) *Ethics and Values in Social Work*. Basingstoke: Palgrave Macmillan. Reproduced with the permission of the British Association of Social Workers and the author.

rules and procedures. State-sponsored services are most likely to be required to work in this mode, which is widely used in education and social work.

Sarah Banks has specialized in ethics for social work and youth workers. She makes a useful distinction between social workers working to serve different goals and from within different models of social work. Table 3.1 distinguishes between social workers who adopt committed/radical, professional and bureaucratic models of practice. It is possible to see parallel distinctions in counselling. Many of the counsellors most concerned about forthcoming statutory regulation fear losing their radical agendas for the people they serve and becoming co-opted into a profession or simply becoming bureaucrats. I think the table is helpful in distinguishing the attention given to the control over the way of working and the outcome. This is strongest in the radical/committed, weakened in the professional and superseded by a centrally determined sense of what is good for the client in the bureaucratic approaches. There are corresponding shift in power between the client, counsellor and agency in each of these positions. It is not unusual for counsellors working in a bureaucratic position to experience conflicts between what their clients consider to be appropriate and what is required of the counsellor.

Professional Codes, Frameworks and Guidelines

Professional codes, frameworks and guidelines are a valuable source of ethical information. They will be the first points of reference for many counsellors. At their best, these documents are a source of collective wisdom validated by a process of consultation and voting during their adoption procedures by the organization that produced them. They often represent a distillation of ethical and legal principles because, even if a code makes no explicit reference to the law, most reputable professional organizations will have sought legal clearance from a lawyer before issuing the code. However, it is the distilled quality of these ethical statements that is also their greatest limitation.

Codes and ethical guidance tends to be written in fairly general and abstract terms in order to condense the experience and thinking behind them and to make them as widely applicable to a variety of circumstances as possible. This means that they are unlikely to be read for their literary quality or narrative pull. Unfortunately, this discourages some people from reading them in advance of an ethical dilemma. This is a pity because the urgency and emotional turmoil surrounding a crisis makes this an inauspicious occasion to read a code for the first time. They are complex documents with many interrelated provisions and need to be understood as a whole before the significance of any of the parts can be fully appreciated. In my experience, moments of high drama tend to complicate gaining an overall understanding of the contents of a code. Counsellors in an ethical crisis tend to clutch at clauses, as drowning men are said to clutch at straws. Extracted from their context, these clauses of comfort can be quite misleading, especially if that is all that someone is relying on.

It is much better to be familiar with relevant codes before the crisis occurs. Often, prior knowledge will enable the crisis to be averted because most ethical guidance forewarns the reader about potential areas of difficulty. Even if the dilemma is not averted, this prior knowledge will usually assist in the interpretation of relevant passages.

One rather off-putting characteristic of codes, perhaps the most authoritative form of ethical guidance, is their tendency to be peppered by 'shoulds' and 'oughts'. These directives sit uneasily with counselling and sometimes seems like a professional organization importing a bureaucratic model into an ethos that tends to be less authoritarian and better adapted to a professional or radical model (see above). Personally, I have preferred to write ethical guidance as frameworks, rather like metaphorical scaffolding in which practitioners can position themselves differently within an overall structure of shared understanding and ethical commitment (see BACP, 2007). The weakening of the authoritative voice is compensated for by greater inclusiveness across human differences and opportunities to take contextual variations into account in resolving ethical challenges.

However, the reality is that any ethical guidance will often be used as the basis for complaints procedures against members of that organization. (No organization known to me will hear complaints against non-members.) To breach the terms of a code by which you are contractually bound is a serious matter and can lead to a formal complaint. However, the level of obligation is seldom such, in my opinion, as to justify blind compliance. That would undermine the ethical basis of the counselling relationship, as it prioritizes the code as more important than the human relationship. Indeed, there may be occasions when the more ethical response is to breach the code, for carefully considered reasons. Some professional practice codes recognize that such dilemmas may occur, inviting the counsellor to carefully evaluate and consider their position.

It strengthens the ethical basis for breaching the code if the counsellor is prepared to enter into a dialogue with the professional body so that the ethical basis of the decision can be examined and, when appropriate, the code can be revised to accommodate the ethical difficulty. The ultimate ethical responsibility must rest with the individual counsellor and her personal and professional judgement. Someone who conscientiously breaches a provision of their professional code for carefully considered ethical reasons is in a much better ethical position than someone who breaches a code through ignorance or reckless disregard of its provisions. Codes, framework and guidelines do not eliminate the need for ethical awareness in interpreting how they apply to particular circumstances. It is salutary to remember that most ethical guidance is seldom comprehensive. For example, most counselling codes are relatively silent about working with young people, in comparison to counselling adults, although this is gradually changing. Ethical guidance can seldom be definitive. It cannot override legal obligations, at least in the eyes of the law. Guidance is also ephemeral, as all codes are periodically revised and updated in response to changes in social circumstances and working practices. However, there is often a time lag between these developments and their incorporation within ethical guidance or requirements issued by any professional body.

In the next chapter I will undertake a detailed analysis of four guidelines produced by national organizations.

Moral Philosophy

Moral philosophy is primarily concerned with identifying what constitutes 'good' and 'bad' and using logical reasoning to consider the implications for ethical dilemmas. A subsidiary area of moral philosophy is professional ethics: this is a rapidly growing discipline within moral philosophy, which also draws on other sources from social sciences and the law. The main focus of professional ethics is an interest in the application of core values that constitute an integral part of professional identity.

Medical ethics are probably the most highly developed professional ethics. The long history and academic ethos of medicine have combined to produce some of the most sophisticated approaches to constructing professional ethical systems and in training professionals in how to combine ethical with technical aspects of their work. Not surprisingly, there is a proliferation of approaches, which reflects the diversity of ethical models within moral philosophy. In Europe and North America, this has typically taken the form of competition between deontological ethics (i.e. ethics of duty and obligation) founded on the ideas of Immanuel Kant (1724–1804) and utilitarian ethics based on the writing of David Hume (1711–76), Jeremy Bentham (1748–1832) and John Stuart Mill (1806–73). The deontological approach is based on deducing ethical obligations from a particular set of beliefs about the nature of reality. These obligations are viewed as universal and can be typified by an emphasis on treating people as ends in themselves. In contrast, the utilitarian approach is founded on an evaluation of the consequences of any action and can be typified by a commitment to achieving 'the greatest good for the greatest number'. The choice between the two systems can be represented as a choice between viewing people as ends in themselves or as means to an end.

The competition between these two ethical approaches has produced several other major responses. One of these has grown out of a critique of the first two as being too founded in the male experience of being an unencumbered individual. This stands in contrast to the female experience of living with the dependency of children, the sick and the elderly. This view of the female experience of ethical responsibility for others has led to the creation of an 'ethic of care', which focuses on the moral implications of the interconnectedness of people. The fourth major approach to current ethics shifts attention from principles to the moral qualities of the person. This has led to a revival of virtue ethics founded on the writing of Aristotle (384–322 BC), which views ethical action as growing out of personal qualities or virtues and is sometimes also referred to as contemplative ethics. Another approach is not so much a single ethic but a group of approaches founded on postmodern doubt that it is possible to produce a universal ethic. From this point of view, ethics are therefore not defined by the production of a distinctive ethical system but by a commitment to engaging in mutually respectful discussion from which ethics appropriate to that context can be constructed. These approaches are sometimes referred to as communicative or narrative ethics.

The existence of these different approaches (and many others) has been a major challenge and stimulus to professional ethics in ways that are analogous to the interaction between the major therapeutic traditions within counselling. There have been those who have taken a philosophically strong approach by arguing that one model is both universally applicable and ethically superior to all others. Others have taken a less dogmatic approach and have sought to draw upon aspects of different models appropriate to specific ethical issues and rejected any hastily reached simplicity in ethics. The most influential ethicists of this kind in medical ethics are Tom Beauchamp and James Childress (2008). Their *Principles of Biomedical Ethics*, now in its sixth edition, has had a major influence on the development of ethical principles for counselling and psychotherapy. They propose four major ethical principles:

- respect for individual autonomy (literally self-government);
- beneficence (a commitment to benefiting the client);
- non-maleficence (avoiding harm to the client);
- justice (a fair distribution of services within society).

It is this combination of principles that is most widely referred to in literature about ethics for counsellors. However, Andrew Thompson, in *A Guide to Ethical Practice in Psychotherapy* (1990), adds a further two principles:

- fidelity (honouring the promises upon which the trust between client and counsellor is founded);
- self-interest (the counsellor's entitlement to all the preceding five principles).

The addition of fidelity as a moral principle is highly compatible with counselling and signals the importance of 'trust' and being 'trustworthy'. This seems an obvious addition that increases the relevance of a collection of principles to counselling. In contrast, Thompson acknowledges that the addition of 'self-interest' is controversial. Nonetheless, he argues strongly for the inclusion of this principle by a combination of ethical and psychological reasoning. He takes the view that self-interest is invariably present in ethical decision-making and can be a distorting influence when it is left as an unacknowledged factor. His reasoning corresponds so closely to my experience as a counsellor that I find it completely convincing. The power of unacknowledged factors in personal decision-making is much greater when they remain unspoken and therefore have a disproportionate and indeterminate influence on the decision-making process.

The use of a combination of ethical principles as a basis for professional ethics has many strengths. The principles act as vehicles for disseminating a terminology and way of approaching ethical problems which takes an integrationist approach to many of the major contemporary ethical models. They act as a metaphorical bridgehead between the different disciplines of moral philosophy and counselling. Arguably, they provide counsellors with a greater level of ethical sophistication than they would be likely to develop by simply reflecting on the ethical dilemmas of their role from a purely practical perspective. In my view, the usefulness of any model for professionals is determined by a combination of two factors that exist in tension with each other. There needs to be sufficient complexity to accommodate a wide range of applications, but also sufficient simplicity for these to be readily recalled and applied by a busy practitioner. The application of the principles by Thompson has that combination of sufficient complexity and simplicity to be useful to counsellors whose primary concern is not moral philosophy but practical ethics.

The presentation of moral philosophy as principles also matches the bureaucratic needs of professional organizations. Principles provide a convenient method for focusing the membership's attention on the rationale for the collective ethic to which they are bound as well as a readily usable method of regulation and adjudication. There is a potentially closer relationship between the expression of individual and collective ethics than would be the case in other approaches to moral philosophy. These positive aspects of the expression of professional ethics in terms of a series of principles has led to some counselling organizations actually promoting them as a method for ethical insight. However, principles are not always easily transferable across cultures.

The New Zealand Association of Counsellors explicitly incorporated these five principles within its 'Code of Ethics' (NZAC, 1998) and has substantially replaced them in the latest 2005 version. The explicit adoption of these principles within a code of ethics that services counsellors in two very different cultures, white European and Maori, disadvantaged one of them. The principles are reasonably acceptable to a modern Westernized culture with an emphasis on individual responsibility, but are almost incomprehensible to a traditional Maori culture where the unit of moral reference is not the individual but the family and the community. This sense of communal identity and morality is conveyed by the phrase 'You hurt my brother, you hurt me.' It is one of the paradoxes of the application of these principles that they provide an ethical basis for a modern Westernized person to relate respectfully to another culture. However, they cannot by themselves form an adequate basis for an ethic of multiculturalism because they do not transfer readily to traditional cultures. This is a significant limitation which suggests that this approach may have to be revised or replaced where counselling becomes a multicultural or global activity. For the moment, the use of a combination of ethical principles remains probably one of the more useful applications of moral philosophy to counselling. However, as ethics for counselling becomes more sophisticated it is likely that other ethical models will become more prominent.

Partly as result of my longstanding interest in the significance of relationship in counselling and the ethical challenges posed by cultural differences in identity and ethical points of reference, I have been turning my attention to a relational ethic based on trust and being trustworthy. I will say more about these developments in the final chapter.

Law

The privacy of most counselling relationships may seem to justify a belief that the law is largely irrelevant to counsellors. This is an illusion. The counsellor and client alike are citizens within a national, and increasingly international, system of law. Being aware of the law has a number of potential gains. Frequently, the law and counselling practice are mutually compatible. A legally well-informed counsellor is best placed to use the law to protect the rights and responsibilities associated with their work. Counsellors seeing fee-paying clients ought to be aware of the law of contract, which can be used to support the counselling relationship and clarify both parties' expectations of each other. Ignorance of the law can be correspondingly undermining and introduce unexpected and unwelcome surprises. For instance, in the absence of a clear contractual agreement between client and counsellor, a court may imply a contractual term. Counsellors seeing non-fee-paying clients have greater difficulty in establishing the legal basis of their relationship and may be subject to greater legal uncertainty. Nonetheless, following the principle that to be forewarned is to be forearmed, all counsellors would be well advised to have at least a basic familiarity with the law concerning contract, negligence, defamation, confidentiality, the protection and disclosure of records and acting as a witness (in civil, criminal and coroner's courts) (see Bond and Sandhu, 2005; Bond and Mitchels, 2008). Depending on the type of work undertaken by the counsellor, it may also be appropriate to consider the law concerning mental health, families and young people. Obtaining this kind of information is becoming progressively easier as new publications appear.

One of the difficulties posed by the law for counsellors is its complexity and the potential for seemingly contradictory legal provisions. Some basic principles of law go a long way towards easing this problem. The law is a hierarchical system. Statute law passed as legislation by Parliament overrides all other kinds of law. In the absence of any statutes, the law may have been created by a system of case law, in which the legal principles developed by the most senior court bind all those below it. Policies adopted by government departments have no legal standing unless they are supported by statute. The courts frequently make the point that government policy by itself is not legally enforceable and that the government has the means at its disposal to make it enforceable if it is so minded.

- Use the most up-to-date law.
- Distinguish between the relevant legislation and case law, as the former overrides the latter.
- Check the legal basis for public or agency policy, especially if this impacts on the relationship between service users and service provider. Following policy alone may lead to acting unlawfully. Be particularly wary of old policy. Up-to-date policy in a legally informed setting is a more reliable guide.
- Seek advice from a lawyer on important issues.

FIGURE 3.2 *Making sense of the law*

It is also important to realize that any contractual term that conflicts with either statute or common law (a form of case law) is unenforceable. This is particularly significant with regard to confidentiality and working with suicidal clients (see Chapters 7 and 10). Another common mistake is to assume that what is good law in one organization automatically applies to all others doing similar work. The legal bases of public sector, commercial and voluntary organizations are quite different. Public bodies can only do what they are authorized to do by statute so may have obligations which would not apply to other kinds of organization. It is also not unusual to find very different kinds of powers and obligations applying to different public bodies. It is commonplace to find that the legal obligations held by social services concerning child protection are wrongly thought to apply to other types of organization. As always in the law, the devil is in the detail, but in Figure 3.2 I have attempted to summarize some basic principles for making sense of the law.

Conclusion

One of my reasons for drawing attention to different sources of ethical insights which are useful in counselling is to challenge the notion that simply relying on a combination of professional code(s) or guidelines and a sense of personal morality is a sufficient basis for ethical standards in counselling. Codes and guidelines are important but in my view they are no longer adequate to meet the personal, social and legal challenge that many counsellors may encounter in their work. The law is an increasingly significant source that needs to be taken into account as it represents a form of national morality within a democracy. Moral philosophy provides a basis for re-evaluating many of the 'taken for granted' aspects of the law and professional guidelines as well as the values implicit within therapeutic models.

As counsellors, we are privileged to witness the moral struggles of our clients as they search for the right thing to do or for moral meaning in what is happening to them. Most of the time, the moral dilemma can be appropriately regarded as falling within the client's responsibility but there are times when the client's moral dilemma creates the possibility of a professional ethical dilemma for the counsellor. A few examples drawn from suitably disguised real-life events will illustrate this point:

- A school counsellor has been approached by a 13-year-old pupil for counselling about family problems. The pupil's teacher supports the counselling but her parents have expressly forbidden the pupil to receive counselling.
- Connie is seven months pregnant and has deeply held beliefs in favour of natural childbirth and against medical intervention. These feelings are being expressed by a refusal to accept a Caesarean delivery in order to protect both the foetus and herself from the consequences of dangerously high blood pressure. She has no illusions about the seriousness of her situation after nearly dying from similar complications in an earlier pregnancy. She has sought counselling to help her resist increasingly insistent offers of medical help.
- Simon is a student in a residential hall. He had become aware that someone living next door to him is heavily involved in selling illegal drugs because people are knocking on his door in error. He has decided not to report the drug dealing but has requested a transfer of rooms to avoid the disturbance from some quite persistent visitors who call at anti-social hours. The student counsellor who saw Simon is aware that the college is seriously concerned to prevent drug use on its premises but Simon is insisting on confidentiality.

Each of these issues posed complex challenges for the ethical standards of the counsellors concerned which could not simply be resolved by a combination of innate personal morality and the published ethical requirements of their respective professional bodies. A securely based ethical decision needs to take into account insights derived from all the sources considered in this chapter. A counsellor's ability to respond ethically and constructively is considerably enhanced by the extent to which she has already actively incorporated these sources into the ethical framework that informs her everyday arrangements with clients. The outline of that framework is given in the next chapter.

4

Framework for Counselling Ethics and Standards

An ethical framework creates a basic conceptual structure within which we can all feel safe and supported to move around freely and make choices. There is enough of a structure to define the available choices and give a sense of distinguishing what is ethically acceptable from the unacceptable or unwise. This can provide essential support and a sense of direction when feeling overwhelmed with ethical uncertainty. On the other hand, the framework creates sufficient spaces to accommodate legitimate differences of opinion. These are spaces where counsellors can position themselves in ways that fit a sense of personal and professional integrity and take account of the needs of clients. The potential for moving around a framework builds in a degree of flexibility that permits changes in position as circumstances change.

> Mutually agreed ethics and acceptable standards of practice in any profession provide the bedrock whereby those practitioners and clients are safeguarded and served within a defined framework and agreed boundaries. In this way the professional search for integrity and credibility is validated. (COSCA, 2009)

This statement draws attention to another aspect of ethical frameworks. They are often the product of collective agreement and endorsed by the members of a profession or professional organization. The most direct sources of the framework are the published codes and guidelines. This chapter is primarily an analysis of the ethical requirements of five major national counselling organizations within the British Isles:

- British Association for Counselling and Psychotherapy (BACP);
- United Kingdom Council for Psychotherapy (UKCP);
- Counselling Psychology Division of the British Psychological Society (BPS);
- Confederation of Scottish Counselling Agencies (COSCA);
- Irish Association for Counselling and Psychotherapy (IACP).

Each of these sources of guidance has been formally adopted by the professional organization as a set of minimum ethical standards that are viewed as important guidance for members. Failure to work within that guidance would be regarded as a legitimate source of concern about the ethical practice of a counsellor which in serious cases could lead to a disciplinary hearing or expulsion from membership.

Comparison between the Statements of Ethical Standards

A comparison between the statements of ethics published by the four national associations reveals considerable consensus around what are the core ethical issues for counsellors (see Table 4.1). All the major professional bodies emphasize a number of ethical concerns:

- client safety;
- professional competence and fitness to practise;
- respect for differences in lifestyles and beliefs between clients;
- respect for client self-determination;
- prohibitions on exploitation of clients;
- contracting;
- confidentiality;
- duty to maintain the profession's reputation.

The ethical touchstone around which all other concerns are organized is the client. It is easy to lose sight of the client because much of the content of ethical guidance concerns counsellor behaviour, but this focus on counsellor behaviour is directed to enhancing respect for clients and protecting them from harm. The emphasis on working with

TABLE 4.1 *Requirements*

Requirements	BACP	BPS	COSCA	IACP	UKCP
Accuracy in statements about qualifications/professional competence	O	O	Implied	O	O
Accuracy in advertising and information about services offered	O	O	O	O	O
Therapist competence					
• working within limits of competence	O	O	O	O	Implied
• adequate training and experience	O	O	O	O	Implied
• CPD to update practice	O	O	O	O	O
• regular monitoring and review of practice	O	O	O	O	Implied
Fitness to practice	O	O	O	O	Implied
Indemnity insurance					
Membership	R	R			O
Accreditation requirements	O				O
Client safety protection	O	O	O	O	Implied
Respect for client autonomy					
• Working with client's consent	O	O	O	O	O
• Non-exploitative	O	O	O	O	O
• Management of dual relationships	O	O	Implied	O	Implied
• Non-discriminatory	O	O	Implied	O	Implied
Conflicts of interest					
Prohibition of taking on working relationship with clients when there is prior knowledge which might cause a conflict of interest	Implied		O	R	Implied
Inform client					
• in advance	O		Implied	Implied	
• as soon as apparent	O		O	O	
Take to supervision	Implied		O	O	
Equal opportunities and non-discrimination	O		O	O	Implied

TABLE 4.1 *(Continued)*

Requirements	BACP	BPS	COSCA	IACP	UKCP
Contracting					
• Clarity about terms	O	O	O	O	O
• Terms communicated in advance or at outset of working relationship	O	O	O	O	O
• Periodic opportunities to review	O		O	O	Implied
Arrangements for breaks and endings	O		O	O	
Confidentiality					
Importance emphasized	O	O	O	O	O
Any limitations to be communicated:					
• in advance	O	O		Implied	
• at client's request			Implied	O	
Sharing information with other professionals requires:					
• client consent or law requires/permits	O	O	O	O	O
• assessment of client interest	O	O	O	Implied	O
• endeavour to inform client where appropriate	R	Implied	O	Implied	
• breach confidentiality only where serious concern about health or safety (client or others) or to prevent serious harm	O	O	O	O	O
Awareness, understanding and consideration of legal requirements and obligations	O	Implied	O	O	O
Supervision					
Regular	O	Where indicated	O	O	
Ongoing	O	Where indicated	O	O	
Not reveal client identity in supervision unless with client consent	Implied	Implied	O	O	

(Continued)

TABLE 4.1   *(Continued)*

Requirements	BACP	BPS	COSCA	IACP	UKCP
Research					
• Integrity in treatment of data	O	O		O	
• Clarity of agreement with participants	O	O		O	
• Consent required: client right to refuse participation	O	O		O	O
• Participant identity to be protected	O	O		O	
• Methods compatible with good standards of counselling and psychotherapy	O	O			
Policy about maintaining reputation of profession					
Serious breach of Code of Ethics or Practice to be reported	O		O		O
Where colleague's behaviour detrimental to profession and discussion has not resolved matters, report to complaints committee/ institute complaints procedure	O	O	O	O	O
Record-keeping	O Unless adequate reasons not to	O	R Information provided about record-keeping	O	
Work environment:					
• safety		Implied	O	O	
• privacy		Implied	O	O	
• avoidance of harassment		O	Implied	Implied	

Sources: BACP (2007), COSCA (2008), BPS (2005), UKCP (2005), IACP (1998)
Key: O = Obligatory R = Recommended
Note: As each professional code covers slightly different aspects of therapy, each expressed in different terms, it is impossible to make precise comparisons. This table is simply an interpretative reflection on common themes within these codes of ethics. Some of the organizations produce additional guidance on specific topics, for example, teaching, supervision, research and other themes, which are not included in this interpretation.

a client's consent and prohibitions on the exploitation of clients is a common theme with all the professional bodies. This in turn influences the management of core issues such as contracting with clients and confidentiality, where an emphasis on working with client consent is the established norm on all ethically significant issues unless there is concern about harm to the client or others.

My intuitive sense is that a greater degree of consensus has grown between the bodies in recent years over what is ethically beneficial behaviour and what is considered unacceptable. This is partly due to each process of revision of ethical guidance having the benefit of seeing how other associations have revised their versions, but also the influence of European law where professional ethics and human rights overlap. Multiple membership also encourages harmonization. Some counsellors belong to more than one professional body and draw attention to inconsistencies between requirements rather than be subjected to contradictory obligations. All these factors combine to promote consistency across the professional bodies in the ways in which they approach ethical requirements. Where differences exist, they increasingly tend to be found in the detail of particular requirements. For example, there are subtle differences over the communication to clients of any limitations to confidentiality or sharing information with other professionals. The extent to which there should be an ethical requirement that clients ought to be informed in advance about sharing information with other professionals varies between a strict obligation (COSCA), a strong recommendation (BACP) or an implied but unspecified obligation (BPS and IACP). This probably reflects differences in types of service and how they have adapted to different settings and client needs. The guiding principle across all professional bodies is acting on the basis of an assessment of the client's best interests in ways that respect client autonomy.

The area of greatest difference with significance for everyday practice concerns record-keeping. Counselling psychologists have an obligation to 'keep appropriate records' (BPS, 2006: s. 1.2 (i)) and to ensure that the 'nature and purpose of records kept and the clients right of access will be made clear [to clients] at the outset of the contract' (BPS, 2005: s. 1.4). Counsellors who are members of BACP are under a general obligation to keep records as a part of good quality of care, although this is not an absolute obligation as it applies 'unless there are adequate reasons not to do so' (BACP, 2007: s. 5). The reasons that would be adequate for not keeping records are not specified. COSCA recommends that records are kept and IACP requires safeguards if records are made. All professional bodies require that any records that are kept are stored securely and their confidentiality is adequately protected. These differences may be greater in the way that they are expressed than in actual practice.

New Developments in Counselling Practice

New developments in counselling practice create new ethical challenges. One of the major new developments is the rapid growth of online counselling using a wide variety of means of communication from text messaging, secure chat rooms, webcam and email. The internet provides a seemingly endlessly expanding range of possibilities which opens up counselling to a much bigger variety of providers and users.

Most of the services of which I am aware appear to be provided by therapists and counsellors who are already trained in more traditional face-to-face work and are expanding their range to include online services. It will take time for these developments to be incorporated into the ethical frameworks of the national professional bodies. Specialist organizations tend to be able to respond more quickly. For example, the Association for Counselling and Therapy Online (ACTO) has developed a Code of Ethics which directs attention to some of the issues which focus on:

- taking the differences between online and face-to-face work into account;
- ensuring clients are suitable for online work;
- recognizing issues of competence and requirements for supervision and continuing professional development;
- appropriate contracting with clients;
- adequate security and privacy for the work;
- the importance of working with attention to issues of consent;
- avoiding exploitation of clients.

In many ways, these are the familiar and well-established ethical concerns that have been restated to meet the challenges of a new range of methods of communication between counsellor and client.

Conclusion

When a professional body publishes a code or ethical framework, it is usually intended for a wide range of people, agencies and organizations. First, any statement of ethics is for the benefit of clients whose interests and rights are being drawn to the attention of the professional. Even though the protection of clients' interests are so foundational, it is ironic that they are least likely to read them in advance of receiving counselling. The primary audience is the members of the professional body who commit themselves to observing the ethical guidance as a condition of membership and may be required to be accountable for any breach in grievance or disciplinary hearings. The third audience is other professionals working alongside counsellors in interdisciplinary teams. They may wish to be informed about the ethical framework to which their colleagues are committed. The fourth audience is the range of gatekeepers and stakeholders in society, such as politicians, policy-makers and commercial managers, who can determine whether or not particular services ought to be funded as credible and useful contributions to society. What unites all these audiences is a concern about the ethical integrity of the service being provided. A published statement of ethical commitment by a professional body on behalf of its membership provides evidence of a collective commitment to being ethical. The degree of consensus across the major professional organizations responsible for counselling in the British Isles suggests that this commitment is both well established and worked out in a reasonable amount of detail.

However, there are changes in process which will affect the ethical landscape for counselling. One of the difficulties for professional bodies is that they appear to have a conflict of interests between protecting the interests of clients and promoting the interests of their members, who are also the service providers. This becomes really apparent whenever a client has a grievance against a counsellor and wants to make a complaint or start a disciplinary case. If the professional body is responsible for investigating and deciding the outcome of the grievance, it is very hard for the client to be convinced that they will get a fair hearing and that the professional body will not 'look after its own'. It is a suspicion that is hard to refute. I am choosing my words carefully because I consider that it is more about suspicion than a bias that exists in reality. I have had a variety of contacts with complaints procedures against counsellors involving all the major professional bodies. This has given me an opportunity to observe what happens first hand. In all cases, the professional body has endeavoured to act with scrupulous fairness between the complainant and its member. It is often the member who is discomforted by the professional body shifting from being part of a network of professional support (for which the member is paying a subscription) to a position of deliberate neutrality between the parties in order to adjudicate the complaint fairly.

The introduction of statutory regulation will change this. It will be the regulator, the Health Professions Council (HPC) in the UK, who will take on the primary responsibility for the protection of the best interests of clients and the professional bodies for the professional development and support of the counsellors providing the services. The first group to be regulated in the UK will be counselling psychologists. They will be subject to a statement of duties as a registrant set out in the *Standards of Conduct, Performance and Ethics* (HPC, 2008). It is envisaged that all counsellors and psychotherapists working in the UK will eventually be brought within the Register, possibly as early as 2011. All registrants will be required to maintain fitness to practise and meet all other require-ments of registration or cease to practise as a counsellor or psychothera-pist. Professional bodies will still have a major contribution to make to the support and development of counselling and to the ethical health of the profession beyond the legal requirements of statutory regulation.

The next section in this book continues with the concern about responsibilities to the client. It starts by looking at issues of safety, negli-gence and insurance.

Part II

Responsibility to the Client

5

Safety, Negligence and Insurance

Responsibilities to the client are usually the counsellor's foremost concern. An important aspect of these responsibilities is to protect the client from any harm which may be caused by attending counselling. As we have seen in the previous chapter, the principle of non-maleficence, i.e. avoidance of causing harm, is not usually presented as the foremost ethical concern. The published ethical statements of national counselling organizations prioritize more positive ethical principles, which by implication assume that avoidance of harm to the client has been taken into consideration in order to achieve these more positive aims. I do not want to present a case for prioritizing avoidance of harm over other ethical principles. My reservations about rigidly prioritizing any of the ethical principles over the others would apply equally to this one. However, I do consider that this is a useful point with which to start. The potential for causing harm can be avoided or at least substantially reduced by considering in advance how the risk of causing any harm may be obviated or minimized so that the way is cleared for more positive ethical aims.

Client Safety

Counselling is primarily a talking therapy. Therefore it is relatively easy to overlook the physical dangers and to concentrate on psychological sources of harm. This could be an unfortunate error, affecting not only the client but also the counsellor. It is in the counsellor's own interests to avoid some of the more obvious sources of legal liability, which, if they arose, could result in the payment of substantial damages to the client. Some fictitious examples will provide examples of the kind of harm that could befall clients.

Physical safety

> Bill was so nervous when he entered the counselling room that he did not notice a shelf at head level. He bumped his head so badly that he required medical treatment.

The risk of physical injury to a client during counselling is usually fairly low, provided that the counsellor has anticipated any sources of danger and removed them. Nonetheless, there is always the potential for a client tripping, falling off a chair, or bumping into something. In these circumstances, the client may seek compensation for any injury, particularly if it appears that the counsellor has not taken sufficient care to protect the client from injury. Normally this claim would be made against the 'occupier', defined in law as 'a person who has sufficient control over premises to put him under a duty of care towards those who come lawfully upon those premises' (Rogers, 2006). Often this could be the counsellor. Normally the claim would be covered by public liability insurance if the counselling is taking place on business or public premises. If the counsellor was held by the court to be in control of the premises and the insurance cover was inadequate, then all or part of the claim might have to be met by the counsellor personally. This has important implications for both counsellor and client. If Bill's injuries were serious or resulted in disability, any award for damages could be substantial.

Many counsellors work from home and may be relying on their household insurance for protection. The counsellor's household insurance company should always be fully informed because failure to inform the insurer about working from home could potentially invalidate an existing household policy. Also, most household insurance policies exclude cover of premises, or parts of premises, used for business purposes, and when informed that the counsellor is working from home, they may refuse cover, impose conditions, or charge an additional premium.

Without adequate insurance cover for public liability, the counsellor could be personally liable to pay damages. It is therefore important, whatever the circumstances of working, that the counsellor seeks advice from a competent insurance broker about whether she requires 'public liability insurance'. This insurance cover is included within the insurance schemes provided in association with BACP and BPS.

Psychological safety

All the counselling models of theory and practice claim that clients will benefit from counselling and usually favour a particular theory and method. In my experience, working with clients is seldom as straight-forward as the counselling models suggest. There are moments when the counsellor is faced with making difficult choices about how to respond and assessing what will be most helpful to the client. Especially in the early stages of a counselling relationship, it is often possible to sense a client's vulnerability around issues that have not yet been declared. It takes time for the necessary trust to develop which will enable the client to voice that vulnerability. One of the differences that I have noticed in supervising trainees and experienced counsellors is the greater confidence of the latter in working progressively and patiently until the client is ready to disclose deeper areas of vulnerability. Inexperienced counsellors are more likely to feel the burden of having to be seen to have something to offer and therefore become more challenging in their interventions than the client's level of trust can sustain. Fortunately, most clients are sufficiently resourceful to protect themselves against such psychologically mistimed interventions whether from inexperienced or experienced counsellors. However, it is unethical to rely on this capacity for self-protection. Any process with the potential for good is likely to have the potential for harm when it is misapplied. In medicine, a subsidiary principle to non-maleficence has been adopted for situations when it is considered that no further help is possible or it is unclear how helpful a particular intervention will prove to be. 'Above all, do no harm.' This sense of respect for the client's situation and proper caution in assessing the appropriate way of responding to the client is fundamental to psycho-logical safety and thus serves both ethical and therapeutic aims. All the published requirements of professional organizations considered in the previous chapters stress that the counsellor should work within her level of competence, which is clearly an essential requirement for avoiding harm to the client. The use of counselling-supervision where these issues can be discussed remains an additional safeguard for clients.

The ethical significance of avoiding psychological harm to a client is barely matched by a corresponding legal obligation. An example will illustrate the sort of situation in which a claim for compensation for psychological harm could arise and the difficulties any client may encounter in obtaining damages.

> Peter approached a counsellor for assistance with a bereavement. Despite the counselling, he felt progressively worse and became more withdrawn. Eventually he was treated for depression by a psychiatrist. On his recovery, he considered suing his counsellor.

If the counsellor has created a contract with the client promising improvements or the absence of deterioration, the client could sue for breach of contract. However, Kenneth Cohen (1992) observed that:

> counsellors and psychotherapists wisely, therefore, tend to be very cautious about predicting outcomes, and the very wisest of them promise nothing at all! Some who do choose to make extravagant claims for their brand of counselling or therapy offer no quibble money back guarantees to disappointed clients: this is a sensible precaution against claims for misrepresentation and breach of contract.

This advice from one of the first lawyers to take an interest in legal issues for counsellors remains highly relevant to current practice.

In the absence of any contractual terms relevant to the claim, the client's case would be based on the alleged negligence of the professional, in this case a counsellor. In order to establish their case, the client would need to show the existence of:

- a duty of care;
- breach of that duty;
- proof that damage was caused by the breach of the counsellor's duty of care (the causal link).

The level of the duty of care owed by a counsellor is the same as that of any other professional. She is required only to exercise reasonable care and skill in rendering her services to clients. The duty of care does not require that there should be no deterioration, or even that there should be actual improvement. Reasonable care will be assessed by a court by examination of the standards of the profession, particularly its guidelines about ethics and conduct, its leading textbooks and the testimony of its leading practitioners. If, as is the case in counselling, there are differences of view about what constitutes acceptable professional behaviour, e.g. variations between theories and methods of counselling, this poses a problem for the court. In these circumstances, the court does not get involved in assessing which treatment is more effective, nor does it regard less effective treatments as negligent. An assessment of effectiveness would be fraught with problems and would leave no room for differences of opinion between conscientious and generally competent practitioners. Courts have therefore adopted a different approach, which is that professional practice is not considered to be negligent if it follows the practice accepted at the time as proper by a reasonable body of professional opinion skilled in the particular form of treatment (Rogers, 2006). The test used to decide whether this is the case was formulated in *Bolam v Friern Hospital Management Committee* (1957), about medical negligence, but now has much wider application. Kenneth Cohen (1992) has indicated the kind of question that a judge might ask him/herself:

Even though there is a body of competent professional opinion which might adopt a different technique, did the practitioner act in accordance with a practice accepted as proper by a responsible body of professional opinion skilled in the particular form of treatment?

If the counsellor can show that he had acted in accordance with a reasonable body of competent professional opinion, then there is likely to be a complete defence, but there are uncertainties about how a counsellor would establish this defence. Courts already attach great weight to medical opinions but the status of non-medical opinions is increasing, where that opinion is given by someone who is sufficiently qualified and experienced to be viewed as an expert witness. Increasingly, courts will also refer to official guidelines for practice, such as those from the National Institute for Clinical Excellence (NICE), Improving Access to Psychological Therapies (IAPT), ethical guidance from a relevant professional body (e.g. BACP's *Ethical Framework* (2007)), and authoritative sources about different approaches to and modalities of counselling.

In order to succeed, the client must also establish that the breach of the duty was the cause of the harm suffered. 'Cause' is defined strictly to mean 'materially contributing' rather than 'determining'. This means that conjectural and speculative explanations of the cause of the harm are inadequate. The question may be put as 'Would the loss or harm have happened but for breach of this duty?' The existence of more than one possible explanation, particularly explanations not involving the counsellor, could discredit or reduce the claim. In Kenneth Cohen's opinion, there may also be an inherent anti-litigation bias within counselling arising from the difficulty the client has in establishing the counsellor's responsibility for the harm suffered in a relationship where the client retains a high level of responsibility for the outcomes of the counselling: 'Many would say that in the long run, a good counsellor or therapist seeks to empower and encourage his client to locate causality operating in her life more and more within herself, rather than others, including in particular the counsellor' (Cohen, 1992). Although the law has continued to develop since he made this observation, it is still generally true. On the other hand, an empowered client might become more active in pursuing grievances against the counsellor if she has been negligent in the way she has worked.

There are other legal rules that may adversely affect a client's ability to sue for negligence. No compensation is available for hurt feelings alone in this kind of case unless they are of sufficient duration and severity to amount to mental illness, see *McLoughlin v O'Brian* [1983] 1 AC 410 at 431. Recent cases have affirmed this general principle.

A client is likely to experience considerable difficulties in bringing a legal action against a counsellor for negligence resulting in psychological harm. This raises the question about whether professional organizations and any agencies providing counselling have a responsibility to hear complaints that receiving counselling has caused serious personal harm. Most of these bodies will hear allegations of harm arising from clearly unethical behaviour, such as the sexual or financial exploitation of clients, but are less likely to consider issues relating to poor practice. It is noticeable that the medical profession is moving fairly rapidly towards creating systems that compare the outcomes of different practitioners by systems of clinical audits and are increasingly concerned to respond to complaints about poor practice. There are significant difficulties in providing these kinds of service even within the relatively regulated world of medicine, and these difficulties are likely to be greater within counselling. Nonetheless, there is a strong ethical case for establishing parallel procedures for counsellors, which is strengthened by the near impossibility of bringing successful legal claims for negligence. BACP, BPS, COSCA and IACP have developed disciplinary and complaints procedures.

In England, I am aware of only one case of negligent psychotherapy recorded in the law reports. In the case of *Landau v Werner* (1961) it was held that the defendant, a psychoanalytically orientated psychiatrist, was liable for negligently causing deterioration in his client's condition by engaging in social contacts with her in a misguided attempt to resolve her transference. Her deterioration had been such that she attempted suicide. The Court of Appeal upheld this High Court judgment. Both courts rejected allegations that the defendant had had sex with his client.

The lack of cases against counsellors based on negligence is in sharp contrast to the USA, where the rules for establishing liability are much more favourable to the client and therefore litigation is a much more frequent occurrence. For a more detailed comparison between the two legal systems regarding various aspects of negligence, see Peter Jenkins (2007: 85–7, 91–3 and 99).

Inappropriate Advice

One of the ways in which clients can be harmed is by being given inappropriate or misleading advice. There are a variety of approaches to the appropriateness of giving advice within counselling. Historically, members of BACP have striven to distinguish counselling from advice-giving. For over a decade BAC (the forerunner of BACP) provided ethical guidance that 'Counsellors do not normally give advice' (BAC, 1997: B.1.3.6). This is probably generally true of all counsellors when it is applied to matters like a decision about leaving a partner, which is usually a personal matter which falls within client autonomy (see next chapter). However, models vary in the extent to which they consider it appropriate for counsellors to give advice or be directive about the counselling. There is some research evidence that counsellors use other types of communication strategy to influence clients, even when they claim to avoid advice-giving (Silverman, 1996). There is also an ethical case for creating an obligation on counsellors to advise clients about the potential risks of seeking counselling where these are reasonably foresee-able by the counsellor. I will consider the case for advice-giving in order to establish that it can be an appropriate activity in certain circumstances within counselling before considering the ethical and legal implications of misleading advice.

Some models of counselling have no reservations about the value of giving advice and advocate constructive directions to clients that might include undertaking specified exercises or activities such as 'homework' between sessions. Cognitive behavioural therapy and many forms of brief therapy take a positive view of appropriate advice-giving. One of the keenest advocates of advice within therapy and counselling was the late Albert Ellis, who asserted the value of talking clients into something that he believes on theoretical and practical grounds will be therapeutic. He is critical of counsellors who avoid challenging inappropriate or self-destructive beliefs and he argues that the timidity of the counsellor is colluding with the client's own maleficence towards themselves (Dryden, 1998). Ellis was an energetic advocate for rational emotive behavioural therapy, the model of which he was the founder and which has influenced other approaches to cognitive therapy. His views directly opposed the established practice of person-centred and psychodynamic approaches to counselling where abstinence from advice-giving is much more the norm. In my view, professional ethics need to avoid being partisan between ways of working that are considered to be valuable within established therapeutic approaches. It would be as wrong to require that counsellors give advice as to require that they abstain from giving advice. The ethical case for giving advice which is consistent with a chosen counselling model is a strong one. In the context of a model which depends upon advice-giving, a counsellor's deliberate avoidance of doing so may harm a client by withholding a potential benefit of counselling and violate the basis on which that client is seeking counselling.

There is another situation where there is probably a general duty on all counsellors to consider giving relevant advice. This concerns informing the client about any potential risks of counselling. For example:

John is a student who is shortly to sit important examinations. He is actively anxious about taking the exams and this anxiety is compounded by a sense that the current stress has re-stimulated early childhood traumas.

It is not unusual for people who are facing major life events also to experience a resurgence of feelings from other aspects of their life, which seem to compound their difficulties. The challenge for the counsellor is finding a way of responding constructively to the life event, such as the forthcoming examination in the example, and assessing whether dealing with the other aspects of the client's issues would be better undertaken before or after the current challenging life event. It is increasingly usual practice among student counsellors to be cautious about starting major counselling work close to examinations. There is a strong ethical case for advising the client to consider dealing with those issues after the examination has been completed and to keep the focus of the counselling on managing the immediate anxiety about the examinations. At least the client ought to be alerted to the possibility that the emotional demands of dealing with other issues simultaneously with a major life event may reduce his level of energy and ability to focus on that life event.

It may also be ethically appropriate to advise someone to seek specialist help other than counselling or in parallel with counselling. For example, someone may present themselves with constant headaches and loss of co-ordination, which she attributes to stress-related problems. Such symptoms could equally well indicate a physical illness such as a brain tumour, where early diagnosis can be critical to the outcome of any treatment. It is ethically appropriate to advise such a client to seek a medical examination to eliminate physical origins of the symptoms or to clarify the nature of the counselling task. The lack of medical training of most counsellors increases the ethical case for maintaining clear boundaries between responsibility for physical and psychosocial issues. People with eating disorders are often reluctant to seek medical help and yet the severer forms of eating disorders can have long-term consequences for health and fertility and can be life-threatening. Again, this is a situation where the counsellor may wish to advise medical checks in parallel with the counselling. It would be inappropriate for a non-medically trained counsellor to be monitoring weight loss but where this is an issue, there are good ethical reasons for at least advising about the consequences of not seeking that kind of help.

The law recognizes the potential harm caused by negligent advice, sometimes referred to as negligent misstatement, and makes the tests for legal liability less stringent than for negligence. Unlike in the action for negligence where the client would have to prove a direct causal connection between the breach of a duty of care and the harm (see previous section), in negligent misstatement the client would simply need to show that the counsellor took professional responsibility for the advice given, and that the client acted in reliance on that advice, to his detriment. Unlike claims for personal injury in negligence, the client would also be able to claim for purely economic losses, e.g. loss of earnings suffered as a result of bad advice, even though there might have been no damage to person or property and/or no legally recognized contractual relationship between counsellor and client. However, there is no liability for advice given informally, for example in a discussion at a social event for which the counsellor took no professional responsibility (Rogers, 2006).

Negligence in the context of counselling practice might take several forms, for example, serious lack of empathy, failure to recognize serious mental illness or suicidality, or giving inadequate or incorrect advice in the context of a modality where advice-giving is the norm. The counsellor's failure to meet their duty of care and their consequent potential liability for negligence in tort will be the same in all these cases.

Counsellors who advise homework for clients (as opposed to facilitating the client setting his own homework between counselling sessions) may incur liability if there is a breach of a duty of care and the client acts on the advice to their detriment. Kenneth Cohen (1992) gives two speculative examples:

> Suppose … a client says in effect: 'I confronted my boss as we agreed I would. But now he's fired me and I wouldn't have lost my job but for your bad advice.' Or suppose a client is arrested by the police for engaging in sexual activities which his counsellor had negotiated with him as homework without realising they are illegal.

These examples illustrate the legal risks of advice-giving and how poor or wrong advice can be deemed negligent in law.

There is a general principle in medical negligence law that failure to advise of risks of treatment can be as negligent as giving bad advice (*Sidaway v Bethlem Royal Hospital*, 1985). However, counsellors are in a different position from medical advisers. They are not usually providing medicines with known potential side-effects or performing physical procedures which often involve some degree of risk, which are recognized by a body of professional opinion that considers that such risks ought to be disclosed. The risks of counselling will depend upon the specific circumstances of each client, and the nature and degree of risk may vary as counselling progresses, for example if the client has unexpected big life events to face, or suddenly becomes psychotic or suicidal. Some clients may need warnings at some point in their therapeutic process, others may never need one. There is no general duty to provide warnings, but in any counselling alliance, a situation may develop in which the therapist has a duty to warn the client, and that duty will depend upon the client's particular circumstances. I consider that the examples given earlier in this section are sufficiently clear to indicate a strong ethical obligation to obtain the informed consent of the client to enter into or continue counselling.

The Importance of Insurance

Some professional bodies require that counsellors have adequate indemnity insurance (BPS, 2008b: s. 62; UKCP, 1998: s. 2.9) or that practitioners are 'strongly encouraged to ensure that their work is adequately covered by insurance for professional indemnity and liability' (BACP, 2007: s. 36). This is a recommendation for members but it is a BACP requirement for accreditation. Although it is increasingly common practice for counsellors to have insurance, there are some who refuse to do so. Their main objections are that the risks of a counsellor being liable for any harm to a client are considerably less than they would be for a doctor or other professions who operate directly on the person's body. From this perspective, counselling is not physically dangerous. (Not everyone would agree with this viewpoint. What if negligent counselling practice leads to physical harm, e.g. anorexic starvation, maiming or suicide, or harming others?) It has also been argued that if counsellors accept a view of their work as potentially dangerous, they are at risk of becoming defensive with clients. A further objection concerns the likelihood that the existence of insurance may encourage litigation by clients seeking financial gain. I think that these arguments are unconvincing.

The risk of legal action against a counsellor is relatively small, which is usually reflected in proportionately small premiums. However, the costs have been considerable where counsellors have been held liable for matters such as clients falling and injuring themselves (public liability), malpractice, errors and omissions (professional liability) or other sources of harm to the client. Professional indemnity insurance (to cover professional liability) and public liability insurance are both necessary. Damages in major physical injury cases, usually arising from car accidents, can exceed £5 million and, at the time of writing a claim for £9 million is subject to appeal. Such severe levels of injury are unlikely to happen as a direct consequence of counselling. If these eventualities were all that insurance covered, then some of the objections would have greater validity. However, no counsellor can be totally confident that a client will not slip on stairs or trip up on a carpet or rug and receive chronic injuries. Whether the injury arises directly as a result of the counselling or is the counsellor's responsibility as the occupier of the premises, it seems to me that there is a strong ethical case for ensuring that the client can be as adequately compensated as possible. The legal purpose of damages awarded to clients in these circumstances is to put them in as good an economic position as if the accident had not occurred. The person who is adjudged to be liable is often responsible for paying both parties' legal costs. Whatever the shortcomings of a rather slow and cumbersome legal process, these are ethically desirable aims. The most practical way of achieving these ethical objectives is through insurance or membership of a professional protection society, unless counsellors have enormous personal resources to indemnify themselves. Addresses of suppliers of both forms of protection are included in the appendix. Howden, who provide schemes for members of BACP, BPS and others, recommend that an adequate policy should include:

- professional liability indemnity (malpractice, errors and omissions);
- public liability cover (includes occupier's liability);
- libel and slander insurance;
- product liability cover (particularly relevant to counsellors who supply items such as relaxation tapes and CDs);
- cover for complaints made against the counsellor to professional bodies and regulators.

The case for having adequate insurance is not simply altruistic, on behalf of the clients. There is also a degree of self-interest. Even the costs of preparing a legal defence to a relatively minor claim can run to several thousands of pounds, which may be prohibitively expensive for the individual counsellor. The payment of relatively modest premiums provides a degree of financial safety for the counsellor as well as protection for the client.

6

Respect for Client Autonomy

Respect for client autonomy is a high priority in most approaches to counselling. Without a commitment to respect for client autonomy or self-determination, counselling would become an ethically compromised and potentially self-diminishing activity for clients. Counselling involves a client being invited to engage in a particular kind of self-talk by a counsellor trained in how to draw someone into this sort of personal reflection. A client is wise to be cautious about engaging in this kind of activity as it has potentially major implications for that person's sense of self-identify and choice of actions. It is also taking place in circumstances where power is unevenly distributed between counsellor and client, in favour of the counsellor. Especially in the early stages of a counselling relationship there is an inherent inequality between the person seeking help and the person offering help. It is arguable that current trends towards professionalization increase that inequality by adding the weight of collective authority to that held by the counsellor as a person. In the absence of a strong and firmly rooted ethic of respect for individual autonomy, the client could be subjecting himself to manipulation according to the counsellor's agenda or for other purposes. As most people seek counselling at a time of personal difficulty, they are more than usually vulnerable and therefore counsellors' professional ethic needs to be correspondingly conscientious about respecting client autonomy.

Autonomy means the right to 'self-rule' or 'self-government'. Raanon Gillon (1985) has provided a more personally meaningful definition which identifies the essential characteristic as 'the capacity to think, decide and act on the basis of such thought and decisions, freely and independently and without, as it says in the passport, "let or hindrance".' However, an emphasis on client autonomy poses several major challenges for the counsellor. How does the counsellor manage the seemingly contradictory expectations of respecting client autonomy while being a constructive influence for the client?

One of the means of resolving the dilemma is to work in ways that enhance client autonomy. This seemingly simple strategy conceals the difficulty of what this might entail, which is probably best illustrated by different metaphorical labels used by counsellors and therapists to describe how they work. It is an issue on which counsellors, recognized for their personal and professional integrity, hold quite different views without necessarily rejecting the importance of client autonomy.

In a seminal book about *Therapists' Dilemmas*, Windy Dryden (1998) interviewed fourteen well-known therapists and counsellors about the challenges of their work and especially those issues which were hard to resolve. A recurrent theme is the challenge of representing accurately the boundary of responsibilities between counsellor and client. Many of the interviewees use imagery and metaphors in order to help them describe their dilemma. I have found it particularly informative to reflect on the differences of view expressed by Albert Ellis, the founder of rational emotive behavioural therapy (REBT) and John Bancroft, a psychiatrist and author of *Human Sexuality and its Problems* (1989). I realize that I am naturally more sympathetic to the evident sensitivity of the latter. His dilemmas are closer to the ones that I experience as a counsellor. However, once I got over my initial irritation with the argumentative way that Albert Ellis asserted his views and his provocatively dismissive attitude to other approaches to counselling, I can see that he approached the problem of respect for client autonomy in a different but perhaps equally ethical way. I will start by outlining their respective views.

The late Albert Ellis conceived the role of therapist as 'scientific healer' with characteristic personal vigour. When interviewed by Windy Dryden he commented on the situation where the practitioner knows the solution to the client's problem:

> why should you waste therapeutic time collaborating 50–50 with the clients when you can effectively help them zero in on what their philosophic problems are? … Indeed, if you do try to maintain a fully collaborative stance, I think you are adopting a hypocritical pretence. … My hypothesis is that many therapists, who are scared shitless of making

mistakes in therapy, like 'full collaboration' because they can cop out of taking risks and of doing a great deal of the therapeutic work themselves. … They are, in a word, afraid of being directive.

He believed that it is unavoidable that the therapists will try to fit clients into their system as opposed to modifying their system to fit the client. He also asserted that it is legitimate to try to talk clients into something that he believed on theoretical and practical grounds is therapeutic. The degree of autonomy he granted the client is the right to consent to therapy on these terms, or to refuse to be persuaded and choose someone else as his or her therapist.

In contrast, John Bancroft experiences the dilemma between being a 'healer' and being an 'educator' quite acutely. He acknowledges the attractions of being a 'healer' and that this image can be effective, particularly in the short term, but he cannot escape from being the 'expert' and implying the message, 'this is what you should do'. He argues that the disadvantage of the healer role arises at the end of the therapy. He comments about his work with couples that,

> If they leave a course of counselling thinking that they have been 'treated', then they are not going to see themselves as equipped with new resources to deal with problems that may arise in the future. So, it is a very important part of my 'educator' role to get the couple, by the time they have left me, to have a clear understanding of what has happened, why it has been helpful, so they can apply these principles themselves. (Dryden, 1998)

He has observed that the association of 'healing' with 'expert' and 'higher dependence' also contributes to a higher rate of relapse following counselling. In contrast, the educator who acts in the role of 'guide' fosters a greater sense of self-reliance with a lower rate of relapse.

At first, I found it so difficult to reconcile these two points of view that I considered that one of them must be inconsistent with an ethic of respect for client autonomy. I no longer hold this view but realize that each of the views is consistent with different views about the robustness of client autonomy and the degree of responsibility and influence held by the counsellor.

Ellis clearly took a robust view of client autonomy and was untroubled by clients who reject his approach to therapy in preference to other methods. He saw his job as getting to the locus of the client's problems, which he described as actively seeking out and disputing the client's self-defeating and irrational thoughts. He was clearly pleased that many of his suicidal clients have done well. He attributed this success to their ability to get over suicidal thoughts and to sustain this position. The two clients who committed suicide some years after therapy are considered outside his sphere of influence or responsibility. By contrast, Bancroft is working directly with people's intimate relationships. The major challenge in his work is not achieving short-term behavioural change, which he regards as relatively easy to accomplish, but how to sustain those changes over time. He is working directly with a wide range of the client's life, and views their vulnerability as compromising their autonomy, hence his concern about being viewed as an expert healer. It is possible that both men modified their views since the mid-1980s when these interviews took place. This does not matter from an ethical point of view because they have provided an illustration of two different approaches to resolving the ethical dilemmas around autonomy.

Respecting client autonomy within the counselling process cannot be resolved simply by following a set of rules or guidelines, such as abstaining from advice-giving. There may be other good reasons for abstaining from advice-giving, especially where it is inconsistent with the therapeutic approach being used, but this does not make all advice-giving inappropriate. Respecting a client's autonomy makes greater demands on the counsellor. It requires communication with a level of authority and personal challenge appropriate to that particular client at that point in the counselling relationship. One factor which the counsellor might wish to take into consideration is the balance between the level of trust that exists between them, and the level of challenge that the counsellor offers. A level of challenge appropriate to a well-established and secure counselling relationship might be profoundly disrespectful, if not bullying, with another client where the relationship is less secure and the level of trust is insufficient to enable the client to counter-challenge the counsellor or express reservations. The counsellor's role is to enhance the client's capacity for personal autonomy, on whatever level that exists. Subjectively, people experience their own sense of autonomy quite differently, according to the general circumstances of their life and the dynamics within specific relationships. Loss of confidence, feeling deskilled or being unable to say what one really wants to communicate, can all be assisted by the counsellor actively working towards enhancing client autonomy. The essential requirement is respecting the client's own sense of what will be helpful to them, whether this involves presenting choice and accepting that the client may prefer to seek help elsewhere rather than follow the counsellor's recommendations or carefully constructing a mutually agreed basis for working together.

A particularly potent combination, which can undermine client autonomy, can arise when the counsellor believes that she knows what is best for the client better than the client does for herself and this is reinforced by the counsellor's determination that the client should comply with the counsellor's prescription. This determination most commonly arises when the counsellor gets satisfaction from exercising power and control over others or zealously wants the client to conform to the counsellor's own personal experience or to a particular theory. For example:

Sue's partner has recently died. Her counsellor frustrates Sue by appearing to expect that the same things that had helped the counsellor in a similar situation will help Sue. Sue also finds that the way she is expected to follow a series of stages in her grieving, which do not fit her experience, is unhelpful. This situation could resolve itself in several ways. Sue could lose confidence in her own experience and start to conform to her counsellor's personal and theoretical expectations. This is clearly a move away from autonomy towards dependency. Sue could abandon the counselling as unhelpful. An opportunity would be lost. Sue could challenge the way in which the counsellor is working, a risky thing to do and she may not have the emotional energy for this course of action when she is feeling so vulnerable. The best outcome is that the counsellor is sensitive to Sue's reactions and invites her feedback, and perhaps with the help of counselling-supervision modifies her approach, thus demonstrating respect for Sue's personal experience and her autonomy.

This example demonstrates the power held by counsellors over vulnerable clients, and how, through too great an enthusiasm for a particular theory or approach, autonomy can be eroded and a client's dependency inadvertently encouraged. The example I have given assumes that the client has sufficiently developed insight to be able to recognize what is happening and has the capacity to take the initiative. Other clients may be so used to having their experiences invalidated that they fail to recognize what is happening to them. The counsellor is then in a very powerful position and this is dangerous unless he or she is aware of the possibility of using this power to undermine the development of a client's autonomy. Alice Miller (1998) characterizes such situations as potentially 'poisonous'. She is especially concerned with the way orthodox psychoanalysis, until recently, dismissed clients' accounts of childhood sexual abuse as fantasy. Psychoanalytic theories had the effect of automatically, and unconsciously, acting as blinkers which exclude from view the real experience of the client's childhood. Almost all counsellors would now accept the possibility that clients may be recalling actual events when they describe childhood sexual abuse. The widespread acceptance of this point of view has taken place as recently as the 1980s. However, it is salutary to wonder whether there are other theoretical 'truths' in the counsellor's repertoire which blinker counsellors against their client's experience. It is important not to exclude something from view that needs to be taken as true if a client's right to act autonomously is to be respected rather than poisoned by a counsellor's disbelief or interpretation. This is not an ethical argument against theory or making interpretations. It is an argument for avoiding investing theories with too much certainty and attempting to impose a point of view on a client, especially if it contradicts the client's reported experience. Both clients and counsellors need a degree of emotional health in order to recognize these situations. In Miller's words, 'Only a feeling person can grasp the way an empty theory may function as a means of power, for he or she will not be intimidated by incomprehensibility.'

The interviews in *Therapists' Dilemmas* suggest that counsellors are most forcefully confronted with what is the appropriate boundary of responsibility in either of two situations. The first arises when the counsellor believes that she can see a solution to the client's problems which has not yet occurred to the client. The second occurs when the client asks the counsellor to express a personal opinion like 'Do you think my marriage is dead?' or 'Do you think I am capable of overcoming this problem?' These dilemmas are intrinsic to counselling and have to be evaluated in the light of the specific circumstances. Part of this involves asking:

- Am I as counsellor taking on responsibilities which are more properly the client's?
- Is there a way I could respond which maximizes the client's autonomy and minimizes his dependence on me?

These are the big questions that clarify ethical choices. However, the questions apply throughout counselling practice and can be just as relevant to more fine-grained and intricate choices. For example, how far should a counsellor present themselves as essential to the therapeutic process or merely as a facilitator of a process in which the client is centre-stage of their own achievements?

Counsellors who systematically ask themselves these questions are much more likely to stay within boundaries that give clients their appropriate responsibility for the outcome of the counselling. John Rowan, a humanistic therapist, has emphasized the importance of how counsellors think and talk about their role. He observes that it is tempting to describe achievements in counselling in terms like:

- Produce a breakthrough in a client;
- Cure client;
- Get client to go from adjustment to ecstasy;
- Ability to facilitate client change of self-direction;
- Ability to get client catharsis/insight/body change/pivotal change.

But these are all, ultimately, things the client does, rather than things the therapist or counsellor does. What I think works on a list like this is to stick to things which the therapist [or counsellor] does. (Rowan, 1983)

This approach to respecting client autonomy is founded on maintaining a clear distinction between responsibility for the counselling process and outcome. The counsellor is viewed as responsible for managing the counselling process. The client is responsible for the outcome(s) of the counselling. This is a widely used distinction that many counsellors apply to their work. The use of this approach clarifies and deepens our understanding of the challenge of respecting the client's autonomy. The *Guidelines for the Professional Practice of Counselling Psychology* (BPS, 2005: s. 1.2) sets out the essential requirements for fitness to practise as including that practitioners will 'always seek to support clients' control over their lives and their ability to make appropriate decisions'. In practice, there are a number of strategies that are commonly used to support the ethic of respect for client autonomy.

Stressing the Voluntary Nature of Counselling

It is a basic principle that counselling is a voluntary activity for the client. In most circumstances this is clearly the case. The client has sought out a counsellor as a matter of personal choice rather than feeling obliged to receive counselling or having been sent for counselling as an alternative to something worse, perhaps disciplinary action.

However, counsellors working in organizational settings report that there are situations where a client may be seeking counselling because they are compelled to do so by someone else. For example, employee counsellors may have someone sent to them as an alternative to disciplinary procedures or as part of a disciplinary procedure. Counsellors in education also experience having clients sent to them, usually to resolve troublesome behaviour, but sometimes because a member of staff has recognized that a pupil is deeply distressed and needs help. Some people seek counselling in all kinds of settings because they feel compelled to do so by partners, friends or their family. Usually the person sending the client is doing so out of a commitment to help and wants to act constructively. However, their action poses a number of difficulties for the counsellor. First, it challenges the client's ability to exercise choice about whether to participate in counselling. Secondly, there may be predetermined expectations about what the outcome of the counselling will be, and these are not necessarily those of the client. This may not be too much of a problem if the aim is to reduce distress, as the client is likely to share this aim. Expectations about changes in the client's behaviour are likely to be much more problematic. For example:

Carl is sent to see a school counsellor to stop what his teacher sees as disruptive behaviour. During the counselling it emerges that Carl feels misunderstood and picked on by his teacher. He wants to find ways of expressing his views more effectively rather than becoming more compliant.

Any attempt by the counsellor to impose the teacher's views on Carl would clearly be in breach of the spirit of the voluntary nature of counselling and indicate a lack of respect for the client's autonomy.

A parallel situation also occurs with adults. Sometimes adults are sent to counsellors by employers as an alternative to disciplinary procedures. Again, this is usually done out of compassion for the client. For example:

Joan is sent to an employee counsellor to help her reduce her lateness at starting work and her unexplained absences. The personnel officer who sent her suspects that she has relationship problems at home and has chosen this course of action rather than dismissing her as she is unlikely to be re-employed by anyone else.

There is considerable potential for confusion over the client's autonomy and the counsellor's role in these circumstances. What if Joan, unknown to the personnel manager, has been preparing to establish her own small business and this is why she is absent and is reluctant to offer an explanation? What if the personnel officer is right about the relationship problems causing the absence but Joan is happy to use them as an excuse and wants to go to counselling as a means of postponing the day of reckoning? In both these situations the counsellor may feel caught between the client's wishes and those of the personnel officer. Certainly, the counselling is unlikely to be effective because the client is not committed to the process; rather, she is using mere attendance as a shield against a less liked alternative. This situation can be avoided by better management systems, which establish a clearer differentiation between disciplinary and counselling procedures. Joan would be in a better position to decide whether or not to attend for counselling had the personnel officer said: 'Unless your attendance record reaches a specified level by a particular date then disciplinary or dismissal procedures will be started. I realize there may be problems which are contributing to your poor attendance record and I would like to help. You may find it useful to talk to the counsellor, who may be able to help you solve these problems. In the end I must act to ensure acceptable attendance levels.' If the choice of whether or not to attend for counselling is put in these terms, it becomes much clearer that the outcome of the disciplinary procedure does not depend on whether Joan attends for counselling, but whether her attendance record reaches satisfactory levels. If she seeks counselling, it will be because she wants it for herself and therefore she is more likely to engage actively in the process.

It sometimes happens that a counsellor is not in a position to influence others in ways that prevent a client being 'sent'. For instance, a client may attend in compliance with a partner's wishes or under threat of someone else doing something that the client wants to prevent. The classic example would be someone accepting a detoxification from alcohol or drugs, which includes counselling, as an alternative to a custodial sentence or imprisonment. Can there be such a thing as a voluntary client under threat of imprisonment? This is one of many situations in which the counsellor cannot assume that it is the client's, rather than someone else's, wish that he receive counselling. It is good practice for the counsellor to help the client establish his options, including not proceeding with the counselling. This may be a very quick process or may involve several sessions of 'pre-counselling' before the client is clear about whether he wants to proceed.

The ethical emphasis on consent as essential to respect for individual autonomy is paralleled by the law. Legally, adults (i.e. over-18 year-olds) are entitled to give their consent or to refuse any form of treatment unless the High Court has made a declaration of lawfulness to impose or withhold treatment. Young people aged 16–18 years old are also entitled to consent to or refuse any treatment, although a refusal to accept life-saving treatment can be overruled by the High Court (see the Family Law Reform Act 1969 s. 8(1) and the Age of Legal Capacity (Scotland) Act 1991).

Below 16 years old, in accordance with the principles set by the House of Lords in *Gillick v West Norfolk and Wisbech Health Authority and Another* [1986] 1 AC 112 a 'Gillick competent' young person of sufficient maturity, understanding and intelligence may give valid informed consent for treatment.

If a 'Gillick competent' young person refuses treatment, then their wishes should normally be respected, but if there is a need for treatment and parents (or others) who hold parental responsibility for the young person disagree with their child's decision or with each other, they can go to court and ask for a Specific Issue order. If the young person is refusing treatment and the matter is serious, they can also apply to the High Court to resolve the issue. Assessing whether someone is of sufficient understanding and intelligence is a matter for an appropriately qualified service provider. For a young person to be competent (in terms of the Gillick case) to make a decision, factors to consider include:

- the age, maturity and understanding of the child;
- the information provided for the child;
- the nature of the decision to be made;
- the seriousness of the decision;
- the consequences of consent or refusal;
- the young person's ability to understand the wider context of the decision to be made.

In Scotland, in making any major decision about a child, a person with parental responsibility shall have regard to the views of the child concerned, and 'a child of twelve years of age or more shall be presumed to be of sufficient age and maturity to form a view' (s. 6 Children (Scotland) Act 1995). However, the ability of the child to express a view is not the same as allowing the child to make an informed decision, which requires 'Gillick competence'.

In both England and Scotland, the consent of a person with parental responsibility is required if the child is not 'Gillick competent' to make a decision. The consent of one person who has parental responsibility is sufficient. If more than one person has parental responsibility and they cannot agree on an important issue concerning their child, they can ask the family court to make an order where necessary.

Failure to have obtained consent before offering counselling can lead to legal action for the civil wrongs (i.e. torts) of assault or, more likely in counselling, false imprisonment (misleadingly named, and better thought of as wrongful restraint). Legal aspects of informed consent are also considered in the context of suicide and confidentiality (see Chapters 7 and 10).

Encouraging Clients to Select Counsellors who Meet their Needs

The rapid growth of counselling means that there are increasing opportunities for clients to exercise personal choice between counsellors. For some clients, the choice will centre on gender, or on the cultural and ethnic background of the counsellor. Often, the client will be looking for someone who is similar to his or her own background, but this is not necessarily the case. I am aware of one major counselling initiative that failed by making that assumption. The counselling service was being established for a large number of female refugees from a central African country. Counsellors were appointed from the same ethnic and cultural background in order to minimize the cultural barriers to potential clients. However, the service was little used until a white English woman was appointed. She discovered that potential clients were deterred by worries about confidentiality and the possibility of details of their whereabouts or circumstances leaking back to their country of origin with potentially adverse impact on family members still living in a war zone. This is one of the clearest examples of the dangers of making assumptions about who will be an acceptable counsellor to other people. Often the criteria for choosing or rejecting someone as counsellor are more personal and concern the potential for forming a constructive relationship.

Increasingly, potential clients are encouraged to 'shop around' in order to find the right type of therapy for them and the best available person to be their counsellor. Experience suggests that someone looking for a counsellor have a number of issues to consider:

1   Being clear about what sort of help you want and the associated costs and
    potential benefits

    • What do you hope to get out of counselling – why are you seeking it?
      How could counselling successfully help you? In what ways could it fail
      you or make your situation worse?
    • Do you want short- or long-term help? How much can you afford?
    • What type of therapy would suit you?

2   Finding a counsellor or therapist

    • Personal recommendations by someone who knows you well and whose
      judgement you trust is a good starting point. It helps if the person
      making the recommendation has used the service or has professional
      knowledge of others being helped by the recommended counsellor.
    • Consult directories provided by major national professional bodies such
      as BACP, BPS, COSCA, IACP or UKCP.
    • Contact organizations specializing in the type of issue for which you want
      counselling to see if they can provide counselling or put you in touch with
      a recommended local counsellor. Good starting points are MIND
      (www.mind.org.uk) or RELATE (www.relate.org.uk).

3   Choosing a counsellor or therapist
    Where possible contact two or three therapists before making a choice and
    ask them:

    • What qualifications do they have, and what sort of training was required
      to get the qualification?
    • How much experience have they in general and with the type of issues
      you want help with?
    • Are they members of any professional organizations? Avoid counsellors
      and therapists who do not belong to reputable professional bodies with
      an active complaints or professional conduct procedures. Counsellors
      who are incompetent or exploitative tend to avoid such professional
      organizations or form small groups of like-minded people.

4   Rely on your instincts

- If you don't like the way a therapist communicates with you, feel uneasy about whose needs are going to be met, or mistrust the other person for any reason, do NOT go to them. You need to feel able to share private feelings and experiences freely with this person and to be confident that they will respect this and you as a person. Therapy is for your benefit as the client and not the other way round.
- If you have any concerns about the way your counsellor is working with you, discuss it with your counsellor at the earliest opportunity.
- One of the advantages of choosing a counsellor from a reputable professional organization is that you can consult them if you have any concerns that your counsellor is acting unprofessionally.
- If you conclude that your counsellor is acting unprofessionally, stop seeing them and report your concerns to their professional body.

Guidance of this kind for people seeking counselling accords well with respect for the client's autonomy. Many counsellors also offer a trial session without obligation to either party to continue the counselling. This practice is a further demonstration of respect for client autonomy.

Providing Pre-counselling Information

The client's choice of counsellor can often be greatly assisted by the provision of written information about the basis on which counselling is being provided. Such information might well provide:

- relevant background information about the counsellor(s);
- a brief definition or description of counselling;
- a summary of what the client can expect of the counsellor;
- the client's responsibilities with regard to receiving counselling;
- any complaints procedure;
- the arrangements for the payment of any fees.

I have seen many such leaflets. Some are beautifully presented with colour graphics and photographs and include statements from former clients. Others are no more than one side of A4 paper with a typed summary of the key points. The quality of presentation is primarily a marketing matter about how to communicate with potential clients effectively. Respect for client autonomy is communicated by the content.

One of the issues confronting anyone writing a leaflet about a counselling service is what to say about confidentiality. It is advisable to avoid statements like 'Counselling is *totally* confidential' because this arguably misrepresents the ethics of counselling and certainly the law (see Chapter 10). It is better to state simply that counselling is confidential, subject to the requirements of the law. If there are known circumstances in which confidentiality cannot be guaranteed, these should be mentioned, or if the circumstances have only a remote possibility of arising, potential clients could be encouraged to raise any issues about confidentiality with their counsellor. This might involve making a statement like:

The counsellors understand that confidentiality can be very important to anyone seeking the counselling. If you would like further information about the level of confidentiality we offer or any other matter, please ask the counsellor about it at the beginning of the session.

The basic principle is that all clients should know the terms on which they are being offered confidentiality. In particular, they should know all the reasonably foreseeable conditions in which confidentiality is *not* possible. Michael Megranahan (1989) made a clear recommendation about the standard of practice for employee counselling which, in my opinion, ought to be transferred to all settings where counselling is offered.

The person seeking help may either directly ask the questions: 'How do I know what I say will be confidential?', 'What guarantees do I have?', or assume that the conversation is confidential. It is essential therefore that the limits (if there are to be any) governing confidentiality are unambiguous, pre-defined and agreed with the employing organization as well as communicated at the beginning of any counselling interview to every person seeking help. The extent of the confidentiality should be public knowledge for every person who has access to the counselling facility and be in writing, e.g. in an employee handbook.

I have often been asked whether counsellors should routinely give clients copies of the counsellor or organization's relevant professional practice guidance or code of conduct as part of the pre-counselling information. On the whole, I do not think this is appropriate. The code is not sufficiently specific to the particular circumstances of the counsellor and client's relationship. I think it is much better that clients are informed of its existence and a copy should be readily available to clients when it is requested. It is much better to produce information that is specific to the counselling being provided and in a style appropriate to the client group. Sometimes this will require providing information in languages other than English. It may also require imaginative use of drawings for clients who are unable to read or the opportunity for preliminary pre-counselling discussions with a receptionist or counsellor about the suitability of counselling.

Clear Contracting

Counselling is not unique in attaching considerable importance to the client's autonomy. There is also an increasing emphasis on autonomy in professions that have sometimes been considered paternalistic in their concern to do good for someone. Nowhere is this change more evident than in medicine. Reiter-Theil et al. (1991) observed: 'Derived from the principle of *respect for autonomy*, informed consent has become one of the predominant rules discussed in medical ethics since the 1970s.'

Informed consent is someone's agreement to treatment after having understood:

- the procedures or methods to be used;
- any risks and benefits; and
- being informed of relevant alternatives.

It must be guaranteed that the client consented without coercion or manipulation and that the client is able to make a rational decision based on the information provided. However, consent is the absolute minimum standard of practice in counselling. It is more appropriate to situations where the person has something done to them, rather than as in counselling where the client is an active participant. Most ethical guidelines for counsellors require a higher standard of actively engaging the client in the contracting process. All the major professional bodies in the British Isles, including BACP, BPS, IACP and COSCA, require that counsellors are responsible for establishing clear and explicit contracts with their clients at the start of the relationship. The BACP *Ethical Framework* views contracting as a core element of client autonomy:

> Practitioners who respect their clients' autonomy: ensure accuracy in any advertising or information given in advance of services

offered; seek freely given and adequately informed consent; engage in explicit contracting in advance of any commitment by the client. (BACP, 2007)

Two issues are frequently raised by counsellors: whether the contract can be based on a spoken rather than a written agreement; and how to manage situations where the client is more concerned to get started with the counselling than to discuss contractual arrangements. I will consider each of these in turn.

There are no ethical or legal reasons that require that the therapeutic contract should be in writing. In many situations an oral agreement is sufficient. However, if there are any reasons for anticipating potential areas of misunderstanding or difficulties over managing the relationship, it may be better to have a written agreement. The contract may serve other purposes in addition to demonstrating respect for client autonomy. It can be a method of reinforcing the agreed therapeutic goals or purpose of the counselling. It may also establish a legally enforceable agreement between counsellor and client. Whenever the client is paying fees or offering a service in lieu of fees, for example gardening or decorating, any agreement between counsellor and client is legally enforceable. It is also arguable in law that a therapeutic contract may be held to exist and be enforceable in some circumstances when counselling is provided to the client free of charge. A written record of the agreement in the form of a signed statement, contemporaneous record in the case notes or a letter sent to the client confirming what has been agreed reduces the risk of contradictory memories arising later. An oral contract is legally enforceable but is much more vulnerable to being contradicted subsequently in any legal dispute or professional complaints procedure.

The ethical emphasis on clear contracting at the start of counselling is sometimes at odds with the practical experience of working with clients. Some clients are committed to starting counselling as quickly as possible, either because of their level of distress or the urgency of the issue that concerns them. In these circumstances, it can be difficult to enter into meaningful negotiations over a contract and the act of doing so may seem disrespectful of a client's obvious wish to get on with the counselling. This is one of the situations which can be eased by providing pre-counselling information and simply checking with the client whether she has read it and is willing to proceed on that basis. The contractual arrangements can be reviewed once the initial urgency has subsided.

It is generally considered good practice to periodically review the contractual relationships with the client. These reviews will probably concentrate on the therapeutic aims and achievements of the counselling but might well include clarification of expectations over confidentiality or practical arrangements. The therapeutic and legal basis of the relationship may be changed by such reviews.

Respecting the Client's Values, Beliefs and Choice of Action

One of the major challenges of respecting the autonomy of clients is offering respect to values and beliefs which may be quite different from one's own or considered unacceptable within one's own social or cultural group. All the ethical requirements of major national counselling organizations are clear on this point. Guidelines for counselling psychologists require that in order to be fit for practice: 'Practitioners will respect the diversity of beliefs and values and will continually review their practice with due regard for changing societal norms' (BPS, 2005: s. 1.2) The use of the word 'respect' in this and other codes suggests a positive commitment to work within and to be supportive of those beliefs and values rather than merely ignoring or tolerating any such differences.

Relationship between the counsellor's and client's autonomy

The optimum standard in counselling is that both the counsellor and client are working together as a deliberate and autonomous choice. This is most likely to happen when they share important personal values. However, this is not always essential. Counselling may take place where there are differences in values, provided the counsellor's personal values are consistent with respect for a client's values, beliefs and choices and a commitment to working within these. In reality, I suspect this is what most frequently happens. Counsellors and clients work together satisfactorily where their personal values are compatible rather than identical. The onus is on the counsellor to provide the client with sufficient space to work within her own value system, with the counsellor's own value system validating this relationship and avoiding the imposition of the counsellor's own personal values. Without the counsellor's commitment to respecting the client's values and capacity for self-determination the relationship lacks integrity. Integrity requires that both counsellor and client are acting autonomously.

However, establishing such a relationship is a high standard to maintain and it is not always easy to do so. What should a counsellor do when he finds himself working with a client whose personal values are so antagonistic to his own that both the integrity of the counselling relationship and the counsellor's own personal integrity are threatened? For example:

Mark is a committed pacifist for religious and personal reasons. He has counselled soldiers recovering from post-traumatic stress disorder who are returning to civilian life. Does respect for a client's values, beliefs and capacity for self-determination mean that he should also be willing to counsel soldiers wishing to return to active military service?

Mark's dilemma is encountered in many forms. To what extent does respect for the client's autonomy require that counsellors work with clients who choose to act in ways which conflict with the counsellor's deeply held views?

When I discussed this issue with ethically-minded and experienced practitioners in BACP, we considered that there is a baseline to good practice which is respectful of the client's autonomy while allowing the counsellor to maintain a conscientiously held moral position. This is the counsellor's willingness to support the client in finding a source of counselling which would offer more support for their chosen course of action when the counsellor has a conscientious objection to the client's proposed actions. Over the years, a number of examples of the application of this principle have been considered. Two have arisen several times.

Pro-life counselling

Some counsellors hold strong personal views against abortion and treat this as a matter of conscience. Such a counsellor may be working in settings where she sees clients about a wide range of issues so that the question of abortion may be raised only infrequently. Alternatively, she may be working in one of the pro-life organizations as a counsellor with the explicit aim of providing alternatives to abortion. What should a counsellor do if a client decides she wants an abortion? It is incompatible with even a minimal level of respect for the client's autonomy merely to say 'I disagree with your choice and can do no more. Come and see me again if you change your mind.' The minimum level of respect is to give the client sufficient information to enable her to implement her choice. Ideally, the counsellor would actively enable a referral to someone who could be more supportive of the client's autonomous choices.

Christian counselling

Many counselling services that identify themselves with the Christian counselling movement resolve the issue of protecting the integrity of their services by being explicit about religious orientation. They may explicitly state that they work 'according to biblical assumptions, aims and methods practised within a framework of Christian commitment, insight and values'. Where these services are provided to like-minded people, the issue of respect for client autonomy is neutralized. However, when these services are provided to the general public, there is a considerable clash between the ethics and values of counselling incorporating a narrowly defined religious agenda and those working within the ethical principles advocated in this book. The principle of autonomy would require the counsellor to work with respect for any religious beliefs of their clients, whether the client identifies with Christian or other religious faiths or has no religious affiliations. This is difficult for anyone to achieve who holds any form of fundamentalist belief.

The type of Christian counselling just described should not be confused with counselling which is provided by someone who has Christian beliefs but respects the client's right to hold different religious beliefs or no beliefs at all. There is a long-established tradition of pastoral counselling which is based on respect for the client's autonomy over religious beliefs (Hiltner, 1949; Wise, 1951; Foskett and Lyall, 1988; Lynch, 2002).

Racist or sexist clients

It is ethically consistent with the core values of counselling of respect, integrity and impartiality that counsellors should strive to provide counselling services on the basis of equality of opportunity for users of the service. A deliberately racist or sexist counsellor could not subscribe to counselling values with personal integrity. This raises the question, how should a counsellor respond to a client who does not share these values? From time to time I have been approached for guidance by counsellors who have been deeply troubled by the racism and sexism of some clients. For example:

Rachel is conscientious in attempting to establish relationships with her clients that have the qualities of integrity, impartiality and respect. Tom, the client, is deeply committed to views that are intolerant and often exploitative of people with different ethnic origins from his own, and these are the basis of his chosen courses of action. How should Rachel respond?

Most of the counsellors with whom I have discussed this issue accept that there can be no automatic duty placed on the counsellor to challenge her client's views. Counselling needs to be provided in ways that permit clients to express views which differ considerably from those of the counsellor. Respect for the client's right to express anti-social views and negative feelings towards others has always been an important part of respect for the client's capacity for self-determination. It is also part of the thera-peutic process, in which such feelings sometimes change. Therefore, the counselling relationship is not an appropriate place for campaigning for greater social tolerance. However, on occasions this effect may be achieved by the resolution of areas of personal pain which fuel intoler-ance. But this analysis does not resolve Rachel's dilemma. She is faced with a client whose personal values are so different from her own that she no longer feels able to offer respect for his capacity for self-determination without sacrificing her personal integrity. In her view, the situation is not resolved by maintaining clear boundaries between her own value system and those of her clients. In these circumstances it seems appropriate to consider discussing the conflict of personal values with the client directly. It is only once the issue has been discussed openly between the counsellor and client that each of them will be in a position to decide whether it is desirable to continue counselling together. How to raise the subject and the timing of the discussion may need to be considered in counselling-supervision. However, to continue without raising the subject is open to objections from both the counsellor's and client's viewpoints. It is not possible to conscientiously help someone to live their life according to their own values when you strongly disapprove of those values. Equally, the client may have valid moral grounds for objecting to being counselled by someone who has kept disapproval of his values secret from him. It could be viewed as covertly undermining his autonomy. The integrity of the relationship requires finding a basis on which both the counsellor and client can proceed by respecting each other's autonomy. Alternatively, it may be better to discontinue counselling and for the counsellor to assist the client in finding an alternative source of help if this is requested.

Issues of this degree of difficulty are best discussed in counselling-supervision or with another experienced counsellor before deciding how to respond to the client. The example given is about racism but could equally have been about prejudices based on gender, disability, sexuality, class, religion or age. Ethically, it is important that the counsellor respond to this dilemma in a way that is both consistent with the counselling model being used and that is respectful of the client's choice of outcome for him or herself. To act otherwise is to move outside the ethical boundaries of relationships in counselling. For example, persuasion and manipulation to seek to change someone's point of view, even for what are widely held to be socially desirable ends, is an intrusion into an area of responsibility which is properly the client's. At times, some counsellors may feel frustration with the need to respect a client's responsibility for the outcome of the counselling. One way some counsellors have found of resolving this ethically is to accept the constraints on their range of personal responses when in a counselling role with particular clients. However, independently of counselling, they offer workshops, lectures, write or campaign to try to change attitudes. There is a tradition within counselling which goes back to Frank Parsons, the probable originator of the term 'counselling', and his campaigns on behalf of the urban poor people in Boston during the early 1900s, which combined counselling with social and political action. In Britain, this tradition has continued in some areas of the country and within movements to empower disadvantaged people, particularly women and gay or lesbian people. Equally, there has been a tradition which is less activist and is politically quietist. It seems to me that both traditions are valid. They present potential clients with a range of choice between a variety of counsellors with different values and personal views about how best to implement those values.

Limitations to Respect for Autonomy

What is the limit of respect for individual autonomy? Both the major ethical systems that have influenced Western society accept that there is a limit to the principle of autonomy. The ethical system founded by Immanuel Kant which prioritizes autonomy over ethical issues and views people as ends in themselves recognizes that there is a point where one person's right to autonomy may conflict with another's. Similarly, John Stuart Mill (1806–73), an exponent of utilitarianism, an ethic committed to achieving the 'greatest happiness of the greatest number', argued strongly for the importance of respecting another's autonomy. However, he imposed restrictions. The person whose autonomy is respected should possess a fairly basic level of maturity and therefore be capable of taking responsibility for his or her own autonomous actions. As a philosopher, Mill was primarily concerned with the rationality of people and this is reflected in his test for an adequate level of maturity, which he defined as a 'a capability of being improved by free and equal discussion'. These two restrictions recur as issues in counselling.

The issue of when one person's autonomy harms another raises questions that have both ethical and legal consequences for counsellors and are considered in Chapters 11 and 15. It is an issue that can pose considerable challenges for the counsellor because it represents a watershed between prioritizing the client's autonomy and best interests in favour of someone else's, which inevitably changes the role of the counsellor and may even destroy the counselling relationship. Counsellors faced with choosing between respect for their client's autonomy and, for example, overriding the client's insistence on confidentiality in order to protect a young person from suspected abuse or to protect an adult from serious physical harm, carry a heavy burden. However, responding to the second challenge of deciding whether or not a client is capable of autonomous decisions is potentially as demanding but seems to be less well recognized.

The suicidal client raises the issue of respect for client autonomy in one of its most acute forms. This is the ethical challenge that is considered in the next chapter.

7

Suicide and Refusal to Accept Life-saving Treatment

Some of the situations which counsellors encounter cause great anxiety. Working with clients who are seriously intent on suicide must be one of the most anxiety-provoking because of the sense of imminent death, which makes any decisions and actions irreversible. The choice between life and death is a stark one. At a time when the counsellor's therapeutic skills are being considerably tested, there are also major ethical issues to consider. The counsellor is faced with a choice between respecting the client's autonomy or seeking to preserve life, either because this is considered to be a fundamental ethical principle or because it is thought to be in the client's best interests. Unfortunately, it is an issue that appears to be surrounded with misunderstanding about both the ethical and legal parameters that apply. I will start by considering general ethical and legal issues concerning suicidal clients before looking at the implications of a recent case that established guidelines about consent which give the client more rights than many counsellors probably realize. As counsellors are increasingly working with psychosocial aspects of physical illness, I will follow my consideration of dilemmas concerning suicidal clients with the client's right to refuse help or treatment. This chapter concludes with a summary of the practical implications for current practice. It is probable that many counsellors and professional agencies will want to review their existing practice in the light of recent clarifications of the law as applied by the English legal system.

The Suicidal Client

A client who is seriously intent on suicide presents the counsellor with an acute ethical dilemma. The choice is between respecting the client's autonomy or intervening in the interest of preserving the client's life. Counsellors are divided about how best to resolve this ethical dilemma.

One view takes the primacy of life as an ethical cornerstone. This is founded on the belief that life is the most valuable thing we possess: life is so obviously good that it requires no theoretical argument to justify its position as a primary value. It is asserted that the sanctity of life is self-evident, especially one's own life. The act of questioning its value is there-fore in itself symptomatic of crisis, illness or abnormality. From this moral perspective it is easy to justify acting to prevent someone taking their own life. The force of this justification would even override a client's autonomous wishes in order to compel a client to accept treatment or confinement without the opportunity to kill themselves. The experience of many mental health professionals appears to match this particular analysis. They report that suicidal feelings are often short-lived and transi-tory. If someone can be protected from acting on these feelings, then the will to live often returns and the problems which have caused this person to become suicidal can be tackled.

There is an alternative point of view that the number of people who continue to commit suicide challenges any claim to the self-evident sanctity of life. Occasions arise when the desire to preserve life may be overridden by a preference for death. From this perspective, suicide is the ultimate expression of someone's choice of how to live or die. It follows that counsellors ought to respect a client's right of choice over their suicide in the same way as they would over other matters. R.D. Laing (1967) also believed that suicide is the ultimate right of any individual. Thomas Szasz (1986) has argued that any attempt at coercive methods to prevent suicide contradicts the concept of individuals as moral agents who are ultimately responsible for their own actions. Some counsellors take this view and apply it consistently to all situations involving suicide. This stance is partic-ularly attractive if, like Laing and Szasz, the counsellor disagrees with medicalization of mental illness and does not accept that that behaviour which others have defined as mental illness erodes an individual's moral responsibility for their own actions. It is also a point of view which appeals to therapists working with the large number of people who go through the motions of attempting suicide but who appear to have no real intention of killing themselves. Known as parasuicide, this is primarily a cry for help. Part of the counsellor's role is to encourage the client to communicate what is wanted more directly and therefore to act with a greater sense of control over his or her autonomy. To rush into a course of action designed to prevent suicide would be counter-therapeutic. It might reinforce any manipulative or 'blackmailing' component in the parasuicide rather than reinforce the client's ability to act more straightforwardly in the quest to resolve their problems.

The proponents of each of these views can argue that their opinions are founded on an ethical analysis and within a constructive framework which enhances therapeutic work with significant numbers of the suicidal. How should a counsellor choose between them? An analysis of the situations in which counsellors encounter clients who are contemplating suicide suggests that the appropriate response ought to be varied according to the client's circumstances. In an earlier edition, I suggested that counsellors who cling exclusively to one opinion or the other do so out of an attempt to control their own anxiety in a potentially extremely anxiety-provoking situation. I also argued that as suicidal intentions occur in such a variety of different circumstances, it is a matter for assessment as to which of the two ethical principles ought to prevail. The law in many jurisdictions has not left matters so open-ended. Different legal systems have tended to favour resolving the ethical dilemma in favour of one or other of the competing ethical principles. English law is no exception to this tendency, as will become apparent. This may provide some relief to those who find uncertainty in these circumstances almost too much to bear.

Suicide as Self-administered Euthanasia

Sally has terminal cancer and has been told by doctors that her illness is well advanced, with an increasing number of secondaries. She has announced to her family and her doctor that she does not wish to battle futilely against her imminent death. She would prefer to die at home at a time of her own choosing. Her family and doctor attempt to dissuade her or suggest alternative ways of providing good quality terminal care but Sally remains committed to her planned suicide and has discussed her plans with her counsellor over several months.

This is the kind of situation where there can be little doubt that the client is making a decision which is authentic, deliberate and clear-headed. She has sustained her point of view over a period of time and is acting under her own volition, not under the influence of others. It may be that the counsellor will want to check that the client is aware of the alternative ways of receiving care during a terminal illness and that her aims would not be better met by home nursing, or the use of a living will in which the client sets out how she wishes to be cared for medically, or going into a hospice. Even if the client is unaware of any of these, or feels that they are inadequate to enable her to take control of her dying, I doubt whether there are grounds for the counsellor to intervene to attempt to prevent suicide (although it would be illegal for the counsellor to actively assist a person in committing suicide). David Heyd and Sidney Bloch (1991) express the view that although doctors will find it psychologically and legally difficult to co-operate actively in such a suicide, no psychiatrist would consider the forced hospitalization of such a person. Under current mental health legislation that applies in England and Wales, the Mental Health Act 2007, there is no provision for compulsory assessment or treatment merely because someone is suicidal. It is well established in English law that adults of have the right to refuse treatment even if to do so would result in their own death. This means that, even if a counsellor wanted to intervene, there would be very little that could be done to override the client's intent.

The counsellor may experience further dilemmas. What if the family seek the counsellor's support in trying to persuade Sally out of self-administered euthanasia? This is a situation where the counsellor needs to consider the nature of the contract with the client and, assuming that this contract is with Sally, the counsellor may have to explain tactfully that her primary responsibility is to Sally, who retains control of the outcome of the counselling. If the family feel unable to communicate their feelings about Sally's proposed actions directly to her, then they may wish to use another counsellor to facilitate such a discussion. For Sally's counsellor to undertake an additional role on behalf of the family could raise all the problems of conflicting loyalties, particularly as there is a substantial difference of view between them.

An alternative possibility is that the counsellor feels strongly supportive of Sally's decision to take control of her own dying. How far should she go in offering emotional encouragement or active support? Legally there are definite limits to how far a counsellor can go without risking prosecution. Unlike Dutch or Swiss law, there is no provision for doctors or anyone else to assist someone to end their own life. The legalization of euthanasia is discussed periodically, but it seems unlikely that it will be legalized in the foreseeable future. Until there is a change in the law, it is a criminal offence to assist someone to kill themselves. Although the Suicide Act 1961 stopped attempted suicide and suicide from being a criminal offence, it also created a new offence. Section 2 states:

> A person who aids, abets, counsels or procures the suicide of another or an attempt by another to commit suicide, shall be liable on conviction on indictment to imprisonment for a term not exceeding fourteen years.

To 'counsel' in this legal context means to conspire, advise or knowingly give assistance, which are not activities usually encompassed within counselling. Although the Mental Capacity Act 2005 strengthens the rights of adults to consent and refuse treatment (see later in this chapter), this legislation explicitly excludes consent to assisted suicide, which remains a criminal offence by the person who offers assistance.

Suicide as an Escape from Problems and Emotional Pain

Another example describes the kind of situation which most counsellors encounter fairly frequently:

Brian is over-burdened by financial problems and social isolation following the ending of a longstanding relationship. He is becoming increasingly depressed and is talking about suicide as a way out of his problems and to escape the emotional pain he is experiencing.

In this example Brian's suicide is not an alternative to an imminent and inevitable death but represents a substantial foreshortening of his lifespan. There is also an element of doubt about whether his choice is authentic, deliberate, clear-headed and rational, or whether he is acting irrationally, impulsively and on the basis of a judgement distorted by extreme personal distress or loss of a sense of reality. Our knowledge of how best to understand and help in such circumstances is becoming better informed by research (O'Connor, forthcoming) and professional guidance (Reeves and Seber, 2007) but is still far from complete. All mental health professionals are faced with complex judgements around the circumstances of a particular person. A key ethical dimension for counsellors in circumstances like these is the choice between respect for the client's autonomy and acting to prevent self-destruction.

It is tempting with such a difficult ethical dilemma to turn to the law as a way of pre-empting the ethical choice. The fear that an ethical dilemma might turn into legal liability makes this a very natural reaction. In my experience, most people turn to the law in the expectation that it will justify an intervention to preserve life and thus end the dilemma. In practice, the law does not provide such an instant solution. For most counsellors there is no clear-cut obligation to intervene on behalf of adults. English law is strongly weighted in favour of respecting individual autonomy unless there is evidence that the person is of unsound mind, that is suffering a diagnosable mental illness, or being coerced. A subsidiary issue arises because the counsellor will not usually have the power to intervene directly. Any offer of treatment in addition to the counselling will require the services of a doctor, psychiatrist, psychiatric nurse or approved social worker. The ethical dilemma is eliminated where the client is willing to seek the help of these services on their own behalf. Many clients will appreciate the counsellor's clear suggestion that there are additional sources of help and that it would be appropriate to contact these. Some clients may request that the counsellor help them to make contact with the service, especially if they are depressed, which is the commonest reason for feeling suicidal. Many counsellors would feel ethically obliged to respond to the client's request for assistance in these circumstances, unless there are good grounds for thinking that this would be inappropriate.

David is a student teacher who has chosen to see a counsellor privately rather than see the university counsellor or the one attached to his doctor's practice. He has made this decision because he wants to protect the confidentiality of the counselling. However, his counsellor insists that he inform his GP or she will do so when he discloses that he is feeling suicidal. David refuses to do so because he does not want his emotional state to be recorded on his medical notes. He is concerned that this might lead to him failing a compulsory medical which he needs to pass in order to practise as a teacher.

A frequent reason for refusing medical assistance in these circumstances is a concern that once the GP is involved the information may be subsequently disclosed in medical reports for employers or insurance companies. It is not only counsellors who have issues around dual relationships and their consequences for service users. Some counselling services have lists of doctors and psychiatrists who will see people privately. Let us suppose that this client continues to reject all suggestions that he should seek psychiatric help. The counsellor points out that both her professional codes and her original agreement with him permit her to breach confidentiality when she considers that there is a serious risk of a client harming himself. He still refuses to allow her to do so. Many counsellors might consider that they are legally obliged to inform in these circumstances and that they will be protected from claims for breach of confidentiality if they do so. These are misunderstandings of the English legal system, which from Magna Carta onwards through a long series of medical cases has protected the adult citizen's right to refuse medical treatment.

The expectation that the counsellor has a duty of care to protect the client from suicidal intent may be based on misapplications of US law. In most states, counsellors are required to breach confidentiality to report a client's suicidal intent. There is no equivalent requirement in Britain. Nor is there any legal protection against an action for breach of confidentiality in the above example. The counsellor could be liable for substantial damages for loss of earnings if the client's career were to be adversely affected by an inappropriate disclosure. Although there is no general duty to intervene, some special circumstances may create such a duty. For example, a counsellor working with patients receiving compulsory psychiatric treatment under the Mental Health Act 2007 may have an obligation to intervene under the terms of their contract of employment or other aspects of civil law. However, this obligation does not automatically transfer to counsellors working independently of the statutory mental health services.

In the case of adults, it is only when the counsellor has reasonable grounds for believing that the client is seriously at risk of committing suicide *and* is suffering a treatable mental disorder, i.e. depression, schizophrenia, that it may be defensible to breach confidence in order to seek an assessment to determine whether the client should be compelled to receive compulsory treatment under the Mental Health Act. This Act explicitly excludes promiscuity and alcohol or drug dependency from its provisions for compulsory assessment or treatment orders. It is defensible to breach confidences where someone is being coerced into suicide in order to prevent a serious criminal offence. However, the current law urges considerable caution with regard to overriding an adult's refusal to permit the counsellor to breach confidentiality in order to protect an adult intent on causing harm to themselves, even if the consequences might be fatal. The law takes a robust view of adult autonomy and will generally protect it unless other people are being placed at risk by the intended behaviour, e.g. jumping from a considerable height on to a public road. The counsellor is permitted to repeatedly offer additional assistance and to try to find a form of help that would be acceptable to the person concerned. Obtaining the client's consent to other forms of assistance is not only the best legal protection but is also the best way of ensuring the client's collaboration in any subsequent treatment. If this seems surprising, it is worth remembering that the Samaritans, who offer a befriending service for the suicidal, will only consider overriding a client's refusal of personal help if he or she loses consciousness, and that this practice is consistent with English law.

The balance of public interest switches more strongly in favour of seeking assistance for someone aged 16–18 in order to avert a life-threatening situation. It is completely reversed in the case of young people of insufficient intelligence or understanding to be considered 'Gillick competent' – see later in this chapter, Chapter 6 and Chapter 10. For young people there are provisions in children and young persons' legislation which provide alternatives to the use of mental health legislation. Further advice can be obtained from the relevant local social services department, NSPCC or MIND.

One of the consequences of this legal protection of adult autonomy is that it places greater ethical emphasis on counsellors being clear about the extent to which they feel competent to work with suicidal clients. The counsellor has a right to withdraw from the counselling when she feels that the counselling is beyond her competence and the client refuses additional assistance or referral. In reaching a decision about whether to work with a particular client or how best to do so, the counsellor may wish to assess the degree of suicidal risk. This is not only to the advantage of clients who are looking to the counsellor to help them overcome self-destructive urges, but is also in the counsellor's self-interest in terms of having some control over the scale of the challenge that she is taking on.

Methods for conducting the assessment may vary between counsellors according to their background, but might well include:

(a) *Suicidal intentions*: strength of feelings about going on or ending it all; degree of planning and preparations already accomplished.

(b) *Mental state*: previous history of mental illness and attempted suicide; any evidence of current mental illness, including depression; current emotional mood.

(c) *Clarification of current difficulties and resources for coping*: exploration of current problems and ways of resolving these; possible sources of acceptable support from other people and agencies; previous strategies for coping with problems.

(d) *Risk factors*: alcohol or substance abuse, bullying, court case pending, being in custody, experience of physical or sexual abuse, social isolation, severe financial difficulties, unemployment.

The assessment procedure often involves difficult decisions. It is in both the client's and counsellor's interests that the counsellor holds appropriate discussions with a counselling supervisor or experienced counsellor and if necessary seeks the opinions of professionals with relevant experience. The purpose of these consultations is to provide support for the counsellor and to clarify issues which require consideration, to provide any additional information not already known by the counsellor or client, especially about the kinds of help available from non-counselling services. Accurate and up-to-date information about these services and counselling helps to ensure the client is in a position to make informed choices about the kind of help that is wanted.

Any consultations by the counsellor with people outside the counselling relationship which are undertaken as part of the assessment stage should either be with the client's consent or be undertaken in such a way that the client's identity is not disclosed. The assumption of respect for the client's autonomy carries with it the high standards of practice concerning confidentiality. These consultations are not an alternative to the client's making these enquiries for himself, which is the usual practice in counselling. It is highly desirable that whenever possible the client make his own enquiries as a means of taking control of his own destiny.

The process of assessing suicidal clients is often therapeutic to clients who actively participate in the assessment procedure. Often what seems an overwhelming and ill-defined sense of hopelessness does change into a differentiated series of separate problems which can seem more manageable. Perhaps most importantly, the counsellor is giving the client permission to explore his suicidal feelings and to discover what they really mean for him, with the possibility of finding alternative outcomes. The assessment process is often a time when clients have a sense of starting to deal with the issues which really concern them. This sense of a new start is often accompanied by a willingness to put suicidal intentions to one side for the time being in the hope of making changes to make life more rewarding. It is sometimes therapeutic to ask that clients commit themselves to not acting on their suicidal intentions for an agreed period of time in order to see how the counselling helps them. It is also appropriate to ensure that the client knows where to get help in an emergency, usually from his doctor, a hospital accident and emergency department or the Samaritans, depending on which are acceptable to the client.

For the counsellor, a systematic assessment procedure provides a means of resolving an ethical dilemma in a considered and conscientious way. Although it is not always possible to be infallible in one's assessments, at least the counsellor knows that she has done all that can reasonably be expected of her and has also maximized the likelihood of the client making an authentic and considered choice. Many counsellors working with suicidal clients would also assert the importance of not taking significant decisions without consultation with at least one other person. If a client does commit suicide, the counsellor may experience regret and concern that, perhaps, something more could have been done to prevent it. It is at times like this that it is useful to know that the decision was not taken on one's own. Consultations with a counselling supervisor, doctor or social worker are a simple way of helping to minimize the inevitable distress following some suicides. In practice many clients consent to these discussions if they can be reassured that they are adequately protected by confidentiality and that they will enhance the quality of the counselling that they receive. In my experience, many clients view this way of working as evidence that you are taking their needs seriously.

Refusal to Accept Life-saving Treatment

Suicide requires someone to take positive action that places his or her life in jeopardy. Counsellors may also encounter situations where someone is facing premature death as a result of their inaction. This may be someone who is refusing medical treatment for a treatable illness which, if untreated, will result in death. Counsellors working with people with eating disorders will be familiar with this situation. Some people with anorexic conditions will refuse all offers of treatment and eventually starve themselves to death. Not all refusals to eat to the point of becoming life-threatening are medically diagnosable. Some people refuse to eat to draw attention to a particular cause, e.g. hunger strikers. Religious convictions may lead others to refuse certain life-saving treatments. The best known of these is the refusal of blood transfusions by Jehovah's witnesses. In contrast to these considered refusals, some people are simply so disturbed or confused that they either fail to understand the significance of not accepting treatment or are incapable of co-operating with any treatment regime on a voluntary basis.

Like suicidal intent, the refusal of life-saving treatment arises from many different circumstances. Assessment of these is an essential component of resolving the ethical dilemma.

Ethically and legally, it is useful to distinguish between adults and young people. One of the characteristics of adulthood is personal responsibility for the way an adult chooses to live, even if this foreshortens life. In contrast, there is a widely accepted social responsibility to ensure that young people reach adulthood, at which point they take full responsibility for their decisions. Of course, the boundary between full adult responsibility and the ethical obligations to protect a young person is not marked by a single life event. There is a progressive capacity by young people to take responsibility for themselves. Any ethical analysis needs to take into account the gradual progression from an ethical obligation for adults to make decisions in the best interests of the child to increasingly showing respect for the young person's autonomy. I will start by considering adults.

Jane is eight months pregnant and has been told that she has pre-eclampsia by her GP and should be admitted to hospital urgently for a Caesarean birth and treatment in order to protect her and the foetus from serious disability or death. Jane believes that serious illness and death are natural events that should not be interfered with. She refuses an emergency admission and instead asks to see the practice counsellor for personal support and insists on minimum medical intervention during the birth should she reach that point.

Here the doctor and counsellor share an ethical dilemma about their obligations to the pregnant woman and to the foetus, which at this point has a reasonable chance of being a healthy baby after birth. If Jane is not mentally ill or being pressurized into this decision by others, then she is in the same position as any other adult with regard to accepting or refusing medical treatment. The doctor's ethical responsibility is substantially discharged by giving the patient adequate information to make an informed decision for herself (the requirements of the Mental Capacity Act 2005 and related Scottish law are considered later in this section). The counsellor's ethical position is no different from providing a service to someone who refuses medical intervention for any other illness. Respect for client autonomy is the ethical norm. However, this need not prevent the counsellor from exploring or even challenging the basis of the client's decision. Standards of practice consistent with the ethic of autonomy require that communicating alternative options takes place within a framework of respecting the client's right to make a decision for herself. It may also be appropriate to offer support in living with the consequences of that decision, as with any other client making a difficult and demanding decision.

The question of ethical obligation to the potentially healthy baby within the mother is a separate issue but one that cannot be considered separately from the mother. Any ethical obligation to ensure the best interests of the foetus can be achieved only at the expense of violating the mother's autonomy and compelling her to undergo major surgery. This is an ethically contentious decision. There are credible arguments in favour of preserving the life of a viable foetus over a temporary violation of the rights of the mother. An alternative view is that the mother's autonomy is the ethical priority and takes precedence over the unborn child. There is no easy way of choosing between these alternatives. Either decision favours one at the significant expense of the other and raises questions about who carries the primary moral responsibility for making that decision. Courts have considered these circumstances. In some jurisdictions in America and Europe, the law prioritizes the preservation of life. In deciding in favour of the preservation of the baby's life, a judge explained: 'Where the harm is so great and the temporary remedy is so slight, the law is compelled to act. ... Someone must speak for those who cannot speak for themselves' (*Winnipeg Child and Family Services v G*, 1997). The English legal tradition has taken different views on this issue.

There was a case which shows how the court was prepared to intervene to save life if the judge could justify it. In *Re T* (Adult: refusal of treatment) [1993] 1 Fam 95, a judge made a declaration of lawfulness for a blood transfusion and a caesarean operation on a woman who was 34 weeks pregnant. She had been admitted to hospital following a road traffic accident. The Court of Appeal justified and rationalized the judge's order on the basis that, although the mother was an adult of sound mind and had refused the blood transfusion for religious reasons, on this occasion she was unable to make a rational decision at that time because she had been given the narcotic drug Pethedine, her mother may have exerted pressure on her, and she had received some misleading responses to her enquiries about alternative treatments.

The Court of Appeal said in their judgment:

> that although an adult patient was entitled to refuse consent to treatment irrespective of the wisdom of his decision, for such a refusal to be effective his doctors had to be satisfied that at the time of his refusal his capacity to decide had not been diminished by illness or medication or by false assumptions or misinformation, that his will had not been overborne by another's influence and that his decision had been directed to the situation in which it had become relevant; that where a patient's refusal was not effective the doctors were free to treat him in accordance with their clinical judgment of his best interests.

In a more recent English case (*St George's NHS Trust v S*, 1998 at 692), the court affirmed other decisions that the mother's rights take precedence:

> In our judgement while pregnancy increases the personal responsibilities of a woman, it does not diminish her entitlement to decide whether or not to undergo medical treatment. Although human, and protected by law in a number of different ways ... an unborn child is not a separate person from its mother. Its need for medical assistance does not prevail over her rights. She is entitled not to be forced to submit to invasion of her body against her will, whether her own life or that of the unborn baby depends on it. Her right is not reduced or diminished merely because her decision to exercise it may appear morally repugnant.

This case is of particular significance to counsellors and other caring professions because it also considered whether two doctors and a social worker had been correct in imposing a compulsory assessment order under mental health legislation and using that as the basis for seeking legal authority from a High Court judge to impose medical treatment. In the process of reaching a decision about these aspects of the case, the Court of Appeal concluded that the professionals had been wrong in law on two counts. First, the Mental Health Act cannot be used to achieve 'the detention of an individual against her will merely because her thinking process is unusual, even apparently bizarre and irrational, and contrary to the views of the overwhelming majority of the community at large'. Unusually in a law report, it is possible to get some direct insight into the personal thinking of the woman who refused treatment as she recorded her objections to receiving treatment in writing. After giving her profession as veterinary nurse and affirming her understanding of the medical consequences of the decision, she wrote:

> I have always held strong views with regard to medical and surgical treatments for myself, and particularly wish to allow nature to 'take its course' without intervention. I fully understand that, in certain circumstances, this may endanger my life. I see death as a natural and inevitable end point to certain conditions, and that natural events should not be interfered with. It is not a belief attached to the fact of my being pregnant, but would apply equally to any condition arising.

Secondly, a woman detained under the Mental Health Act cannot be forced into medical procedures unconnected with her mental condition unless her capacity to consent to such treatment is diminished. For example, a man suffering from schizophrenia has been legally supported in his decision to refuse to have a gangrenous leg amputated in the face of a medical consensus that it would be in his best interests and life-saving.

The importance of making a record of the basis on which it is decided that someone has the capacity to give or refuse consent to a proposed course of action also emerged in this case. The judgment criticizes the doctors for failing to attend to their patient's capacity to consent or refuse consent to treatment. They concluded: 'None of the contemporary documents suggest that this factor was given express attention during the decision-making process.'

One of the aims of the Mental Capacity Act 2005 in England and Wales and the earlier Adults with Incapacity Act 2000 in Scotland was to clarify the law and to ensure compatibility with human rights law. This legislation sets out some core principles. A person over age 16 must be assumed to have capacity to give valid consent until it is proved otherwise. This includes the right to refuse treatment for all persons over 18 years and some rights to refuse for people aged 16–18. Someone must be supported to make a personal decision, as far as it is practicable to do so. Someone is not to be treated as lacking capacity simply because of making an unwise decision. Nor is capacity to be regarded as fixed or determined by a particular physical or mental characteristic or general ability to make decisions. Each assessment of someone's capacity must be made in the context of the decision to be made and may vary between different decisions. Any relevant information to assist the making of a decision must be presented in ways that are appropriate to that person's circumstances. The assessment of whether someone has capacity depends on whether someone can retain the information for long enough to make a decision and whether a person is able to weigh it in order to arrive at a choice. Finally, someone must be able to communicate a choice even if it is restricted to blinking an eye to communicate 'yes' or 'no'. This development in law demonstrates a strong respect for individual autonomy and a robust protection of that right even when someone is in difficult circumstances due to illness or other limitations of their mental capacity. Further information can be found in Bond and Mitchels (2008), where capacity is considered in the context of client confidentiality and record-keeping, where consent is a fundamental issue. Updates and guidelines from government and charities can be found on the web.

The issue of a young person's right to refuse treatment is complicated by the progressive shift from total dependence on adults to self-reliance as adulthood approaches. Where the young person is considered incapable of giving or withholding consent, the responsibility for that decision rests with someone holding parental responsibility. Where parental consent is being exercised against the young person's best interests or is unobtainable, the High Court may decide the appropriate course of action. Section 8 of the Family Law Reform Act 1969 gives 16–18 year-olds the right to consent to or to refuse medical investigations and treatments. The courts have generally upheld these rights but have sought reasons to override the right to refuse treatment for life-threatening conditions. In *Re W* (1992), the Court of Appeal was considering the refusal of a

16 year-old suffering from anorexia to be transferred from one unit to another for treatment. The court decided that they could order her immediate transfer because they considered that anorexia distorts the young person's ability to comprehend sufficiently to be able to rebut the rights given to her under the Family Law Reform Act. A similar decision was made in *Re J* (1992) where the issue of the power of a young person's ability to override parental consent was considered. In this case, J was suffering from anorexia nervosa of such severity that there was a serious risk of irreversible damage to her brain and reproductive organs and her life was in danger. The Court of Appeal granted an emergency order enabling J to be treated despite her lack of consent. Although J maintained her refusal to consent, she accepted that the court order would have to be complied with. The Court of Appeal explained the decision in the following terms:

> No minor of whatever age has the power by refusing consent to treatment to override a consent to treatment by someone who has parental responsibility for the minor. Nevertheless such a refusal was a very important consideration in making clinical judgements and for parents and the court in deciding whether ... to give consent. Its importance increased with the age and maturity of the minor. (*Guardian Law Reports*, 1992)

This view is consistent with an increasing emphasis in the law that the young person should be consulted and their views taken into account on any major decision about their best interests, even if they are deemed incapable of giving or refusing consent in their own right.

Below the age of 16, the ability to refuse investigations or treatment depends on an assessment of whether the child is of sufficient 'understanding and intelligence' (i.e. Gillick competent) to give or refuse valid consent. A fuller discussion of the assessment process can be found in Chapter 10 in relation to confidentiality. In the situation where a 'Gillick competent' young person gives consent, that consent cannot be vetoed by someone with parental responsibility. Conversely, a young person who is not considered to be 'Gillick competent' cannot veto a valid parental consent. The counsellor or anyone else who provides a service or treatment on this basis is protected from legal action that might be brought on the grounds of invalid consent. The Master of the Rolls reiterated the protection given by a valid consent in the face of other objections to the proposed course of action (*Re W*, 1992 at 767). The valid consent may be withdrawn and this protection would cease unless other valid consents applied.

The legal framework creates a series of principles which have resulted in an increasing recognition of the ethical value of respecting a young person's autonomy while balancing that with a general responsibility to act in the best interests of the young person. A theme which runs throughout the courts' decisions is a reluctance to impose hard-and-fast rules that might be inappropriate to some cases. The decisions about the 'best interests of the young person' are made by consideration of all the relevant circumstances. Similarly, where an assessment of a young person's 'competence to give valid consent or refusal to consent' is required, that assessment would take into account the gravity of the decision to be made. In contrast, adults' right to refuse treatment is largely resolved by an ethic of respect for individual autonomy.

After a Death

It is increasingly common practice for counsellors to be called to give evidence in coroner's courts, especially about deaths where there is the possibility of suicide. The main aim of the court is to establish the identity of the deceased and to determine the cause of death.

If a counsellor is summoned to appear, it will usually be in order to establish the cause of death. This means that the counsellor will need to decide how much she is willing to say in open court. The central issue will be the agreement about confidentiality made with the client. It is accepted practice among counsellors that agreements about confidentiality continue beyond the client's death.

It is often easier to discuss the nature of the ethical difficulties outside the public hearing. For example, a counsellor might feel willing to answer questions in general terms about a client being depressed because of relationship difficulties but may know there are some things which the client had stressed as being confidential, such as specific feelings about a named sexual partner or a relative. Most coroners will use their discretion in order to respect the ethical integrity of a professional witness where this does not compromise the purpose of the hearing. The coroner, who is usually a local doctor or solicitor, has considerable discretion about how he conducts the hearings. If any difficulties cannot be resolved by a preliminary discussion, it is advisable to seek legal advice and to be legally represented in court.

After a suicide it is not unusual for relatives to want to discover whether everything had been done that could be done by those caring for the person who committed suicide. If they were unaware of the mental and emotional state of the person who died, they may also want as much information as possible. Out of their anger and grief they may wish to show that the counsellor was either incompetent or uncaring. This can lead to some challenging questions, either in court or elsewhere. It goes without saying that a counsellor who has been clear from the outset with a client about her qualifications, experience and policy over respect and autonomy or intervention to prevent suicide is in as strong a position as it is possible to be in these circumstances, particularly if she has also conducted an appropriate assessment in consultation with others and then acted on it. Evidence of clear agreement that either the client would abstain from suicidal attempts for the duration of counselling or that the client would contact specified people or organizations should he become suicidal helps to add to the credibility of the counsellor and to an understanding of the counsellor's position with regard to client autonomy. Members of the general public, and particularly distressed relatives, may wrongly assume that a counsellor has a clear duty to intervene in all circumstances to prevent suicide and may also have unrealistic expectations of what could have been done, even if the counsellor did attempt to intervene.

The issue of keeping written records is highly relevant to any situation which might result in a court appearance. This is discussed in Chapter 13.

Conclusion

In this chapter, I have made extensive reference to the law. It is in the courts that the practical issues around the responsibilities of professionals towards people who are suicidal or are refusing life-saving treatment have been extensively examined. The courts have, in effect, become the venue for deciding public morality on these most contentious of cases. Different national jurisdictions have varied in the priority given to the ethical principles of respect for client autonomy or the preservation of life. Just as there is no universal agreement about which ethical principle should prevail in law, there are comparable divisions of opinion between counsellors about how best to respond. For some counsellors, the laws will reinforce their ethical convictions. Others will find the legal requirements contrary to their ethical convictions. However, I am not aware of any jurisdiction that treats the ethical issues as a matter of conscience for individual counsellors or other professionals. Counsellors working in Britain need to take into account the legal framework that has been developed over many centuries since the assertion of personal liberty contained in Magna Carta. There is no general or automatic legal obligation to intervene on behalf of an adult who is suicidal or refusing medical treatment. Counsellors are working in a legal system that will usually support adults' rights to make decisions for themselves. The two most common circumstances likely to be encountered by counsellors where this is not the case concern adults who lack the capacity to give or withhold consent to psychiatric treatment due to serious mental disorder under the provisions of mental health legislation or the complex provisions relating to young people and children. In Britain, the law favours an ethic of respect for adult autonomy and protects an individual's right to consent to or to refuse treatment as the usual basis for managing these difficult personal and social dilemmas.

The law that forbids actively assisting suicide, even in cases where someone is dying and wishes to void uncontrollable pain or loss of control of their most basic bodily functions is challenged in the media with increasing frequency but there is little sign at the time of writing that assisting someone's autonomous choice to control the end of life can overcome concerns about the preservation of life or the risk of vulnerable people being pressurized into ending their lives.

This ethical analysis of how to respond to suicidal clients is organized around the principle of client autonomy, which helps to decide how to respond ethically and lawfully but cannot eliminate the unavoidable anxiety and anguish that is so often associated with death, especially for surviving relatives and social contacts.

8

Counsellor Competence

A commitment by counsellors to work within their competence is widely recognized as fundamental to working ethically. It is one of the ethical requirements that not only recurs in the ethical guidance of national professional organizations (see Table 4.1, pp. 58–60) but cascades down through agency policy and expectations that others hold of counsellors. Failure to work within one's own competence as a counsellor undermines many of the ethical principles considered essential to counselling. Clients are rendered vulnerable to additional emotional distress and psychological harm, the opposite of a commitment to doing good (beneficence) and avoiding doing harm (non-maleficence). The basis of trust between counsellor and client is undermined and, with it, the principle of fidelity. Any claim to respect for client autonomy is discredited by the lack of basic respect being shown to the client's desire for enhanced self-determination. The counsellor is also working against his own interest by contradicting the ethical basis on which he might expect the client to show respect for his need for autonomy, beneficence, non-maleficence and fidelity. There are few acts in counselling which compare to working outside one's competence for simultaneously undermining so many ethical principles.

What is competence? Professional competence requires having adequate skills, being properly qualified and trained, effective and working ethically. The responsibility for ensuring competence rests on the individual counsellor in the last resort. No one else is better placed to monitor and evaluate whether counselling is being provided to adequate standards. It is not a purely personal self-assessment, but will be informed by feedback from clients, colleagues and professional mentoring or supervision. Some counsellors, especially those working in agencies, may use systematic audits of the client experience to inform awareness of issues of competence and where updating or training may be required. Competence is only a minimum standard for acceptable practice by the good enough counsellor. Many will aspire to something above this level to achieve a standard between competence and excellence out of a sense of personal vocation or commitment and to obtain work in a competitive environment.

As a counsellor, trainer and supervisor, I am aware of several complications in achieving competence. First, there is the process of becoming competent. A novice or trainee counsellor experiences the challenge of becoming competent most acutely and how does someone know that they have reached this standard. Assessments by a trainer, service manager and/or supervisor are good guides as well as self-monitoring. There is also that rather tricky transition to becoming competent between knowing enough to start seeing clients but still requiring support from someone who is more advanced in their development as a counsellor. The delivery of a competent level of counselling rests on a combination of individual ability and a systemic infrastructure of personal and professional development so that responsibility for a competent service depends on several people, including the counsellor, until the counsellor is ready for more autonomous practice. This is not the end of the story when a counsellor has become competent and had that validated by qualification and accreditation. Every time someone moves into a new area of practice the cycle of learning begins again, from 'not knowing' to competence.

Sustaining competence requires a willingness to be self-critical and an awareness of changes of knowledge and practice in the field of counselling. After nearly thirty years of practice, I find myself asking myself whether I am generally competent in my practice and more specifically with individual clients and in particular moments within sessions. The quest for competence is not a 'once in a lifetime, achievement but recurs throughout the lifetime' of counselling. It has to be assessed against a changing background of clients' needs and expectations in response to changes in society. Social changes around gender, sexual orientation, family relationships, ethnicity and disability over my working life have had a profound influence on what clients bring to counselling.

New technologies have opened up possible ways of delivering counselling that were inconceivable when I first started. Not only is the context within which counselling takes place changing but so is the professional knowledge base and infrastructure to support competent practice. There is a perpetual need for updating, especially in the knowledge and skills base for practice, and increasingly to meet the demands of professional accountability.

Externally Determined Aspects of Competence

Professional counselling organizations frequently make an important distinction between their criteria for membership of a professional body, accreditation as a practitioner and competence as a counsellor. The former is used as a strategy to bring some order to an ill-defined field and to set minimum entry requirements or thresholds appropriate to that professional organization. Accreditation ensures that someone's suitability to practise has been externally validated against publicly declared criteria by the professional body. In earlier editions I have offered a comparison between the criteria for accredited practitioner status in the major national professional bodies. There appears to be so much change in prospect at the moment that any comparisons may be misleading.

The impending regulation of psychologists within the Health Professions Council (HPC) and the real possibility of future statutory regulation of counselling and psychotherapy is causing all the professional bodies to review their minimum entry requirements and potentially their accreditation criteria. The best way of keeping up to date with developments is through updates on key organizations' websites. The British Psychological Society (BPS) is furthest into the process of statutory regulation and therefore a good indicator of the sorts of issues that the other professional bodies may face.

Was My Counsellor Competent?

In recent years, professions like medicine and law have begun to implement procedures that respond to significant but less serious concerns about competence. These concerns are more easily dealt with when they involve matters such as failure to keep appointments, undue delay, poor financial management or failure to provide a service that was promised. In contrast, concerns about professional judgement or incompetence are more problematic. In any profession, there will be a range of opinions about what constitutes satisfactory practice. This is particularly true of counselling and can be illustrated by the difficulty of answering the straightforward question, 'Was my counsellor competent?' Whether or not a particular intervention is likely to be judged competent will depend on the context and the counsellor's theoretical orientation.

For example: 'Kate is distressed by her counsellor telling her that he feels antagonistic towards her when she does or says certain things. She asks is it appropriate for a counsellor to disclose that he feels angry and frustrated or is he being incompetent?' The answer to Kate's question depends on the theoretical orientation of the counsellor. Out of the 400 or more models of counselling in current use, I shall restrict myself to four major models.

From a psychodynamic perspective, such an intervention would be judged counterproductive. In order to help a client gain insight into her transferences, the counsellor deliberately keeps him or herself, as a human being, in the background. Michael Jacobs (2004) states that transference is partially resolved because

> the counselling setting provides a chance for strong feelings to be expressed [by the client] for as long as is necessary, until they cease to exert so much pressure on the client. ... It is frequently the fear that love or hate drives others away that leads people to push down their strongest emotions. As they realize in counselling that the counsellor is not shocked, is not hurt, is not put off, does not misuse the client's feelings, or does not respond in any other inappropriate or damaging way – in other words, does not repeat the reaction which the client has experienced in the past – the very strength of the feelings can diminish.

The counsellor's interaction is therefore an act of incompetence in psychodynamic counselling.

However, this is not the view of a person–centred counsellor, whose objectives and methods are rather different. The person–centred counsellor focuses attention on the quality of the relationship between counsellor and client. Congruence is an essential quality in this relationship. Brian Thorne and David Mearns (2007) observe that, 'The counsellor is "congruent" when she is openly being what she *is* in response to her client ... when her response to her client is what she feels and is not a pretence or a defence'. Therefore the intervention could be highly appropriate and competent provided the counsellor's feelings are genuine and spontaneous, and communicated appropriately.

In rational emotive counselling this kind of disclosure would be more likely to be viewed as irrelevant. The type of self-disclosure recommended by Windy Dryden and Michael Neenan (2004) is directed towards encouraging clients to internalize a new rational philosophy. The counsellor 'is to disclose not only how you as a counsellor have experienced a similar problem in the past, but also how you overcame it. Thus, for example, I sometimes tell my clients how I overcame my anxiety about having a stammer and therefore stammered less.' The counsellor's self-disclosure to Kate is not of this kind and is therefore irrelevant in rational emotive counselling. This sort of intervention would act as a distraction in cognitive behavioural counselling where the primary focus would be the client's cognitive processes (Trower, Casey and Dryden, 1988). To the extent that the intervention disrupted the rapport between Kate and her counsellor, it could be judged more severely as both counterproductive and incompetent.

Not all counsellors are purists in the sense of adhering to a single model. Some, like Sue Culley and myself (Culley and Bond, 2004), seek to integrate skills drawn from a variety of models in a systematic way. From this viewpoint, the counsellor would be acting competently provided the counsellor was acting within the specific guidelines for the use of immediacy. If, on the other hand, the counsellor was randomly eclectic, there might well be no criteria for determining whether the intervention was competently executed.

The theoretical orientation of the counsellor is only one of the contextual variations which might be relevant to assessing the competence of a particular intervention or method of working. The cultural setting, the needs of particular client groups, whether the counselling is one to one, with couples, or in groups, may also be relevant. What is competent in one context may be incompetent in another. This makes it difficult to generalize and to be specific and precise at the same time. Guidelines intended to have a wide application are of necessity written in general terms. For example, a general guideline 'Counsellors should only disclose their immediate feelings about their clients when it is appropriate' might alert counsellors to a potential issue but because it is written in terms which are intended for universal application, it gives little actual guidance. It is easier to become much more specific once the context and particularly the theoretical orientation of the counsellor are established.

The Law and Competence

Any profession can learn from the experience of those courts that have long experience of hearing negligence claims that someone has provided seriously unsatisfactory service. 'Competence' is not a term that is much used in law. Lawyers have approached the issue of identifying adequate standards of practice from a different point of view. It is defined in terms of the service provider, including counsellors, having a duty to exercise 'due care', 'reasonable care' and/or 'reasonable skill'. It has been important in deciding claims for negligence to determine whether 'reasonable skill and care' has been used. Many of the leading cases relate to medical negligence where the courts have been faced with differences of view about what constitutes reasonable skill and care. Counsellors are not unique in having several established, but conflicting, views about how best to work.

What is *reasonable* skill and care? The same standards are not expected of a passer-by who renders emergency first aid after an accident compared to the skill of a qualified surgeon. Someone who is acting in a voluntary capacity may not be expected to show the same level of skill as someone who is working for reward. If someone practises a profession or holds himself out as having a professional skill, the law expects him to show the amount of competence associated with the proper discharge of that profession, trade or calling. If he falls short of that standard and injures someone as a consequence, he is not behaving reasonably (Rogers, 2006).

How does a court assess what is a reasonable standard? The court will look to see if the counsellor explicitly promised a result as a term of the contract with the client. This is one of the reasons why counsellors are wise not to make such promises, e.g. to alleviate depression, anorexia, etc., within a fixed time limit. In the absence of such a promise within the contract, the court will assess what constitutes a reasonable standard by using one of two procedures which vary according to whether the court is dealing with professional or industrial procedures. It seems most likely that it is the professional procedure which would be used in cases relating to counselling.

If, as in counselling, there is no agreement about a universal standard of what is proper, then the court will not get involved in choosing between differences of professional opinion. The test is: did the counsellor act in accordance with a practice accepted at the time as proper by a responsible body of professional opinion skilled in the particular form of treatment? It does not have to be a majority opinion in order to be valid. It is sufficient if the practices have been adopted by a minority of practitioners as demonstrating a reasonable level of care. Two other legal points may be particularly relevant to counselling.

First, the standard of reasonable skill and care requires striking a balance between the magnitude of the risk and the burden placed on the counsellor to avoid the risk. This may mean that a higher standard of care is required when the counsellor is working with issues about significant mental illness, HIV infection or abortion (or a high risk of potential suicide?) compared to assertiveness or bereavement.

Secondly, there is a legal preference for associating a standard of care and skill with the post rather than with the individual who occupies it. In other words, courts expect the same minimum standard of a newly qualified counsellor as they would of an experienced practitioner in the same post. Similarly, no allowance is made for domestic circumstances or financial worries, or other factors which might contribute to error. This means that organizations are well advised to set the same standards for similar posts throughout the organization. For counselling in general, it is becoming increasingly important to establish a series of nationally recognized standards appropriate to different kinds of counselling posts.

In actual practice, the courts are much less likely to become involved in hearing claims of negligence against counsellors than against services involving physical interventions, such as medicine, for the reasons outlined in Chapter 5. Even in the USA, where the law of negligence is constructed in favour of greater liability, legal action against counsellors for negligence is relatively rare (Syme, 1997). It is interesting to note, as Peter Jenkins (2007: 76) points out, referring to medical practice, 'that there has been a substantial increase in medical claims against the NHS, which increased from £53 million in 1990 to £500 million in 2005'. He adds, however, that: 'There is, in fact, no real evidence yet of a "medical malpractice" crisis in the UK.'

Referring specifically to therapy case law, Jenkins notes that:

> In the UK, the number of cases involving professional negligence by therapists is still small, with one key case being recorded in detail

at the Appeal Court level, namely *Werner v Landau* (1961). There is a second relevant case, that of *Phelps v Hillingdon London Borough* (2000), which concerns the failure of an educational psychologist to carry out proper tests for dyslexia in assessing a school pupil with educational difficulties, but this relates to a breach of statutory duty rather than to a breach of the duty of care as a therapist. (2007: 79)

The difficulty that clients have in pursuing concerns about incompetent practice by counsellors through the courts and professional organizations places a considerable ethical responsibility on counsellors individually to assess whether they are working within their competence. The method of analysis used in law can help to inform the self-analysis process but is insufficient by itself, without the support of other strategies.

Enhancing Self-assessed Competence

One of the challenges faced by counsellors in determining adequate subjective standards of competence is the privacy of their work. Although the requirement of privacy is a widely-held norm for counselling, it leaves the counsellor vulnerable to becoming isolated from the practice and ideas of other counsellors in a way that is unlikely to happen in team settings where people work together. Therefore, it is desirable to develop strategies which help to counteract the counsellor's isolation in standard-setting and to encourage the counsellor to inform his self-assessment by reference to other counsellors.

The distinctive strategy, which characterizes most of the reputable counselling movement, is an emphasis on receiving regular and ongoing counselling-supervision. This way of working together is distinguished from managerial supervision in order to create a relationship where the counsellor can talk frankly about issues of competence, personal doubts and vulnerabilities. As counselling-supervision is such a distinctive ethical feature of counselling in Britain, it is discussed at greater length in Chapter 12.

Additional information about acceptable practice can be obtained from discussions with counsellors working in similar settings or with similar client issues. Membership of counsellor networks and associations takes on an ethical significance for counsellors who are working in isolation as a way of keeping in touch with acceptable practice.

All the major professional organizations emphasize the importance of continuing professional development, which is usually achieved by periodically attending training conferences and courses. Further sources of information about what is currently considered to be competent practice are journals, books and, increasingly, the internet.

Counsellors with Impaired Functioning

One potentially very difficult situation has arisen from time to time and is therefore worth considering specifically. Like anyone else, counsellors are vulnerable to all the frailties of the human condition, and these may affect their competence. Therefore, it is good practice that counsellors should not counsel when their function is impaired due to personal or emotional difficulties, illness, disability, alcohol, drugs or for any other reason. It is reasonable to assume that most counsellors know whether they have been drinking alcohol or taking drugs, medicinal or otherwise, which impair their functioning. Occasionally counsellors are unaware of the effect of this consumption, particularly if they are becoming addicted.

There is another situation in which a counsellor's functioning may become impaired. This is the insidious erosion of ability due to illness or disability:

Trevor has a progressive illness that affects his conceptual abilities and he appears unaware that his interventions are increasingly confusing for clients. What is the responsibility of his counselling supervisor?

It is widely accepted that the counselling supervisor has a responsibility to raise the concern with Trevor and perhaps advise him to withdraw from counselling. Fortunately, this is a rare occurrence but there is a much more frequent variation of this situation which is less clear-cut:

Margaret has recently been bereaved by the death of her last surviving parent. She knows she is preoccupied with her loss. Should she withdraw from offering counselling?

This is the sort of situation which ought to be discussed in counselling-supervision. Usually it is raised by the counsellor but sometimes the discussion is initiated by the counselling supervisor. There are four possible assessments of the situation:

1   The counsellor is able to use her current experience of bereavement as a resource for her clients, particularly those also experiencing bereavement.
2   The counsellor finds it too emotionally painful to function with recently bereaved clients but is able to continue working with other clients on non-bereavement issues.
3   The counsellor needs to withdraw temporarily from all counselling.
4   The counsellor needs to withdraw from providing counselling indefinitely or permanently.

Sometimes counsellors in situations such as those of Trevor or Margaret are more optimistic about their ability to function than their counselling supervisor. Where there is substantial difference of opinion and the counselling supervisor believes it is necessary to take positive action in the interests of protecting clients, the following procedure has proved useful:

1   The counsellor is told by their counselling supervisor of any reservations about competence to practise, in writing if necessary.
2   If the counsellor and counselling supervisor cannot agree about the counsellor's competence, the opinion of a mutually acceptable third person is sought to make an assessment.
3   If the situation remains unresolved, the counselling supervisor may withdraw from that role, giving reasons, which would usually be in writing.
4   The counselling supervisor may raise the issue with the counsellor's professional association or, in the last resort, implement the complaints or disciplinary procedure.

It would be inappropriate if someone should withdraw from counselling merely because of disability or illness. The test is whether the counsellor's circumstances impair his or her functioning as a counsellor. There are many effective counsellors who have restricted mobility, or are visually handicapped. Some counsellors with hearing difficulties are able to overcome this by the use of hearing aids, lip reading or counselling using sign language. Some counsellors have managed to turn what might at first sight seem to be a hindrance to their functioning as a counsellor into an advantage.

Conclusion

This brief review of ethical and legal significance indicates the advantages to counsellors and clients alike where counsellors can agree national standards for specific voluntary and professional posts. Guidance from professional bodies, latest research and current textbooks are all relevant sources for determining what is a reasonable level of practice.

There will always be a need for counsellors to monitor their own level of competence and to be willing to be accountable to clients and other counsellors for their practice on a day-by-day basis. What can a counsellor do in these circumstances? Probably the minimum standard every counsellor should aspire to is:

(a)   Know why you are doing or saying something to your client.
(b)   Be sure you are saying or doing what you intend.
(c)   Know what its effect is likely to be.
(d)   Adjust your interventions according to the client's actual response.
(e)   Review your counselling practice regularly in counselling supervision.
(f)   Develop strategies for keeping up to date and seek continuing professional development opportunities.
(g)   Assess whether your level of skill is the same or better than that of other counsellors offering counselling on similar terms or holding similar posts.

Simple as these principles are, they can act as the foundation of competent practice.

9

Avoiding the Exploitation of Clients

It is widely accepted that exploitation of clients is ethically incompatible with counselling. The use of the word 'exploit' carries with it strong negative moral overtones when applied to people, and especially when the exploitation takes place in a relationship founded on trust, respect for autonomy and serving the best interests of the client. The difficult task is identifying the different forms of exploitation that can occur. The identification is much clearer when someone deliberately overrides their professional values and ethics but is less readily apparent when the exploitation is less premeditated or even wholly unintentional. The conventional classification of exploitation distinguishes between financial, sexual and emotional (BACP, 2007: s. 18). To this list, I propose to add ideological exploitation, by which I mean the imposition of interpretations on a client's experience in order to validate the counsellor's belief system, whether that be political, economic, therapeutic or otherwise. I realize that this addition to the usual categories of exploitation may be controversial. It has grown out of my reflections on the false memory debate, which raged in the mid-1990s in the USA and Britain. I consider that the ethical implications are of wider significance so I will start with this issue before turning to financial, sexual and emotional exploitation.

Ideological Exploitation

It is unrealistic to expect the counsellor to perform the impossible task of suspending all personal beliefs in the interests of respecting the client's autonomy over her own beliefs. Any belief system pervades our experience of other people and ourselves, as well as influencing the way that we construct communications about these experiences. Some aspects of our belief systems must be present as an unseen influence between counsellor and client. There may well be influences the other way, from client to counsellor, but the primary ethical interest, with regard to exploitation, is from counsellor to client. This raises the question of how these beliefs should be managed within counselling. There is a strong ethical argument that making therapeutically significant beliefs explicit is more respectful to the client than leaving them ill-defined in the undergrowth of the relationship, especially if communication of the counsellor's beliefs acknowledges the possibility of the client holding different beliefs. An example may illustrate the point:

Clive is in the midst of a painful separation from his partner that has led him to doubt his previously strong religious convictions. As he had contacted his counsellor through a religious network, he appears to assume that the counsellor is committed to the beliefs that he is now questioning. This assumption seemed of marginal significance when working on the break-up of the relationship, but the counsellor senses that Clive's assumption about his counsellor's beliefs may be discouraging Clive from exploring what his new beliefs might be.

The client is clearly at a critical moment of personal transition when his own beliefs are fluid and not yet secure in their formulation. This points to the need for care in how the counsellor influences the client's development of his beliefs. The counsellor needs to be wary of viewing the client's dilemma as corroboration of her own beliefs. If she were a strong believer, it would be ethically inappropriate to link the client's emotional pain with his crisis in faith and to suggest that renewing his commitment to his former beliefs would alleviate the pain. This would be disrespectful of client autonomy and could be ideologically exploitative if this interpretation grows out of the counsellor's needs for bolstering her own belief system. Conversely, it would be inappropriate for a counsellor who had abandoned her previously strong faith, to seek to influence the client in that direction. The more appropriate responses will depend on the therapeutic orientation of the counsellor. A psychodynamic counsellor may concentrate on exploring the significance of the client's assumption and fantasies about the counsellor's beliefs without either corroborating or disavowing these projections. The aim would be to legitimize the client's ownership and responsibility for developing his beliefs with greater insight into his own personal process. Humanistic and cognitive behavioural counsellors would be similarly interested in exploring the client's assumptions but might well follow this by some personal disclosure of the counsellor's beliefs in the spirit of defusing the influence of the unknown and emphasizing the client's responsibility for reaching his own conclusions. Any or all of these interventions are fundamentally respectful of the client's autonomy and trust in the counsellor. It is arguable that passively continuing with the influence of the client's assumptions left unexplored is a less seriously exploitative act than co-opting the client's experience to corroborate the counsellor's beliefs, but it is a minor exploitation nonetheless. The client's autonomy would have been partially undermined and doubts would have been raised about the competence of the counsellor. Questions about competence and autonomy are often entangled in any consideration of whether exploitation has occurred.

The first example of possible ideological exploitation has been chosen deliberately to focus on beliefs that might well be considered extraneous to counselling as it is usually practised. It is easier to see the ethical issues in these circumstances than where the belief system is intrinsic to the therapeutic model or position adopted by the counsellor. The ethical challenge posed by the 'false memory' versus 'recovered memory' debate concerns the counsellor imposing a predetermined view that abuse has or has not taken place as a matter of personal belief or idealogy in ways which pre-empt the client's own search for memories and their interpretation. The pre-empting tendency is so powerful in this instance that there is no widely accepted term for a client who discovers previously 'lost' memories of sexual abuse, within counselling or therapy. As Peter Jenkins (1996) pointed out in his informative analysis of the ethical and legal implications of the debate surrounding this issue, both 'false memory syndrome' and 'recovered memory' are terms with inbuilt persuasive tendencies towards partisan positions within the debate. The former seeks to exclude the possibility that any such memory could be based on actual instances of sexual abuse and usually attributes the phenomenon to the insidious influence of the counsellor or therapist who implanted the memory and its interpretation, leading to false accusations against family members. Conversely, the term 'recovered memory' suggests acceptance that the memory is invariably based on historical fact. In the absence of less loaded terms, I prefer to use 'tentative' and 'corroborated' to distinguish between memories that have an unknown historical basis and those that can be shown to be based on a historical event which has been confirmed independently of the client. A typical example might be:

Angela reveals during her counselling that she has some 'blank periods' in her memory of her childhood when she cannot recall where she was or what happened. She has a sense that something terrible happened and has heard from friends that this could be an indication of having been sexually abused. She realizes that these 'lost memories' coincide with her mother ending a relationship with her natural father and starting a relationship with her stepfather, with whom she has never had a close relationship. As a result of her concern about the significance over the 'blank periods', the relationship with her stepfather has worsened from merely being distant to open hostility, with negative effects on her relationship with her mother. She wants to resolve the issue of these missing memories.

In a situation like this, there is no corroboration of any sexual abuse. The client has some symptoms that may indicate some form of trauma which need not necessarily be consequences of sexual abuse. Few counsellors can come to situations of this kind without being mindful of the controversy evoked in our own profession by Sigmund Freud changing his views from hysteria being founded on historical events of abuse to having its origins in fantasy (Masson, 1985; Mitchels, 2006: 76–9). Awareness of the early history of psychoanalysis and its societal and subsequent theoretical struggles with the possibility of sexual abuse indicates the level of difficulty that suspicions of sexual abuse pose for therapy. It is possible to overreact to the apparent historical denial of childhood sexual abuse in the origins of therapy by a counsellor being totally and uncritically accepting of the historical basis of any memories of abuse. On the other hand, knowledge of the Ramona case in the USA, in which a father successfully sued a therapist for 'implanting false memories of sexual abuse into his adult daughter' (*Ramona v Rose*, 1994), points in the opposite direction. The British inquiries into social work practice over child abuse in Cleveland and Orkney (Butler-Sloss, 1988, 1993; Asquith, 1993) also suggest that considerable caution and expertise in responding to any allegation of child abuse is required. Sadly, there are also cases where suspicions of abuse have been founded in reality, but as a result of an inadequate response to investigating the allegations, the allegations may remain unproven and/or the child may not be protected, to the detriment of the child concerned, e.g. a long string of cases, including most recently Victoria Climbié and Baby P. However, it is not the history of the disputes and difficulties surrounding this issue that makes this a fraught area of work. Personal experience is also very powerful, perhaps the most powerful influence on the counsellor's predisposition towards seeking to corroborate or doubt the occurrence of sexual abuse. It seems to me that a counselling ethic does not prevent a counsellor holding strong personal convictions about this or any other issues. However, the application of counselling ethics would point to the importance of keeping any personal convictions bracketed out of helping the client resolve her lost memories. Memories are often fragmentary, especially at the point when they are emerging and can be prematurely foreclosed by a desire to find consistency between different elements of the memory or racing to an interpretation before the memory has been as fully recalled as possible. Awareness of the ease with which memories can be influenced emphasizes the importance of working conscientiously in an open-minded way. Arguably, this is fundamental to demonstrating respect for the client and her process of reconstructing her own history.

One of the more challenging aspects of my own work as a counsellor has been working with a small number of people who are aware of having no memory of periods of their life as young people. Less frequently, I have counselled people who are worried about a loss of memory concerning a significant location in childhood, usually the childhood home. In each case, my client was aware that this might be an indication of sexual abuse and in some cases this awareness was the source of the anxiety rather than the loss of memory which had prompted them to seek counselling. It was the first of these clients that alerted me to the dangers of prematurely offering an explanation for untypical areas of blank memory. She had been to see a therapist who insisted that the loss of memory in combination with an eating disorder indicated that she had been sexually abused. My client was a professional with a scientific training who was disconcerted that someone could be so certain about the meaning of a negative phenomenon when negative findings in most other contexts are recognized as being notoriously difficult to interpret. She was uncertain about whether she had been abused as a child, but she felt in immediate danger of being abused by a dogmatic therapist. Over a period of systematically reviewing her childhood, in an open-minded way, tentative memories started to emerge, some of which seemed to be more suggestive of abuse than others. Taking my lead from her, I avoided suggesting that there might have been abuse or supporting other explanations as they seemed to emerge. My role was to remain even-handed between all possible explanations and to support my client in seeking additional information from relatives and childhood friends.

As with other clients, the process of recall was a progressive discovery of fragments of memory, which in the early stages were like a small number of jigsaw pieces of uncertain relationship to each other. They could have been forced together but only at the price of losing the emergence of a more complete picture, once better fitting pieces had been found. In the end she proved to have been right in seeking to protect her exploration of lost memory from premature interpretation as she eventually pieced together memories of a childhood trauma involving an accident, which was confirmed by relatives. In other cases memories of sexual abuse have been recovered, some confirmed by others who had been abused by the same person. However, during the process of reconstructing, I doubt that I could have predicted which memories would eventually point to abuse or other traumas. Some of these other lost memories appear to have their origins in distressing childhood illnesses. Others have involved accidents, usually including a blow to the head or physical shock, which have been confirmed by relatives or medical records. Another was the result of a traumatic event in the family witnessed by the child, which had remained unspoken until my client started to ask questions. Those memories that could be checked with others who had been present often contained elements which were corroborated but also had the characteristics of a child's perspective which were different from the understanding of the adults who were present.

One of the more rewarding aspects of this work is to be reminded how different the world can seem from a child's point of view and how it is this perspective that is recorded in memories that have been left unexamined since the originating event. Sometimes the strong emotions aroused at the time of the originating event appear to have compounded the trauma. For example, one adult realized that the tears that he was weeping in his distress, when his dog went missing temporarily, limited his ability to see who took him home. He was surprised to find that someone who was remembered as shadowy and terrifying was in fact a person he loved and trusted and who many years later could recall how unusually distressed he had been.

All the resolved memories appear to have been rooted in trauma, although I remain open-minded about whether this must always be the case, as some of the unresolved ones could have other explanations. Useful guidance on working with recovered memories has been issued by the British Psychological Society (2000), which reminds practitioners of the need for both counsellor and client to learn to tolerate uncertainty. I mention my experience of working with clients in order to indicate how, if we are sensitive to the concerns that clients voice, we can not only enhance the therapeutic dimension of our work, but also gain new ethical insights, and that the two are very closely connected. A more ideologically committed stance runs the very real risk of only meeting the needs of clients whose needs conform to our own personal and therapeutic ideologies and, perhaps more seriously, risks distorting our client's memories so that any historical origins become irrecoverable. If this analysis is correct, the adoption of a committed stance in favour of either side of the false/recovered memory debate does represent a form of ideological exploitation when it is imposed on clients. Avoidance of ideological exploitation is only the first step in working effectively in this contentious area of counselling. It requires knowledge and appropriate expertise in patiently allowing memories to become established and tested.

It is not only the process of regaining memories that is particularly vulnerable to ideological exploitation. I have also found a similar range of issues around eating disorders. I have encountered mental health workers, not necessarily counsellors, who hold the view that all eating disorders have their origins in sexual abuse and, more specifically, that all bulimia (i.e. gorging and vomiting food) is the result of oral sexual abuse. I have the same ethical reservations about working with clients on the basis of these beliefs as I would have about 'lost memories'. Eating disorders may or may not be associated with sexual abuse. It seems equally important to avoid contaminating a client's material by imposing this interpretation in order to sustain a therapeutic ideology. It is ethically better to bear in mind the many different theoretical explanations of the origins of eating disorders and to be open-minded as to which one will most closely fit any particular client's experience.

Ideological exploitation is not only harmful to clients and others who may be implicated by invalidated accusations, but also discredits the validity of counselling and therapy. My reason for dealing with this issue within a wider category of ideological exploitation is to indicate that the ethical learning from that controversy extends beyond that debate to other issues raised by clients. Whenever a therapeutic theory suggests a general belief that 'a is caused by b', there are ethical issues about the application of that theory in work with individual clients and the degree of respect shown to clients in determining whether that belief is confirmed or contradicted by their experience.

Financial Exploitation

The potential for financial exploitation in counselling occurs in a number of ways. The most common source of complaint arises from lack of clarity about the financial costs incurred by clients. For example:

Stephanie seeks counselling and agrees to monthly payments of £60. After the first two months they agree to meet more frequently and change from fortnightly sessions to weekly. The discussion about the new arrangements was hurried and at the end of a session. Some time later, Stephanie is perplexed and shocked to receive a bill for £160 at the end of the next month. She had wondered what the cost would be, but had calculated that the maximum charge would be for four weekly meetings at £30 pounds, a total of £120. When she raised the issue, her counsellor explained that his charges had gone up to £40 per session at a point during the first two months of seeing her and, as this was a new arrange-ment, he felt obliged to charge at the higher rate.

This is a classic example of where lack of clarity about fees, prior to the client incurring costs, can lead to misunderstanding and can even destroy trust in the counselling relationship. It would have been better if the original arrangement had been an agreed fee for a fixed amount of counselling expressed in hours or sessions. This would have removed uncertainty about the implications of any changes in arrangements. In my opinion, any increase in charges without notice and charged retrospec-tively is exploitative. It is also unenforceable in law. One of the basic requirements of a legally valid contract is prior agreement about its terms.

Clients are entitled to feel cheated if, after reaching an agreement about the payment, the counsellor is bad at time-keeping, particularly if this results in the client paying a full fee for a session when they have only received part of one. Habitual bad time-keeping is almost certainly an indication of low standards of practice by a counsellor. However, like anyone else, a counsellor can be unexpectedly delayed by an accident or for some other reason. What should a counsellor do in these circumstances? The obvious course of action is to reduce the fee in proportion to the time missed. If, however, the purpose of the session has been frustrated by the shortage of time, then it may be more appropriate to make no charge. If the client has incurred costs or been inconvenienced to attend a session which has been adversely affected by the time-keeping of the counsellor or even the total absence of the counsellor, then it may be more appropriate to reimburse those costs and sometimes to pay compensation. One way of minimizing inconvenience to a client is to have a prior agreement about how long the client should wait for the counsellor before assuming the session is abandoned. Such an agreement would only apply when something unexpected has intervened. It is much better to avoid such situations and if a session needs to be rescheduled to have reached an agreement about the new arrangements as far as possible in advance.

Counsellors who charge fees for their services are vulnerable to the suspicion that they keep fee-paying clients on longer than is strictly necessary. There are two opposing views about who is responsible in this situation. Some take the view that it is the client's responsibility to monitor whether or not they want to continue counselling and whether they are getting value for money. This seems appropriate when the counselling is clearly provided on this basis and the counsellor does not express an opinion about the desirable duration of the counselling relationship. It is arguably another way of respecting the client's auton-omy. However, in practice, matters are not always as clear-cut as this. For example:

Polly values her counselling sessions, which started when she was having difficulties due to bereavement. She asks her counsellor how long she is likely to benefit from counselling. He replies that in his experience of comparable situations six months would be the appropriate length. In the event Polly makes more rapid progress and after two months has begun to use the sessions to consider other aspects of her life. She is fee-paying and always pays willingly, which is a relief to her counsellor, who is experiencing financial difficulties.

In these circumstances it is more appropriate for the counsellor to draw attention to change in purpose of the sessions and to reach a new agreement. The temptation is to allow the counselling relationship to extend itself by the counsellor's inaction to the end of six months or indefinitely. The tendency to extend contracts with wealthy clients is not always deliberate. One way counsellors can check whether this is actually happening is by watching whether they give wealthy clients longer contracts than their poorer clients, and by periodically reviewing this issue in counselling-supervision. Incorporating periodic reviews with clients about their counselling contracts also acts as a safeguard. It is a test of the counsellor's integrity whether he can set aside his financial needs in order to negotiate the duration of the counselling relationship so as to take into account the client's best interests.

Sometimes clients want to give their counsellor a gift. This raises issues that involve both the integrity of the counselling relationship and of the counsellor. For example:

Elsie is alienated from her relatives and wishes to leave her counsellor a substantial sum of money in her will.

This situation could threaten the integrity of the counselling relationship if the client's conscious or unconscious intention is to buy the counsellor's loyalty or manipulate the relationship in some way. On the other hand, it could be a straightforward way of acknowledging the personal value the client places on the counselling, which will only take effect once the relationship is over. The risk to the counsellor's integrity is the suspicion that she may have used her influence to obtain the gift. For all these reasons, counsellors are wise to be cautious about accepting gifts and to refuse to do so if the gift would compromise the counselling relationship. If there are no obvious reasons for declining the gift, it is a sensible precaution to protect the counsellor's reputation to discuss it in counselling-supervision and in the case of a substantial gift, to discuss it with their counselling association. Often it is more appropriate to encourage the client to make a gift to charity rather than to the counsellor personally.

Sometimes financial exploitation may arise from dual relationships operating concurrently between the counsellor and client. For example:

Douglas, a car dealer, knows that his counsellor wants to buy a car. After some negotiation, the counsellor agrees to purchase a car from Douglas. In the event, the car turns out to be faulty and they are unable to agree how to resolve it. The counsellor sues Douglas.

This case reveals that there are as many dangers in dual financial relationships. At the very least the counsellor has left herself vulnerable to the suspicion that she has used her role in relationship to Douglas to obtain a more favourable deal from Douglas than she could obtain elsewhere. Even if this were not the case, the potential for the business transaction undermining the counselling relationship is a high one if grievances arise in the commercial relationship. It is very unlikely that the dual relationships, counselling and financial, could be kept separate. In the example, it is the client's part of the deal that is problematic, but the effect would be much the same if the counsellor had difficulty making payments or if any of many other possibilities arose.

Sometimes counsellors enter into dual relationships out of the best intentions. For example:

Jon is a fee-paying client in the middle of his counselling when he is made redundant. His counsellor agrees to Jon's offer of doing odd-jobs for him instead of paying fees.

There are dangers in this situation for both the counsellor and client. What if the counsellor is dissatisfied with Jon's work? On the other hand, what is a reasonable rate of pay from Jon's point of view? The potential difficulties are such that both these situations need to be considered in advance of entering into such an arrangement. Some counsellors prefer to avoid the risk of such complications by using a sliding scale of fees that could be adjusted according to Jon's circumstances, or by continuing counselling without any charge.

Bartering goods is sometimes considered as an alternative arrangement in circumstances similar to Jon's. What if Jon agrees to give the counsellor an ornament or some other possession as an alternative method of payment? Again, the problems are similar to bartering services. The counsellor needs to consider in advance what would happen if the object exchanged turns out to be damaged or faulty. Jon needs to be confident he is getting value in the exchange. Probably an independent valuation is required as the starting point for any agreement. So far as I know, there are no British guidelines for situations where fees are paid by barter (although there might be professional ethical considerations around the existence of dual roles). In the USA these issues have received more extensive attention (see Herlihy and Corey, 1992). The American Counselling Association makes the following provision about bartering in its *Code of Ethics*:

> Counselors may barter only if the relationship is not exploitive or harmful and does not place the counsellor in an unfair advantage, if the client requests it, and if such arrangements are an accepted practice among professionals in the community. Counselors consider the cultural implications of bartering and discuss relevant concerns with clients and document such agreements in a clear written contract. (ACA, 2005: A.10.d)

Sexual Exploitation

Social awareness of sexual exploitation and harassment by people with power over others has increased dramatically over the last decade. It is widely accepted that there is a significant amount of sexual abuse of children by adults, often members of their own family. There is also a growing realization that members of the caring professions, including psychiatrists, psychologists, social workers and counsellors, have also engaged in sexually inappropriate behaviour with their clients (Rutter, 1989; Russell, 1993, 1996; Jehu, 1994).

There are no means of knowing accurately how frequently clients suffer sexually inappropriate behaviour but there are indications that it is sufficiently frequent to be a real cause for concern. In the USA, it was estimated that sexual contact occurs between male therapists and clients in about 11 per cent of cases and between female therapists and clients in 2–3 per cent of cases (Pope and Bouhoutsos, 1986). A subsequent downturn in self-reported cases by therapists may indicate that increased awareness of the issue has been successful in reducing sexually inappropriate behaviour. On the other hand, it may be the result of a less candid self-reporting (Pope and Vasquez, 1991).

In Britain, the incidence is less certain. They are a significant but minority source of complaints in BACP professional conduct procedures 1996–2006 (Khele et al., 2008). It appears that incidents are under-reported. Judging by the number of clients who have approached me about their distress about sexual relationships with counsellors who turn out not to be members of BACP or any other reputable counselling body, it is my impression that sexual misconduct may be even more common outside the membership of the large professional organizations. Even if the incidence of sexual misconduct by counsellors turns out to be lower than in the USA, and there is no evidence to suggest that this is the case, we need to do everything we can to reduce it further. The effect on clients is so devastating that their reactions have been linked to the victims of rape, battering, incest, child abuse and post-traumatic stress syndrome. Kenneth Pope (1988) has described the therapist–patient sex syndrome as involving many of the features of these other traumas.

- *Ambivalence*: a state of fearing separation or alienation from the counsellor, yet longing to escape the counsellor's power and influence. For as long as the ambivalence persists, the client may not report the counsellor out of a sense of loyalty and fear of destroying his or her professional reputation.
- *Guilt*: this arises because the client may feel responsible for not having stopped the sexual activity or for having initiated it. However, it is the counsellor's responsibility to monitor the boundaries, even if the client does act seductively, and it is the counsellor who is responsible for maintaining the appropriate level of personal/professional distance, not the client. The client's sense of guilt is often similar to the feelings associated with child abuse and there is a similar sense of responsibility for what happened on the part of the client.
- *Emotional lability*: a long-term consequence of counsellor–client sexual involvement can be a sense of being emotionally overwhelmed during the relationship, which may be followed by periods of emotional instability. Sometimes the emotional volatility occurs inappropriately with sexually appropriate partners.

Other responses identified by Pope include: identity/boundary/role confusion; sexual confusion; impaired ability to trust; suppressed rage; cognitive dysfunction; and, increased suicidal risk. I have spoken to several clients, who have experienced deep emotional distress and turmoil, sometimes for several years, following sexual relationships with their counsellor, before they have felt able to discuss their experience confidentially with someone else. Sometimes it takes years before someone feels able to make a formal complaint. I am sure many complaints are not brought forward because of the fear of having to relive the painful experience of the original relationship.

The risk of serious emotional distress to the client is only one of the reasons why BACP, from its early beginnings onwards, adopted a prohibition on sex with clients. There are other reasons why sex between counsellors and clients is considered dangerous. Clients are vulnerable to exploitation because of the inequality of power that is inherent in a counselling relationship. Inevitably, the helper will hold more power than the person being helped will. It is the difference between being the provider and the needy. Psychodynamic counsellors have also pointed out the likelihood of a powerful transference growing between the client and counsellor arising from the client's childhood. When this occurs, the client is relating emotionally to the counsellor as a child would to an adult or to a parent. If the counsellor enters into a sexual relationship, it is experienced as sexual abuse or incest. This may explain the level of distress experienced by some clients.

It is sometimes suggested to me that there are situations where it is appropriate for an adult client to take some responsibility for any negative feelings that result from engaging in sex with a counsellor. I think this must be so if the client is acting as an adult out of an adult psychological state. However, the client does not have the counsellor's additional responsibility of monitoring and maintaining safe boundaries within the counselling. So, even if the client is an adult in an adult psychological state and therefore carries some responsibility, the greater responsibility rests on the counsellor. If the client is regressed to an earlier childhood state or the methods used evoke childlike behaviour or feelings, then there is an even greater responsibility on the counsellor to avoid sexual relationships with clients.

The risks inherent in sex with clients are not confined to the client. The public reputation of counselling in general is at stake. The public must have confidence that they can approach counsellors and discuss personal issues in a safe environment. As part of the counselling process people often become emotionally vulnerable and expose themselves psychologically to their counsellor. Therefore, it is important that the counsellor maintains an appropriate boundary in the relationship to provide the client with safety. The 'no sex' rule for counsellors is out of respect for the clients' psychological vulnerability in the same way as doctors need to respect their patients' physical vulnerability. The prohibition on sex with clients therefore both protects current clients and also protects the reputation of counselling in the public mind so that future clients feel able to take the risk of approaching a counsellor.

What is sexual activity?

The prohibition of sexual activity with current clients was adopted in the first BAC *Code of Ethics and Practice for Counsellors* in 1984 and repeated in subsequent ethical guidance not only from BACP but also from COSCA, BPS, IACP and UKCP. This has inevitably raised the question, what is sexual activity or relationship? The phrases imply that the ethical concerns extend beyond sexual intercourse involving penetration to include other behaviours, such as masturbation, 'heavy petting', etc. But where is the boundary between sexual activity and hugging and kissing, which are activities that may or may not have an obvious sexual component? The sexual ambiguity of these activities means that it is impossible to produce a definitive definition of what constitutes sexual activity. With some activities, it will depend on the intention of the people involved and, just as importantly, the interpretation of the person on the receiving end. Counsellors are wise to be cautious in situations where their actions can be misunderstood.

'Sexual activity' covers many different categories of activity. Three are of particular concern when they arise in a counselling relationship. Sexual assault implies a deliberate attempt to force a client into sexual activity against their will. It is a criminal offence. Sexual abuse may involve force but is more likely to be manipulation into sexual activity under the pretence that it will be therapeutic. It is characteristic of abuse that it involves an abuse of power. Sexual harassment consists of deliberate or repeated comments, gestures or physical contacts that are unwanted by the recipient or expressed in a relationship where the recipient is in a less powerful position than the person making them. In terms of helping counsellors to think through the issues around sex with clients it is useful to separate these different activities and to realize that any sexual activity with a client is likely to fall into one of these categories. It is an aspect of the difficulty of counteracting the inherent power imbalance between the counsellor and client.

'Sexual activity' also has positive connotations. It is associated with intimacy, physicality and relationship, and outside the counselling relationship can be extremely positive and life-enhancing. The prohibition on sex between clients and counsellors is not based on latter-day Puritanism but on the hope that both counsellor and client will find sexual fulfilment independently of each other. My experience of counsellors who have entered into sexual relationship with clients is that they fall into several distinct categories. I think there are a few who deliberately use counselling as a means of obtaining sexual contacts and who appear relatively indifferent to what happens to the client afterwards. Their motivation and behaviour is pathological. More often I encounter counsellors who cross the boundary because of a lack of satisfactory emotional and sexual relationships in their own lives. Such a person may well use clients (and trainees) as a source of social company and hence the possibility of sexual relationships is increased. Counsellors behaving in this way often have considerable confusion over issues to do with personal boundaries, which may permeate much of their life and their work with clients. The best way a counsellor can avoid this situation is to explore their own sexual needs and to ensure that the forum for meeting these is outside the counselling relationship. A counsellor who has done this is in a much better position to deal with sexual attraction that will inevitably arise from time to time.

Sexual attraction

Sometimes it is the client who feels the sexual attraction most strongly and who clearly takes the initiative in attempting to seduce the counsellor. When this happens the counsellor needs to be clear about his or her role. Rather than comply with the client's overtures, it is better to acknowledge openly what appears to be happening and to explore what the client wants from a sexual relationship with the counsellor. If this situation is handled well, it often marks the movement into a new phase in counselling where both the client and counsellor feel able to discuss their feelings about each other more directly. It is often a time when the client is willing and able to disclose personal needs more frankly, which are not being met elsewhere in their lives. For the counsellor, it is important that this kind of situation is discussed in counselling-supervision so that he or she feels clear and supported in maintaining an appropriate professional boundary. Any alternative approach is usually less satisfactory.

To pretend to ignore the client's advances represents avoidance of where the greatest energy in the relationship may be currently operating and with it the greatest motivation to work on real needs and issues. To comply with the advances and become involved in sexual activity not only defuses and misdirects potential therapeutic energy, but carries with it personal risks for both the counsellor and client. For the counsellor, in the event of a complaint, there is also the possibility of expulsion from counselling associations.

Counsellors sometimes experience a powerful sense of sexual attraction towards a client. It is still probably taboo to talk about such feelings (Pope et al., 2006). If you have not experienced such feelings, you can imagine the feelings you might experience if you encounter a client who is your sexual ideal and who also has personal qualities you admire. Sometimes extremely strong sexual attractions develop in longer counselling relationships of a psychologically intimate nature. The desire to move into a sexual relationship may be enormous. It is not unethical to feel attraction to a client. The ethical response is to acknowledge the feeling to yourself, and to consult a counselling supervisor and colleagues about the situation as quickly as possible. The decision about whether to tell the client about your feelings of attraction will be a matter of judgement depending on the circumstances and the model of counselling being used. Sometimes seeking your own counselling is useful. So far as I know, very few counselling training programmes include formal training in how to recognize and respond to sexual attraction in counselling. This is a serious omission.

Sex with former clients

It is only relatively recently that the issue of sexual relationships with former clients has started to receive serious consideration by counsellors on both sides of the Atlantic. There has been considerable debate, particularly during the mid-1990s, within BACP (Bond, 1994) and BPS (Jehu, 1994). BACP's current position is summarized in its *Ethical Framework* for counsellors:

> Practitioners should think carefully about, and exercise considerable caution before, entering into personal or business relationships with former clients and should expect to be professionally accountable if the relationship becomes detrimental to the client or the standing of the profession. (BACP, 2007: s. 18)

One of the challenges in reaching an agreed policy was an issue that divides counsellors according to the nature of the work they do with clients and the counsellor's theoretical orientation. Some examples may illustrate these different widely-held opinions.

Lesley seeks counselling to help her to manage a conflict between her and a colleague at work better. A combination of problem-solving and assertiveness techniques is successful. After two counselling sessions she has resolved her problem and the counselling stops. Six months later she bumps into her counsellor socially at a party and after a pleasant evening together they decide to meet socially. Neither person is in a relationship with someone else. Some weeks later they start a sexual relationship.

In this example, the counselling work is unlikely to have involved much intimacy or intensity as the theoretical orientation has a strong behavioural component and the focus of the work is outside the immediate counsellor–client relationship. The meeting that precedes the sexual relationship occurs in a setting unconnected with the counselling and on equal terms. It seems inappropriate to prohibit two adults from continuing to develop their relationship in the way that they want in these circumstances. It has been argued that to be too protective of clients is to infantilize them and constitutes erosion of their autonomy. Counsellors who believe this situation is typical argue against any restraint on sex with former clients or for minimal restraints.

David uses counselling to explore his difficulty in having close relationships that last longer than a few months. During the counselling, which was weekly over five months, attention is paid to his feelings towards his counsellor, Sarah, who points out when she feels David is trying to distance himself from her. As a result, David becomes aware of how he pushes people away and how this re-enacts a painful period during his childhood. Six months after the end of the counselling David meets Sarah at a charity event and suggests they meet again for a meal. Both of them realize that there is a mutual sexual attraction. What should Sarah do?

In this example the counselling was more intense, intimate and longer-lasting. This is the kind of situation where powerful transferences and countertransferences are likely to arise, whether or not the counsellor is using a psychodynamic model. Considerably greater caution is required before a sexual relationship is started, if ever. For example, members of the British Association of Sexual and Marital Therapists have adopted a lifetime ban on sexual relationship with former clients. They believe this is essential to protect the integrity of counselling on these sorts of issues. There is anecdotal evidence that some clients are deterred from seeking counselling about marital and sexual issues because they are not confident that counsellors will not engage in sex with them. Many practitioners with a psychodynamic orientation also doubt whether it would ever be possible to enter into a relationship that is truly free of the transferences and power dynamics of the original counselling. This is the focus of one of the debates that is currently taking place. Should the prohibition on sex with former clients be absolute and for ever? Alternatively, is it possible that in some situations transferences are resolved and therefore it becomes a matter of judgement whether sex with a former client is permissible? The kinds of criteria to be taken into consideration are:

- Has sufficient time elapsed to mark a clear boundary between the counselling and the new relationship? (The American Counseling Association requires a minimum of five years (ACA, 2005: A5b).
- Have the dynamics involved in the counselling, particularly with special attention to power and transference, been given careful consideration by the counsellor, and are there good reasons for believing these are resolved and no longer influential in the proposed relationship?
- Have the risks to the client been explored with him or her?
- Has the issue been discussed with the counselling supervisor and his or her support for the relationship been obtained?

If the counsellor decides to go ahead with starting a sexual relationship after satisfying these requirements, she or he needs to be aware of the possibility of the former client experiencing many of the symptoms of the therapist–patient syndrome described earlier. Because of this, most prudent counsellors would prefer to avoid sex with former clients unless the counselling relationship had been extremely brief, lacking in emotional intensity and therefore not involving the dynamics of transference and power which might persist or recur in a subsequent non-counselling relationship. Using these criteria, it would be personally and professionally prudent of Sarah to avoid entering into a sexual relationship with David.

Counselling in an appropriate environment

John Rowan (1988) has drawn attention to the way the furnishings of a counselling room communicate to a client what is expected of them. He suggests, for example, that 'Cushions on the floor give much more flexibility and a suggestion that it is alright to be childlike or even childish. And a couch or mattress lends itself to fantasy, dreams, deep regression and loss of conscious rational control.' In contrast, it is argued that chairs suggest rationality and the straighter the chair, the greater the emphasis on rationality. Similarly, the presence of a box of tissues may be perceived as indicating that others have used the room for crying and that the counselling room is a safe place to cry in.

Without wishing to press these observations too far, I think most counsellors would recognize a degree of reality in them and acknowledge the conscious and unconscious influence of the physical environment in which counselling takes place. One of the obvious questions which follows is, why do some counsellors see clients in either the counsellor's or the client's bedroom? This must send mixed messages about the counsellor's intentions. I think it is better to avoid counselling in bedrooms altogether. If this is not possible, it is better to use a room that is not being used regularly by the counsellor or client, such as a spare room and optimally a dedicated room for counselling that is appropriately furnished for the type of counselling to be undertaken. An obvious exception to this is counselling someone who is confined to bed because of illness.

Emotional Needs

Much of what has already been said about sexual exploitation is directly transferable to emotional needs. If the boundary in sexual activity is sometimes hard to identify, this is even more so with emotional needs. I cannot imagine that anyone continues with providing counselling unless it is meeting an emotional need of some kind. This is not problematic if the need is complementary to the client's use of counselling and is sufficiently within the counsellor's control to avoid distorting the counselling relationship. A counsellor's emotional needs are not always counterproductive. Sometimes a counsellor's neediness or vulnerability can be used as a resource in order to enhance a client's understanding of her own situation or to break down a sense that the client is unique in having a particular vulnerability. This often represents a high standard of practice and is within the tradition of the 'wounded healer'. The problem arises when the counsellor's neediness is such that the client's needs are eclipsed, or under the pretence of working to meet the client's needs, the counsellor is really seeking satisfaction of her own. This can occur in a vast variety of ways. The most obvious are counsellors who cannot end relationships with clients because they are a source of regular companionship and a substitute for the counsellor developing friendships with people who are not their clients. Perhaps a little less obvious is the counsellor who has such a sense of personal unworthiness that she chooses to work with the most socially stigmatized and disadvantaged clients available to her on the basis that at least they will be grateful for help. Often they are not grateful or appreciative, and the counsellor's disappointment and sense of rejection can become the dominant emotional force in the relationship rather than the client's feelings of vulnerability.

Good practice with regard to emotional exploitation requires that counsellors periodically review what their emotional satisfactions and needs are. It is important that the counsellor has alternative sources of emotional satisfaction from outside counselling for most of their deep needs. Good quality counselling-supervision is invaluable in helping counsellors address this issue.

Responding to Exploitation by Counsellors

Exploitation involves meeting the counsellor's needs or someone else's at the expense of the client's. Exploitation may be deliberate or unintentional but it is always unethical. What should a counsellor do when she suspects another counsellor of exploiting clients? The course of action must depend on the circumstances in which the suspicions arise if the client is not to be subjected to further harm.

For example:

Marjorie seeks counselling because she feels troubled by her experience with her previous counsellor. She had been having a sexual relationship with her counsellor, which had started while she was receiving counselling. She is aware that this is a breach of the counsellor's code of ethics but does not wish to make a complaint.

In these circumstances the counsellor ought to be bound by his agreement with Marjorie about confidentiality and can only act with Marjorie's consent. He may actively seek this consent or encourage Marjorie to pursue her own complaint, but if he does more than this he will inevitably compromise his own relationship with his client by failing to work within an agreement about confidentiality and to respect her autonomy. Even though the counsellor may feel uncomfortable with his knowledge, there is little else he can do; otherwise he will compound the original harm, increasing the client's vulnerability by a further breach of confidence. The client's needs ought to have priority.

What if the client reveals in confidence a situation where a counsellor is repeatedly exploiting many clients? It will then be a matter of judgement whether it would be better to respect an agreement with an individual client about confidentiality or whether it would be better to report the situation in order to prevent further harm to other clients. The significance of considerations of acting to promote the 'public good' with regard to confidentiality is considered in Chapter 10. This is an extremely difficult situation because there can be no hard-and-fast guidelines. Each person has to assess the situation according to the known circumstances.

An alternative situation could be as follows: 'Sandy, a counsellor and colleague, tells you confidentially that he has started a sexual relationship with a current client.' Here there is a crucial difference. The counsellor, not the client, has approached you directly. Notwithstanding the agreement about confidentiality, it is probably better to encourage the counsellor to report the circumstances to his professional association and seek their guidance and, if this does not happen, to take the initiative yourself. A counsellor who actively seeks assistance for himself is likely to be viewed more favourably than someone who waits to be reported. However, even in this situation, because the counsellor has approached you in confidence, there should be no automatic breach of confidence. Again, it is a matter of weighing up whether you are more likely to promote the 'public good' by breaking confidence or by keeping confidence. This constraint does not operate if you are told of the sexual relationship without any preconditions relating to confidentiality.

Sometimes allegations of exploitation occur as rumour. For example: 'You are at a party and you hear allegations that a counsellor you know well and have worked with is financially exploiting her clients.' There must be some doubt about the credibility of such a rumour because you do not have direct personal evidence. If you think that it is unbelievable, then you may wish to let the counsellor know about the existence of the rumour so that she can choose what to do about it. If the counsellor admits to you that the rumour has an element of truth, you are in a similar position to the second example. If, on the other hand, you have reason to suspect the rumour might be true but the counsellor denies it, then it is a matter of personal judgement how to proceed or whether to wait and see whether your suspicions are confirmed or disproved.

All the major counselling organizations place an obligation on counsellors to challenge any suspected malpractice by other members of that organization and to report the malpractice when this is appropriate. The act of reporting a fellow counsellor can seem extremely daunting and full of potential conflict and embarrassment. However, these are seldom sufficient reasons for not doing so. Far more important as the basis of your decisions is the appropriate protection of clients' rights and, ultimately, the members of the public who seek counselling.

Conclusion

The exploitation of clients raises important issues for counsellors. It is not merely a matter of harm to the clients most directly concerned but to the reputation of counselling as a whole. When I am consulted about situations which might turn into formal complaints, I am constantly reminded how hard it is for counsellors to make judgements about others and perhaps themselves. Counsellors tend to value diversity in people and relationships. When faced with clear examples of exploitation it is all too easy either to under-react by maintaining an inappropriate level of non-judgmentalism or to over-react with excessive zeal. Neither of these responses is helpful. Exploitative practices must be challenged and eliminated but as this chapter has shown, it requires great care to assess the issues involved in specific situations and to be fair to the client and everyone else involved.

One issue that recurs for any counsellor considering how to respond to situations of exploitation relates to the management of confidentiality. This is the subject of the next chapter.

10

Confidentiality

Confidentiality is probably the single issue that raises most ethical and legal anxiety for counsellors. It is an issue over which practice has evolved from a total commitment to the client's privacy and confidentiality to something which requires active management by the counsellor and may involve making difficult judgements. These changes have taken place in response to a greater appreciation of the ethical complexities of providing counselling, but also have been driven by changes in the law.

The Importance of Confidentiality in Counselling

Confidentiality is considered fundamental to counselling because, by its very nature, counselling is an intimate relationship which often involves the client in divulging information about their current and past situations as well as their opinions and innermost feelings (Bond and Mitchels, 2008). This can only take place in a relationship based on trust. In particular, a client needs to feel that whatever has been disclosed will not be used in ways that will harm them. This usually means that disclosures in counselling are made by clients on the assumption that what is said remains confidential between the counsellor and client.

Confidentiality acts as a shield to protect the client's autonomy by putting them in control of how they use their counselling in their everyday life. Confidentiality protects against unwelcome intrusions from the counselling room into other areas of the client's life. It also provides protection against any stigma associated with having sought help (Holmes and Lindley, 1998).

One meaning of confidentiality is 'strong trust' (from the Latin *con-fidere*). High levels of trust are necessary to create the conditions in which clients can strive for the levels of personal truthfulness necessary to address the issues that are causing them concern. It requires corresponding levels of trustworthiness on the part of the counsellor. For these reasons, protecting confidentiality is a high ethical priority in counselling and requires sound ethical reasons for confidentiality to be curtailed in any way. However, professional attitudes to confidentiality have changed over time in the face of other competing ethical demands, particularly the protection of vulnerable people and children from harm.

The Historical Commitment to Total Confidentiality

Psychoanalysis has traditionally taken a very robust view of confidentiality and protection of clients' privacy. Some psychoanalysts have been prepared to risk prison in order to protect confidences. In a remarkable account of being summoned to court to give evidence, Anne Hayman described how she successfully persuaded a judge to exercise his discretion to allow her not to give evidence. She appeared in court with her own legal representation and presented the following argument for refusing to disclose her patient's confidences even though she had the patient's permission to do so:

> Suppose a patient had been in treatment for some time and was going through a temporary phase of admiring and depending upon me; he might therefore feel it necessary to sacrifice himself and give permission, but it might not be proper for me to act on this.
>
> This example involves a vital principle. Some of the United States have a law prohibiting psychiatrists from giving evidence about a patient without the patient's written permission, but this honourable attempt to protect the patient misses the essential point that he may not be aware of unconscious motives impelling him to give permission. It may take months or years to understand things said or done during analysis, and until this is achieved it would belie all our knowledge of the workings of the unconscious mind

if we treated any attitude arising in the analytic situation as if it were part of ordinary social interchange. If we allow and help people to say things with the ultimate aim of helping them to understand the real meanings underlying what may well be a temporary attitude engendered by the transference, it would be the crassest dishonour and dishonesty to permit unwarranted advantage to be taken of their willingness to avail themselves of the therapeutic situation. It would be as if a physician invited a patient to undress to be examined, and then allowed the Law to see him naked and arrest him for exhibiting himself. Where no permission has been given, the rule to maintain discretion is, of course, similarly inviolable. Patients attend us on the implicit understanding that anything they reveal is subject to a special protection. Unless we explicitly state that this is not so, we are parties to a tacit agreement, and any betrayal of it only dishonours us. That the agreement may not be explicit is no excuse. Part of our work is to put into words things which are not being said. We are the responsible parties in the relationship, so surely it is we who should pay, if there is any price to be paid, because something has not been said clearly. (Hayman, 1965)

What is remarkable about Anne Hayman's level of commitment to absolute confidentiality is that she was prepared to accept the consequences of refusing to give evidence.

I complied with the subpoena by attending Court, but I decided I could not answer any questions about the 'patient', and I made all arrangements, including having a barrister to plead in mitigation of sentence, for the possibility that I should be sent to prison for contempt of court. In the event, although my *silence* probably did constitute contempt, the judge declared that he would not sentence me, saying it was obviously a matter of conscience. In this he was acting within the discretion the Law allows him. Though I had no legal privilege, I was in effect given the same freedom to remain silent usually allowed to priests for the secrets of the confessional. It is possible that the judge was partly moved by the idea that any evidence I could give might only be of marginal relevance to the case. (Hayman, 1965)

In the late 1980s counsellors shared with other members of the psychological therapies an instinctively protective approach to clients' confidences. For example, Hetty Einzig (1989), in the first edition of *Counselling and Psychotherapy – Is It for Me?*, a publication designed to inform potential clients, stated: 'all counselling is totally confidential'.

However, there is also some limited evidence from that time that some services were promising higher levels of confidentiality than they were prepared to deliver. When the Children's Legal Centre conducted a survey of over 100 counselling services for young people, they found that although many initially considered that they were committed to 'total confidentiality many changed their view on further consideration'.

> There are some agencies who do guarantee absolute confidentiality (although it is debatable whether some of them, on further questioning, would have acknowledged extreme circumstances in which even they would feel forced to breach confidentiality – what if a child comes in and shows a counsellor a bottle of deadly poison which they intend to pour into the city's water supply …). Others had carefully defined exceptional circumstances. But a sizeable number showed a worrying degree of confusion – suggesting an answer to one question that they did guarantee confidentiality, and then proceeding to indicate very wide exceptions (e.g. if a client child was thought to be 'at risk'). (Children's Legal Centre, 1989)

This is the heart of the ethical problem. How far can a counsellor go in making confidentiality a priority over all other ethical concerns, such as the protection of others from serious harm? Counsellors have not been alone with this ethical dilemma. Finding a way of reconciling conflicting pressures in favour of privacy and confidentiality while requiring or permitting ethically desirable disclosures of confidences has been accelerated by developments in law applicable to all citizens. These developments have resulted in both greater legal protection for client's confidences and also greater clarity when breaches of client's confidences may be required. However, there are still areas of law which require counsellors to make carefully considered judgements as to what is the best outcome and to be legally accountable for these decisions. I will begin by considering legal obligations to protect a client's confidentiality and privacy.

Legal Protection of Confidentiality

The protection of a client's confidences and privacy is a legal obligation required by several levels of law. In this chapter, I can only summarize the bare bones of the law of confidentiality. For a fuller consideration of how the law impacts on practice see Bond and Mitchels, *Confidentiality and Record Keeping for Counselling and Psychotherapy* (2008).

The Human Rights Act 1998 created legal obligations for all 'public authorities' and is therefore directly applicable to all counselling provided in statutory services such as health, education and social services and indirectly reaches wider than this. Similar measures apply across the whole of the European Union. Article 8 concerns the protection of privacy and is set out in two parts. The first part establishes the general right to privacy and the second sets out the limits of these rights.

> Article 8.1   Everyone has the right to respect for his private and family life, his home, and his correspondence.
>
> Article 8.2   There shall be no interference by a public authority with the exercise of this right except as in accordance with the law and as is necessary in a democratic society in the interests of national security, public safety, or the economic well-being country, for the prevention of disorder or crime, for the protection of health or morals, or the rights and freedoms of others.

This sets the right to privacy and confidentiality within the wider social context of the structures required to protect a democratic society. This is the wider legal context that is easily forgotten when sitting in the counselling room with the door closed against the outside world. All the people in the room are citizens and subject to law which both protects confidences disclosed in that room but may limit that protection.

The Data Protection Act 1998 is also applicable across the European Union. It covers a wide range of requirements to do with record-keeping, many of which are considered in Chapter 13. Almost all counselling records will fall within 'sensitive personal data', which is the category stipulating the most stringent requirements for confidentiality and the safe storage of any records.

Common law applies in any circumstances not covered by statute. The obligation to protect information given in confidence is established where the recipient of the information knows or ought to know that the other person can reasonably expect his privacy to be respected, see the case of *A v B plc and C* ('Flitcroft') [2002]. Therefore, it follows that counsellors owe their clients a legal duty of confidentiality.

Exceptions to a Duty of Confidentiality

There are number of exceptions to a general legal duty of confidentiality for counsellors. These can arise where the client waives a right to disclosure by giving consent to disclosure, where the law recognizes a countervailing factor that outweighs a right to confidentiality, or where there is a legal obligation to disclose. The first of these provides a practical basis for involving the client in deciding how to resolve many ethical dilemmas over confidentiality.

1. The obligation to protect confidential information ceases if a client (who is the subject of that information) consents to disclosure. Typically, the consent will be to disclose specific information to specified people or organizations or for specific purposes. Going beyond the client's conditions for granting consent will amount to a legal breach of confidence unless there is some other legal justification. Seeking a client's consent to making a disclosure is the best way of overcoming any ethical difficulties. Oral consent is sufficient but a record of the consent made as close to the time of the consent as possible provides additional protection to client and counsellor in case there is a later disagreement about what the client consented to. This record should include any conditions required by the client that limit his or her consent to what may be disclosed. A later record of what was disclosed and to whom it was disclosed is further protection and demonstrates ethically and legally informed practice.

2. The balance of public interest is probably the most important criteria for overriding confidentiality, especially if this is against the client's wishes or it has not been possible to obtain consent. The counsellor is required to balance the public interest between the public good served by preserving confidentiality and the public good served by breaching confidentiality. The protection of members of the public from serious physical harm would usually tip the balance in favour of disclosure. For example, the courts found

in favour of Dr Edgell when he broke both his common law and contractual obligations to preserve confidentiality in order to prevent the release of a patient from a secure psychiatric unit because he considered the patient to be dangerous to the public. The court considered that the risk of harm to the public outweighed the obligations in favour of confidentiality. There are a number of criteria that a counsellor would be wise to consider before breaching confidentiality on a balance of public interests. In our analysis (Bond and Mitchels, 2008), we recommend consideration of:

(a) *The degree of risk*: a real risk of harm weighs towards breaching confidentiality. A client who has made similar threats but not acted on them would represent a lower risk.
(b) *The seriousness of the harm being prevented*: the risk of serious physical harm, rape and child abuse would be of sufficient harm to be weighed in favour of breaching confidentiality. The prevention of psychological harm without any associated physical harm would not usually be sufficient for protecting adults. It would require the client's consent.
(c) *Imminence*: time to prevent the harm is running out.
(d) *Effectiveness*: there is a reasonable probability that the breach of confidentiality will prevent the harm.

In order to protect the disclosure from legal action for breach of confidence, any disclosure should be made to someone or an organization capable of preventing the harm; the information disclosed should be restricted to what that person needs to know to prevent the harm; and should be made on an explicitly confidential basis. Making a record of the decision-making process and why it is considered that the balance of public interests favours disclosure is considered good practice. This might include any professional and legal guidance sought to inform the decision where the circumstances permit this. A record of when it was disclosed, to whom, what has been disclosed, how the disclosure was made, and the reasons for the disclosure is also considered good practice. (Marginal decisions to preserve confidentiality on the balance of public interest are probably also best recorded.)

3. The prevention and detection of serious crime. There is no authoritative definition of serious crime that would justify breach of confidence. The Department of Health guidelines (Department of Health, 2003: 35) suggest that this category would include murder, manslaughter, rape, treason, kidnapping, child abuse, and other cases where individuals have suffered serious harm. It probably includes harm to state security, public order and substantial financial crimes. It would not usually include theft, fraud and damage to property where the losses are less substantial.

Legal Obligations to Disclose Confidences

These include:

1. Court orders: a counsellor can be ordered to appear as a witness or to provide all records concerning named clients to a court (called a *subpoena duces tecum* – an order to 'attend and bring the documents with you'). This is a formal order and should not be confused with requests for information from a solicitor, which can be refused. Solicitors tend to send out standard letters requesting 'all notes and records', but they may accept an offer from the therapist of a report instead. This might obviate the need to provide all the records and is a commonly accepted practice by psychologists and psychiatrists. If a report and/or notes are refused, a solicitor may seek a court order where necessary. For further guidance, see Bond and Sandhu *Therapists in Court: Providing Evidence and Supporting Witnesses* (2005).

2. Statutory obligations:

   (a) *Terrorism*: there is general duty to report information that assists in the detection or prevention of terrorism and it is a separate offence known as 'tipping off' to give anyone information about the disclosure that might interfere with an investigation (Terrorism Act 2000).

   (b) *Child protection*: counsellors working in statutory services, such as health, social services and education, may be required to provide information to authorities responsible for the prevention and detection of child abuse. Some counsellors working in non-statutory services may be required to make disclosures through their contract of employment. The level of difficulty encountered by any single professional adequately assessing the degree of risk to a child creates a strong ethical case for conforming to legal obligations under the Children Acts 1989 and 2004 and voluntary co-operation where there is no strict legal obligation to do so. For non-statutory guidance, consult www.everychildmatters.gov.uk or search the internet for basic guidance in the government publication *What To Do If You Are Worried that a Child is Being Abused?* (Every Child Matters, 2006a) and more detailed guidance in *Working Together to Safeguard Children* (Every Child Matters, 2006b). Wherever possible, such referrals should be made with consent unless it could compromise the safety for the child or young person. Further consideration of issues relating to consent can be found in Chapter 6.

Contractual Obligations to Disclose
Confidential Information

A breach of confidence would not be justified simply because it was required by a contract of employment. The Law Commission on *Breach of Confidence* (1981) considered a situation that is relevant to counsellors.

> A doctor or a psychologist employed in industry is faced with the demand by his employer for the disclosure of medical records relating to other employees of the firm who have frankly discussed their personal problems with him on a confidential basis and without any express or implied understanding that the information would be made available to the employer.
>
> Assuming that no question of the public interest is involved (as it might be, for instance, if the health or safety of other employees was at stake), we think that the doctor or psychologist must preserve the confidences of those who confide in him. Of course, if he only accepts the confidence on the express or implied understanding that, pursuant to his contractual duty, he may disclose the information to the employer, this would constitute a limitation on the scope of the obligation of confidence to which he is subject.

This guidance requires the counsellor to have sought the client's consent to disclosures that are not a statutory requirement or can be justified on the balance of public interest. Failure to do so places counsellors in a 'catch 22' situation where they are forced to choose between breaching an obligation of confidentiality or their contract of employment. Whichever way is chosen is likely to incur legal penalties and may also result in professional conduct proceedings. Planning ahead to meet all one's legal obligations by ensuring overall compatibility between them and ensuring that clients are adequately informed about the terms on which counselling is being offered is the only way of avoiding these legal difficulties. The employer should be made aware of the deterrent impact of restrictions to confidentiality and the ethical significance of confidentiality in counselling so that all restrictions are purposeful and kept to a minimum.

Suicidal Clients

In UK law there is no general duty to report suicidal risk or serious self-harm concerning adults. There is long tradition that any adult may refuse treatment for physical illness for good reasons, irrational reasons, or no reasons. A counsellor is legally obliged to respect the wishes of an adult client with mental capacity who is contemplating suicide and actively forbids the counsellor to seek additional help. Public policy in favour of reducing levels of suicide would justify the counsellor in using all their powers of persuasion avert the suicide or to obtain permission to get additional help. Where mental illness is suspected, it may be appropriate to consult the client's GP (if known), social services or a psychiatric service to see if the client meets the requirements for a compulsory admission to hospital for assessment or treatment under mental health legislation. Where counsellors are working in some statutory services or on behalf of public bodies, there may be duty of care to take reasonable steps to prevent suicide, particularly in residential settings, or it may be included as a duty in the contract of employment. Knowing your agency requirements and making compatible agreements with clients is the best way of managing legal requirements and any constraints on confidentiality associated with suicide and self-harm. See Chapter 7 for further discussion.

Where the method of suicide risks serious physical harm to others, for example by jumping off a bridge into traffic or jumping off a building over pedestrians, the balance of public interests would usually favour breach of confidence if the risk is real and imminent.

The law relating to young people under the age of 18 with life-threatening conditions is more protective of their ongoing survival than adults as a matter of public policy. There is a presumption in common law that favours enabling young people to reach adulthood. The balance of public interest (see above) would probably favour breach of confidence to obtain advice or services where there is an imminent risk of suicide or death due to self-harm, especially if there is no other reasonable way of preventing it. Depending on the availability of local services, it may be possible to obtain advice from social services, child and adolescent mental health units, or voluntary organizations specializing in supporting young people. The practical difficulty facing anyone seeking help and advice is the comparative shortage of services to protect young people from self-harm in contrast to the growth of services to protect young people from abuse and neglect by their carers and others. The imposition of treatment against a valid refusal of consent by a young person or someone with parental responsibility would require either legal authority from mental health legislation or an order from the High Court.

Does the Client Have a Duty of Confidentiality?

At workshops I have often been asked about whether a client is bound to keep everything that happens in the counselling confidential. Two arguments in favour of expecting clients to observe strict confidentiality are usually offered. First, total secrecy helps to mark a boundary between the counselling and the rest of the client's life. The existence of this boundary may increase the intensity of the personal experience of counselling and therefore its effectiveness. It may also prevent interference from partners and friends. Secondly, counsellors may be quite disclosing about themselves during counselling. This is an issue of particular importance for the users of the person-centred approach and related methods that require the counsellor to be self-revealing.

Although these are strong arguments, I think the adverse effects of attempting to impose confidentiality on a client counter them. First, on ethical grounds it would be limiting the client's control of the outcome of the counselling and would be difficult to enforce without undermining the counselling by putting the counsellor in the conflicting roles of counsellor and enforcer. Secondly, the issue of confidentiality is complex enough for the counsellor without the need to develop parallel standards for the client. Thirdly, most clients have considerable emotional barriers against seeking counselling because of the necessity of acknowledging their own neediness. To impose confidentiality on clients could increase these personal barriers because of a widespread cultural tendency to associate secrecy with shame. Therefore a general principle of client secrecy seems inappropriate.

Occasionally, it may be appropriate for the counsellor to say something in confidence to a client. Usually this would be because the counsellor is about to say something which is personally sensitive about herself and wishes to retain control of whom she informs. For example, a counsellor with relevant personal experience who is working with a sexually abused client may wish to say something about her own experience of being sexually abused and how she overcame it. The counsellor needs to be aware that any attempt to enforce confidentiality on the client would raise the ethical difficulties already mentioned. Therefore, counsellors do sometimes have to accept that some clients might break confidences and the counsellor is unlikely to be able to do much about it. Both client and counsellor take a risk in confiding in each other. Observance of ethical guidelines by counsellors minimizes the risk to clients but counsellors are not protected in the same way. Counsellors need to assess which clients to confide in and to recognize that there is some unavoidable risk of the confidence being broken

In child care cases, the family court can make orders about the retention and confidentiality of documents in the case, which might include therapy reports and records. This power may also apply in some circumstances to certain criminal cases where confidentiality is necessary in the public interest.

Collaboration between Professionals

Counsellors increasingly work in teams or agencies with other counsellors or in settings like primary care or education where collaboration between professionals with different functions is considered desirable. Where information is shared on a strictly confidential basis within the boundaries of a team, clients may benefit from:

- minimizing the repetition of what may be a painful history or event being told repeatedly to each member of the team;
- better co-ordination between the people delivering services;
- greater opportunities for service providers to pool knowledge and expertise and enhance the quality of service offered;
- the opportunity to be involved in decisions about what information is shared and with whom. Clients may be deprived of this opportunity where exchanges of information are informal or *ad hoc*, and thus outside their awareness.

Recent developments in new technology have extended the possibilities from consultations and discussions between staff to data-sharing, particularly of computerized records.

In 1997, the Caldicott Committee produced a report which recommended six principles for information-sharing in the NHS and between the NHS and non-NHS organizations. The six Caldicott principles are:

1. Justify the purpose(s) for using confidential information.
2. Only use when absolutely necessary.
3. Use the minimum that is required.
4. Access should be on a strict need-to-know basis.
5. Everyone must understand his or her responsibilities.
6. Understand and comply with the law.

The personally sensitive nature of information disclosed in counselling suggests that clients should know what is being shared and with whom and for what purpose, and have the opportunity to consent to this.

This principle of respecting client autonomy by putting them in control of what is communicated about them should arguably also be applied to information-sharing to conform to professional standards such as ongoing and regular counselling-supervision or seeking a client's consent to be presented for training purposes.

There has been one inquiry which considered the responsibility of counsellors working in health care teams following the murders of his mother and stepbrother by Anthony Smith while suffering from paranoid schizophrenic delusions. An inquiry into the care of Anthony Smith was commissioned by Southern Derbyshire Health Authority and Derbyshire County Council (SDHA, 1996). Prior to this tragedy, he had been receiving counselling in his GP's practice and a range of community- and hospital-based psychiatric services. The report considers many different aspects of his treatment and makes a large number of recommendations that extend well beyond counselling. With regard to counselling, the report is critical of the caution with which counsellors manage confidentiality. In particular, it argues that there ought to be an ethical obligation to breach confidentiality to the extent of having confidential discussions with other members of the clinical team where the counsellor suspects that a client is becoming seriously mentally ill and poses a threat to themselves or to others. It also recommends that counsellors should be trained in the recognition of mental illness. These recommendations undoubtedly deserve serious consideration when developing agency policy and implementation in ways that are compatible with the Caldicott principles published a year later. The general principle that there should be clarity about management of confidentiality and communications between team members is one that merits wide support.

Penalties for Breach of Confidence

The remedies and penalties applied indicate the level of seriousness with which courts view breaches of confidence. The court may issue orders (i.e. injunctions) to prevent a proposed disclosure of confidential information. These only work where the person affected has prior notice of an intention to breach confidence. After a breach of confidence has taken place, the court may award damages and this is the most likely outcome, especially if the client is fee-paying. The damages may be substantial if it can be shown that there was damage to social reputation, severe injury to feelings, job loss, reduced prospects of promotion or other losses. Damages may be awarded even if the client has not suffered any economic loss because there may be no better way of acknowledging the harm that has been done. Imprisonment is also a possible outcome. A judge has speculated that imprisonment would be an appropriate penalty for a health worker who leaked the names of doctors with AIDS to the press (*X v Y*, 1988).

Alternative ways for clients to resolve breaches of confidentiality are to seek a Data Protection Compliance Order if the professional is a data controller, which would usually be the case if the counsellor (alone or jointly) determines the purposes for which the data is processed. A client may also bring a complaint against the counsellor to an employer or any professional body to which the counsellor belongs.

Conclusion

Although the law of confidentiality is complex, it is broadly compatible with ethical analysis. Confidentiality is a high ethical and practical priority in order to avoid deterring clients from taking up counselling and to create the conditions that make counselling effective. However, confidentiality is a secondary requirement to make primary ethical concerns possible, such as respecting client autonomy, fidelity or honouring trust and doing good and avoiding harm. When understood in this way, confidentiality is not an end in itself nor should it be the primary ethical principle to guide all actions.

There are situations where offering total confidentiality would compromise the integrity of the counsellor. Counsellors may find themselves faced with difficult ethical decisions to protect their own integrity and that of counselling. Where does integrity lie if a client insists on the counsellor respecting his autonomy by maintaining confidentiality in order to enable him to violate someone else's autonomy by causing them serious harm or committing a serious crime against them? Similarly, ought clients to be able to insist that a counsellor remains trustworthy by protecting their confidences when a client is being seriously untrustworthy to others by exposing them to serious harm? The law goes a long way to protect confidentiality and establishes criteria by which a counsellor would be expected to justify any breaches of confidentiality. In most situations, it ought to be possible to find a way of reconciling law and ethics.

Part III

The Counsellor and Others

11

Responsibility to Oneself, Colleagues and the Community

Responsibilities to the client are the primary concern of the counsellor but they are not the only responsibilities. There are other categories of responsibility. Any or all of these may impinge on how the responsibility to the client is implemented or occasionally may even take priority. Each of these is considered in turn.

Responsibility to Self as a Counsellor

The ethical principle of autonomy is usually referred to in terms of respect for the client's capacity for self-determination. However, autonomy also applies to the counsellor. This is one of the components in Andrew Thompson's principle of 'self-interest' (see Chapter 3, p. 51). Like clients, counsellors should only enter into a counselling relationship on a voluntary basis and as a result of having made a deliberate choice to do so. Counsellors also have an obligation to exercise care of themselves. Sometimes the ethical desirability of maintaining their own effectiveness, resilience and ability to help clients is understood solely as ensuring that the counsellor is competent to provide counselling and has the personal resources to do so. But behind it is an even more important principle. Counselling places considerable demands on the counsellor, There is always the risk of emotional burnout when working closely with the pain and problems of others. Counsellors have a responsibility to monitor their own responses and to protect their own well-being by avoiding excessive working and by making use of regular counselling-supervision. Counselling-supervision has a supportive role but this is only one of the tasks addressed in supervision. Sometimes, it is useful to supplement the support offered in supervision with personal counselling.

I think these are minimum standards of self-care. The optimum standard would include periodic reviews of whether providing counselling enriches the counsellor's quality of life. A great deal is said and written about the demands on the counsellor, but if the only effect is personal depletion then why continue to do it? It is important to the mental health of the counsellor that there is also personal satisfaction in providing counselling.

Indemnity insurance

The importance of indemnity insurance from the client's point of view is considered in Chapter 5. There are also gains to the counsellor in terms of peace of mind. Even though the risks of having a claim made against a counsellor appear to be relatively small, should it arise, the sums of money required even to obtain legal advice can be quite large. Adequate insurance helps to reduce the risk that the counsellor will incur unanticipated expenditure to compensate a client, and some insurance schemes also include free legal advice.

Personal safety

Fortunately, it is rare for counsellors to be physically or sexually attacked by clients but it is not unknown. On very rare occasions, a client has killed a counsellor. A recent tragedy involved an experienced female counsellor seeing men who had recently been discharged from prison, some of whom had been serving sentences for serious offences against people. The exact circumstances of the killing appear to be unknown. However, this tragedy indicates that some aspects of what is generally thought to be good practice add to the potential seriousness of the situation. For example, the counselling will usually take place away from other people in order to give the client confidentiality and privacy. This makes it harder for the counsellor to call for help. It is also not unusual for counselling rooms to be sited well away from busy areas to reduce extraneous noise. The same situation may arise if the counsellor is working in her own home. This means that there may be no one close by to hear cries for help. The usual practice of taking clients who are not previously known to the counsellor, in order to maintain clarity about the nature of the relationship and professional boundaries, also creates an element of unpredictability and risk each time a counsellor takes on a new client.

Counsellors should organize their work in ways to reduce the risk of assault on themselves. Counsellors who are vulnerable to assault have adopted some of the following strategies, which can be implemented without compromising the ethics and standards of practice intended to protect the client:

- taking referrals through someone else, e.g. GPs, voluntary organizations or colleagues, rather than seeing clients who walk in directly off the street or respond directly to advertisements;
- making telephone contact whenever possible with clients before the first meeting. This provides a basic check on their physical location and gives the counsellor an opportunity to make a preliminary assessment.

Counsellors working with some client groups may not be able to implement any of these safety measures. For instance, counsellors who see clients with alcohol and drug problems may find that the potential benefits of a referral system for the counsellor's safety are outweighed by the deterrent effect it has on clients seeking counselling. Some clients do not have telephones or do not wish to have telephone calls from a counsellor because of the risk of someone they live with discovering they are receiving counselling. For example, a client seeking counselling about an extra-marital affair or a violent partner may have good reasons for not wanting the counsellor to make phone calls to their home.

However, all counsellors can take a number of basic precautions once the client arrives by:

- avoiding seeing new clients, or existing clients if there is any risk of assault, in an empty building. It is better to have someone around who can be alerted by shouting or any unusual sounds. This is one of the advantages of counselling services that have receptionists or where counsellors share premises;
- providing the counselling rooms with telephones with outside lines. If counsellors are seeing clients in premises with a switchboard operator telephone service they may need a direct line to the public exchange when they see clients outside the usual working hours of the switchboard;

- installing an alarm or 'panic button': this may be particularly useful if there is a high level of risk to the counsellor;
- letting someone know in advance a specific time when the counsellor will contact them and giving them instructions about what to do if the counsellor fails to make contact. It is much easier to handle a dangerous situation if all you have to do is to contain it until help arrives, rather than having to take action to obtain help which may provoke the other person.

These strategies may not prevent an assault but they increase the chance of obtaining assistance.

A sense of personal safety is important if the counsellor is to feel secure enough to work creatively with clients. Sometimes counsellors experience a sense of danger without any attack actually occurring. These feelings ought to be taken seriously and discussed in supervision. The sense of threat may arise from real danger, or a counsellor picking up a client's sense of threat to himself, or the re-stimulation of something from the counsellor's past. Whatever the cause, there is no ethical requirement that the counsellor continues to see clients who evoke such feelings. The counsellor may refer the client to another counsellor if taking reasonable steps to promote safety is insufficient to reduce the sense of danger to acceptable levels.

Clients who harass counsellors outside the counselling relationship

It is rare for counsellors to be harassed by clients making nuisance phone calls, sending frequent unsolicited correspondence or making unwelcome visits to the counsellor's home. However, 'stalking' and harassment of counsellors does happen from time to time. These are extremely distressing incidents for the counsellor when they occur. The distress is compounded by the ethical constraints of confidentiality. Although ethical guidance seldom explicitly considers this kind of situation, a number of strategies are consistent with the ethics of counselling. These are as follows:

- Counselling-supervision is important in providing emotional support for the counsellor as well as for reviewing potential courses of action.
- Medical and legal opinion may be sought about the client at an early stage. Providing the client's identity is not communicated, there is no breach of confidentiality. These consultations should take place with people who are unlikely to know the client.

- If the client is making public statements which are untrue and to the detriment of the counsellor, it may be appropriate to write to the client by recorded delivery in the following terms: (a) any repetition of the statements by the client will be taken as an indication that the client regards the issue as no longer requiring confidentiality; (b) the counsellor will feel entitled to put her side of the story to those directly involved; and (c) the counsellor may contact solicitors, police, doctors, etc., as appropriate.
- If the client persists after receiving a letter from the counsellor, then it is appropriate to consult solicitors to take action on the counsellor's behalf and sometimes it may be appropriate to contact the police.
- Events which happen outside the counselling relationship or after the counselling relationship has ended need not be treated as confidential.

I know that some situations have been resolved by the combination of a solicitor's letter and a refusal by the counsellor to enter into any further communications. All subsequent telephone calls and letters were ignored and eventually they stopped. The persistence of some clients is remarkable and, unfortunately, as distressing and disruptive to counsellors as any form of persistent stalking or harassment. In these situations, it may be necessary to seek legal advice about how best to stop the harassment.

These actions should be reserved for extreme situations. Counsellors do have to accept that from time to time clients misrepresent what has happened within a counselling relationship. This most often happens when the counsellor is seeing one partner about difficulties in their relationship. Sometimes clients will attribute to the counsellor things that they are afraid to say for themselves. For example, 'My counsellor says we should separate'. I have known college students tell their parents that their counsellor says they should give up their course when this has not been said by the counsellor. These situations are clearly potentially difficult, especially if the partner or parent approaches the counsellor directly. Nonetheless, the counsellor must maintain confidentiality by neither admitting nor denying what has happened in the counselling. (If a serious concern is being raised about the welfare of a young person, then it may be appropriate to follow agency policy where this exists, for example by making a referral, and to inform the inquirer of this policy but without breaching the confidentiality of the young person.) Such incidents are on quite a different scale from a situation where the client is seeking out the counsellor's colleagues or friends, or is persistently phoning late at night, or sending letters in disguised handwriting to ensure they are opened by the counsellor.

Responsibility to Other Counsellors

Undermining public confidence in counselling

Counselling is only possible in a relationship of trust. The public reputation of counselling can create circumstances in which it is easier or harder to establish trusting relationships. In order to protect the collective reputation of counselling and the reputation of members of any counselling organization there is a shared interest in protecting the public the reputation of counsellors. Most counselling organizations attempt to protect their reputation for supporting good practice by requiring members to report concerns of any misconduct by other members and will expel members for behaviour that brings counselling into disrepute. The seriousness of what has occurred is also relevant in deciding whether public confidence in counselling is undermined and brought into disrepute. In my opinion, a fairly robust view has to be taken. For instance, two counsellors engaged in a heated public debate would not fall into this category unless either party became personally abusive and defamed the other, or violence resulted.

Can a counsellor bring counselling into disrepute by activities unrelated to counselling? For example, if someone who works as a voluntary counsellor in his own time is convicted of fraud at his place of work, would this amount to bringing counselling into disrepute? Most professional organizations require members to notify them of criminal convictions and will consider whether the conviction is compatible with continued membership of that organization. Insurance companies will ask for information about any convictions and this may impact on the cover given or the cost of the premium. Recent criminal convictions, especially those involving deception or violence, can bring disrepute on the profession.

Responsibility to Colleagues and Members of the Caring Profession

Accountability to others

Counsellors working on their own in private practice are free of the need to be accountable to anyone other than their client and can discuss any difficulties with a counselling supervisor. However, counselling is increasingly provided within organizations involving more complex patterns of accountability to managers, committees and others.

There have been situations in which it has seemed that counsellors have wanted to use confidentiality as a shield to protect them from appropriate accountability to colleagues. For example, confidentiality has been used as an excuse for avoiding disclosure that a large number of clients are missing their appointments, or to avoid accountability for resources being used. This is an abuse of confidentiality. However, the methods used in being accountable should be consistent with the ethics and standards of practice of counselling. What this means in practice is considered in detail in Chapter 14.

The counsellor's responsibility to increase colleagues' understanding

Counsellors report that the voluntary nature of counselling and the need for confidentiality are the two aspects of counselling which most frequently give rise to misunderstandings. It takes positive action by counsellors working in organizations to develop appropriate expectations of counselling.

Sometimes clients and colleagues have inappropriate expectations of the counsellor's role. For example, a tutor may refer a young person with an eating disorder for counselling and assume that the counsellor will also monitor the client's weight and general health. These are inappropriate expectations. The weighing of the client and health checks would need to be carried out by someone with medical or nursing qualifications.

Responsibility to the Wider Community

The ethical focus is usually on the client–counsellor relationship rather than on social units like the family, except for counsellors working primarily with families or the wider community. However, there are situations where the counsellor is faced with dilemmas concerning responsibilities to the wider community.

One recurrent issue is what to do if a client talks about committing or having committed serious crimes. For example:

Sheila talks about her distress at being involved in a robbery in which someone was injured. She also mentions plans for another robbery in one week's time. What should the counsellor do?

Does the counsellor have a duty to report the crime that has been committed? There is no general duty in criminal law to report to the police or anyone else that a client has committed a crime. Statutory exceptions are considered in Chapter 10. There is no general duty to answer police questions about a client. A polite but clear refusal to answer is all that is required. However, to give false or misleading answers can amount to the offence of wasting police time or obstructing a police officer in the execution of his duty.

Does the counsellor have a duty to prevent crime? There is no general duty under criminal law to prevent someone committing a crime outside the counselling room (with the exception of statutory requirements to notify the authorities of information held about particular offences like terrorism (see Chapter 10).

If the crime is being committed within the counselling session, then the legal position is rather different. A counsellor who failed to prevent or take reasonable steps to prevent an offence in the counsellor's presence may have committed the offences of aiding and abetting, or 'counselling' (in the criminal law sense of being an accomplice to a crime). This would arise only if the counsellor's inactivity amounted to a positive encouragement. A counsellor is most likely to be charged with these offences when a client assaults another, uses illegal drugs or attempts suicide in the presence of the counsellor.

There is a right, but not a duty, to use such force as is reasonable in the circumstances to prevent crime. Some crimes are not serious enough to justify the use of force. Illegal drug use may come into this category. The use of more force than is reasonable is in itself a crime. Therefore the use of physical restraint to stop someone hitting another person is usually reasonable, but the use of a weapon would not be. Because suicide is no longer a crime, there is no general right to use reasonable force to prevent suicide attempts or suicide (see Chapter 7 for further discussion of this issue).

Could the counsellor inadvertently incur liability for a client's acts? The answer is 'yes'. An example illustrates how a counsellor could commit the criminal offence of incitement.

Suppose the counsellor honestly but mistakenly believes that it is not illegal for his 15-year-old male client to engage in sexual intercourse in private with another consenting adult of the same age. Consequently, the counsellor encourages and supports his client in sexual experimentation of this nature as part of his 'homework' assignment.

It is not necessary for the counsellor to know that the activity is an offence for the counsellor to be guilty of incitement. (The current age of consent for homosexual acts between men is 16 years old in England, Wales, Scotland, the Isle of Man and Jersey; 17 in Northern Ireland and Eire; and 18 Guernsey and Gibraltar.) The counsellor may not want his client to break the law. It is sufficient that the law has been broken for the offence to have been committed, although the counsellor's mistake about the law and lack of deliberate intention to incite an offence would be taken into account in sentencing. It is therefore wise to be cautious when setting the client tasks between sessions, a technique frequently used in behavioural methods of counselling. Windy Dryden and Michael Neenan (2004) caution: 'Whatever behavioural assignment you negotiate with your client, ensure it is both legal and ethical.'

A counsellor can also incur civil liability for inciting or encouraging a client to break a contract with a third party. For example, a counsellor encourages his client to change jobs without giving the contracted amount of notice to the first employer or to stop supplying goods that the client has contracted to provide. If the client carries out the act, which has been encouraged, the counsellor may become jointly liable for any resulting loss to a third party. It is also possible that the counsellor could be jointly liable for a client's breach of confidence that has been incited by the counsellor.

Although I am not aware of any counsellor being prosecuted or sued for incitement of a client's wrongdoing, this is a theoretical possibility. At a workshop, Kenneth Cohen cautioned counsellors to be careful when using empathic responses with a client who is intending to commit an unlawful act. The counsellor has to choose between being empathic, which the client often interprets as encouragement, and the possibility, albeit a remote one, of incurring legal liabilities as a consequence of the client's subsequent acts or withholding empathy.

So far I have concentrated on the counsellor's legal responsibilities to the wider community and the potential consequences of these. However, ethical dilemmas that do not necessarily involve the law can also arise. For example:

Edward uses counselling to ease his guilt about deceiving his partner about his frequent sexual relationships with other people. Sheila, the counsellor, feels increasingly concerned on behalf of his wife.

The ethics of respecting the client's autonomy and confidentiality would prevent the counsellor from communicating her concern to the wife directly. But what if Edward has a life-threatening illness with which he could infect his wife? This makes the ethical dilemma much more acute. This has arisen in HIV/AIDS counselling. The general practice has been to respect the client's control over confidential information but to work in ways which make it easier for him to tell his wife, including offering to be present when he tells his wife. Occasionally, counsellors have told partners with the client's consent or at the client's request. Alternatively, clients have, often of their own volition, chosen to abstain from doing anything which would put their partner at risk of infection until they feel able to tell them about their health problem. Some clients prefer to abstain from sex or other activities that would put their partner at risk for the rest of their lives, rather than tell a partner. But what if the client deliberately and recklessly continues to put a partner at risk of infection? This would appear to be a situation in which, after consultation with the client and other experienced counsellors, the counsellor might decide it is defensible to break confidentiality to warn the partner (see Chapter 10). There has been an increasing tendency to prosecute people who knowingly put others at risk of HIV infection. The seriousness of the situation for everyone involved means that the counsellor needs to be sure that there is no alternative possible course of action.

Conclusion

The management of conflicting responsibilities is particularly challenging for a counsellor. Whenever possible, it is better to anticipate what these might be and to find ways of avoiding them. If the conflict of responsibilities cannot be avoided, then it is important that the client knows of this so that either the contract between the counsellor and client can take them into account or the client can seek counselling elsewhere. These situations are much easier to handle prospectively than retrospectively.

One of the best ways to be forewarned of potential conflicts of responsibility is to discuss situations with an experienced counsellor working in a similar situation. This is one of the important functions of counselling-supervision.

12

Counselling-supervision

Supervision has along history that goes back to the origins of the talking therapies. Both the early Freudians and Jungians appear to have developed forms of supervision to support psychoanalysts and therapists with the dynamic aspects of their work, particularly the unconscious elements at work between the therapist and client. It is as true now as it was in the origins of psychoanalysis that it is considered helpful to have someone familiar with the psychology of relationships and human interactions to assist therapists in understanding their work with clients. Many counsellors would not use psychoanalysis directly and prefer other approaches to their work, but recognize the value of an ongoing working relationship with someone to discuss their counselling. Most professional bodies for counselling require that counsellors receive regular and ongoing supervision (BPS, 2005; BACP, 2007; IACP, 2007). Ongoing supervision has been widely accepted as an essential protection of professional and especially ethical standards. However, there are critics of supervision requirements, especially for experienced counsellors. I will return to the issue of whether supervision ought to be an ongoing requirement later in this chapter. I am not aware of anyone disputing its value in the early stages of a counsellor's career. Therefore, I will start by exploring what is supervision and how it supports ethical practice throughout the early stages of a counsellor's career before turning to the more problematic aspects of supervision.

What is Counselling-supervision?

Most definitions of supervision have several elements in common, even if the precise words are different. Counselling-supervision is characterized by:

- being primarily directed to the enhancing the service to clients, although operating indirectly through the counsellor;
- a degree of formality with explicit agreements about the working arrangements for the supervision, including the regularity of sessions, the allocation of responsibility for the client work, confidentiality and any payments;
- protecting ethical standards both individually and collectively for counsellors;
- protecting and enhancing standards of practice;
- operating largely independently from direct line management or accountability to professional bodies in order to provide sufficient privacy for the counsellor to work with the personal issues involved in the work. Exceptions to this are usually clearly defined and usually only arise when there is sufficient cause for concern about the counsellor's practice to justify notifying an employer or professional body.

All these elements are brought together with varying degrees of emphasis in the following definitions:

> Supervision is a formal arrangement for therapists to discuss their work regularly with someone who is experienced in both therapy and supervision. The task is to work together to ensure and develop the efficacy of the therapist/client relationship. (BACP Information Service, 2008b)

> Supervision support is a contractually negotiated relationship between practitioners for the purpose of supporting, evaluating and developing professional practice. Supervision is designed to offer multi-level support in an atmosphere of integrity and openness for the purpose of enhancing reflective skills, maximising the effectiveness of therapeutic interventions, informing ethical decisions and facilitating an understanding of the use of self. (BPS, 2007: s. 2.1)

> The purpose of professional supervision is for counsellors to reflect on and develop effective and ethical practice. It also has a monitoring purpose with regard to counsellors' work. Supervision includes personal support, mentoring professional identity development and reflection upon the relationships between persons, theories, practices, work contexts and cultural perspectives.

Professional supervision is a partnership. It is a contractual, collab–orative and confidential process, based upon informed consent. (NZAC, 2003: s. 9)

International Variations in Approaches to Counselling-supervision

Different countries have developed counselling–supervision in distinctive ways. In the USA, counselling–supervision is primarily directed at devel–oping trainee counsellors and is replaced by a system of consultation with experienced colleagues when supervision is no longer required after quali–fication. It is very closely associated with the education of counsellors and is adapted as counsellors move from the dependence and naïvety of a novice towards independent practice through a developmental approaches to supervision (Stoltenberg and Delworth, 1987). The British approach to supervision is different. It is envisaged that supervision will continue throughout the working life of the counsellor, both as form of professional accountability in the interests of clients and for the professional and personal development of the counsellor.

Hawkins and Shohet (2007) identify six levels of supervision which capture different elements of the triangular relationship between client, counsellor and supervisor. These concern:

1. Reflection on the content of the counselling session, especially what was said by the client.
2. Exploration of the counsellor's interventions and the use of techniques and strategies.
3. Exploration of how the client and counsellor interact and their relationship.
4. The counsellor's feelings towards the client, especially countertransference responses and any personal issues stimulated by contact with the client.
5. What is happening between the supervisor and counsellor and how this relates to the work with the client. To what extent can the current interac–tions be distinguished or are they interrelated in some ways that reveal 'parallel processes' which, if resolved in the supervisory relationship, would assist the counselling?
6. Examining the supervisor's countertransferences towards the counsellor in order to capture what is not being consciously put into words by the super–visor or counsellor in order to examine their implications for this relationship and the work with the client.

This focus on process is also evident in the other widely-used model of supervision in the UK, the cyclical model of Page and Wosket (2001), which describes the reflective space offered by supervision in terms of a cycle of five stages. These are:

1. Contracting about ground rules and expectations of each other.
2. Agreeing a focus.
3. Making a space for reflection.
4. Building the link between supervision and work with the client.
5. Review and evaluation.

They envisage that the counsellor and supervisor will keep revisiting these stages in a cyclical manner thus strengthening both the supervision and the counselling.

In both the UK and the USA, it is assumed that the supervisor will be from within the profession of counselling and suitably trained in both counselling and supervision. European traditions appear less restrictive and are more open to supervision across professions. Supervisors are not restricted to work within their own professions but apply their skills and knowledge of supervision across a wide range of different types of workers with people (Carroll and Holloway, 1999).

International comparisons between approaches to supervision reveal another distinction which I will return to later in this chapter. The movement of people between countries means that counsellors increasingly face the challenges and opportunities of working with clients from outside their own cultural background. Counsellors in New Zealand appear particularly aware of this challenge because of the sensitivities and tensions between the Maori as the longstanding inhabitants of those islands and the Westerners or 'pakeha' in a constitutional framework of biculturalism. In reality, New Zealand is becoming rapidly multicultural as people from other cultures in Asia and the Pacific settle alongside Maori and Europeans. The implications of providing counselling across cultural differences are also particularly evident in North America. The ethical challenges of cultural difference are taken sufficiently seriously for supervision to be seen as having a major role to play developing culturally appropriate services and supporting counsellors in understanding the unfamiliar. In some cases, the supervisor will be selected because of specific cultural knowledge and background, and will fulfil all the functions of supervision. Alternatively, the cultural supervision may be provided to supplement the usual counselling-supervision from within a specific cultural identity. This use of supervision to address cultural differences is not wholly absent from UK approaches to counselling, but is much less prominent in published ethics by professional bodies in the UK in comparison to New Zealand and North America.

The Tasks of Counselling-supervision

Counselling-supervision is intended to make a major contribution to the ethical integrity of the work with clients but this is only one of several functions. One of the pioneers of supervision training in the UK developed supervision to address three core tasks:

1 *Normative*: establishing and protecting professional ethics and standards of practice.
2 *Formative*: enhancing the aptitude, knowledge and skills of the counsellor – a form of continuing professional development focusing on work with current clients.
3 *Restorative*: supporting the counsellor with the personal effects of working closely with people who may be experiencing considerable distress or difficulty. The preventative function is to reduce the counsellor's risk of burnout or secondary traumatization. Providing a degree of personal support is also intended to prevent the counsellor from becoming so self-protective against emotional pain that they are unable to form empathic or effective relationships with the client. It also works positively to affirm the value of this type of intervention to keep the counsellor motivated and energized for providing counselling.

As a result of researching counsellors working in multidisciplinary teams (Bond, 1991b), I have added:

4 *Perspective*: an opportunity to see the counselling in the wider professional context of other services and social systems and to reflect on how to maximize any benefits to the client. (See Table 12.1.)

Counselling supervision is about much more than ethics. It is a mixture of ethics and 'practics', in which the overall impact comes from the supervisor modelling good practice that influences the counsellor positively (Houston, 1995). Modelling is a very powerful influence that operates both consciously and subliminally and can enhance good practice. Unfortunately, poor modelling in supervision can also undermine

TABLE 12.1   *The tasks of counselling-supervision: template for dividing tasks*

| | | Undertaken by | |
| | | | Counselling supervisor/ consultative |
Task	**Description**	**Line manager**	**support**
Formative	Skill development Reflection on experience New understanding New knowledge about counselling process, client group, specific issues raised by client		
Normative	Counselling: standards; ethics and practice Agency: standards; ethics and practice Monitoring the quality of counselling Consideration of feedback from client		
Restorative	Dealing with personal issues and stress arising from counselling Validating achievements		
Perspective	Overview of total counselling work Relationship between counselling and other methods of client's obtaining help Relationships with counsellors and with members of other professions		

good practice and encourage poor practice. I will touch on this again in some of the examples.

Ethical Dimensions of Counselling Supervision

Boundaries between professional and personal relationships

Maintaining boundaries between the supervisor and supervisee have long been considered as important as between counsellor and client.

There are probably two main reasons for this. The first is sustaining a model that supports the management of boundaried relationships between counsellor and client. Behavioural modelling is a powerful way of reinforcing or undermining learning for other relationships. The second reason is that a substantial part of the justification for the supervisory relationship in counselling is one of professional accountability and such accountability can become clouded by possible confusion with line management issues, divided loyalties, friendship and close personal relationships. Some supervisory relationships can start out with clear relational boundaries but may become closer over time. For example:

Sheila has supervised Bob's counselling for over three years. They have developed a mutual respect for each other and have successfully managed encountering each other in a local counselling association at training events and have been able to keep a boundary between being sociable in these local events and working in greater depth in supervision. They both enjoy walking and without any knowledge of each other's arrangements have booked on the same ramblers' weekend, staying in the same hostel. When they discover this, they start to question where the boundaries lie in the relationship for supervisor and supervisee.

This would be an appropriate point to review how far it is possible to maintain the boundaries in the supervisory relationship in ways that are professionally credible to others regardless of how scrupulous the two people concerned are. Some people are better than others in maintaining boundaries. Even if there is no intention for the friendship to develop further, it may be worth considering the supervisee finding a new supervisor and reflecting on how future social contacts with the former supervisor will be maintained. Where this is not practical, perhaps due to a shortage of suitable supervisors, it may be wise to adopt deliberate strategies to ensure clearer boundaries between the professional and personal roles. Some approaches to counselling are more open to combining friendship with a professional role in a considered way in comparison to others. All these factors need to be taken into account. This is the sort of situation that requires careful consideration by the people involved and may be relatively unproblematic on some occasions and possibly quite problematic in others.

Who is responsible for the counselling delivered to the client?

The general principle is that there is a chain of responsibility from the client to the counsellor and then from the counsellor to the supervisor. Supervisors do not normally assume a direct responsibility to a client. They work to enhance the counselling work and the benefits for a client through the supervisee. The following example raises the issue of whether this ought to be the approach to responsibility for the work with the client.

Hubert is a trainee counsellor who is developing good basic skills but is not yet confident in moving from what clients say to selecting the most appropriate counselling actions to help them. He presents a case in supervision where he considers that the client and he are going around in repetitive circles and the client's circumstances are deteriorating. As Hubert's supervisor, Pam is sufficiently concerned for the client that she is questioning her responsibilities to the client and the trainee counsellor.

A great deal will depend on the modality of the practitioner and expectations of therapy, the degree of vulnerability of the client and the severity of the client's problems. If we suppose that the client's deterioration is putting the client seriously at risk of self-harm, and Hubert, as the counsellor, seems both overwhelmed and helpless, in such circumstances, a supervisor may feel that the normative and protective functions of supervision ought to carry greater weight than the formative support of the supervisee. An experienced supervisor will explore a range of possible options before taking the exceptional act (see later) of intervening directly by offering to see the client personally. It may be that Hubert can be supported in seeking additional support or making a referral to a more experienced or suitable counsellor. Such an approach would have the advantage of supporting Hubert in recognizing the boundaries to his competence and how to manage such situations in future. However, this will only work if there is a real prospect of meeting the client's needs at the same time as developing the trainee counsellor. Similarly, there may be resources on Hubert's course that could be brought into play or, alternatively, from within the counselling service where Hubert is seeing the client. In an extreme situation, the priority ought to be the protection of the client's best interests. In the absence of any other possibility, it may be justified for the supervisor to arrange a meeting with the client through

Hubert in order to undertake an assessment to ensure that the client's needs can be met by a suitable referral or through a better-supported Hubert. One of the difficulties thereafter is that the supervisor takes on potentially conflicting responsibilities to the client and the trainee. In order to prevent such an eventuality, most supervisors of trainees will ensure that the counselling agency and the training course take primary responsibilities in backing up the work of the trainee where a client is considered to be at risk. The arrangements for communicating any concerns would have formed part of the working agreement between the supervisor and supervisee and ought to be consistent with the agreement between the client and the trainee. In the example, the concerns were raised through the trainee counsellor. What if they had been raised by the client directly? A concerned client ought to be directed to raise their concerns with the counselling agency in the first instance rather than with the training course or the supervisor.

Some clients are faced with deteriorating circumstances that may be beyond any reasonable expectations of a trainee counsellor or even beyond the range of a competent experienced counsellor. A sound assessment procedure before allocation minimizes such occurrences but cannot wholly eliminate them. Life happens. In fairness to both clients and trainees, it is important to have plans for such eventualities in place.

Supporting supervisees taking on new approaches to providing counselling

It is increasingly common for clients to want to communicate with their counsellors using electronic technology. For some clients, this may be simply arranging appointments by email or text, but what if this is wanting to receive counselling electronically rather than face to face. Similarly, growing numbers of counsellors are also interested in offering services to people by taking advantage of new digital means of communication, for example by webcam, a dedicated chat room or as a virtual client in 'Second Life' (a virtual world in which participants create avatars of themselves). These are natural developments in view of the increasing availability of the technology and the widespread and growing familiarity with it. The technology opens up the possibility of counselling for people who might not be willing to see a counsellor face to face in an office. In this example, the supervisee is more familiar with new technology and its possibilities than the supervisor.

Jane is a competent face-to-face counsellor and very capable with new technology in other areas of her life. She has a young family and is looking for ways to be able to work from home in dedicated blocks of time around her support with childcare. She greatly values her supervisor's insights and has found that her current supervision greatly enhances her work with her face-to-face clients. She is not in a position to take time out for substantial further training but would like to develop an online counselling service for mothers with young children. She raises this possibility with her supervisor, who is doubtful about the potential of online counselling.

This is a situation which challenges both counsellor and supervisor alike. The ethical issue for both is offering services within their competence. How far is it feasible or ethically acceptable to offer services in a new format without any training? Training does not have to be within a classroom at some inconvenient distance from the home. It can be online and in these circumstances may be the most appropriate way forward. As the counsellor has demonstrated a good basic competence in face-to-face counselling and an openness to learning, it may be that other forms of informal learning will also be highly appropriate, such as reading around the growing literature (Anthony, 2007; Evans, 2008; Jones and Stokes, 2008) and discussing this as a part of supervision. The supervisor is also faced with questioning his conservatism or willingness to innovate and what are the boundaries of his competence. Is it possible to supervise competently in areas where the supervisor has no previous experience? There may also be some gendered prejudices about the opportunities available to women with families. If the supervisor is at the edge of his comfort zone and competence, it may be more appropriate for the supervisee to seek a new supervisor for this component or all her supervision. One possibility would be online supervision.

However the supervision is carried forward, there will be a need to consider the appropriate online methods for offering counselling, developing the relevant skills (e.g. how to communicate core counselling skills in text rather than in person), developing contracts appropriate to the medium of working, ensuring confidentiality and security, meeting data protection requirements and the other issues that will inevitably arise. Whether or not it is supervisory role or some other form of support, there is strong case for the counsellor joining a network of like-minded counsellors to accelerate her familiarity with the issues and how they can be resolved. (For further guidance, see Anthony, 2007; Evans, 2008; Jones and Stokes, 2008.)

Working with clients across cultural differences

The more that I work with people from different cultures in counselling and other roles, the more I have come to appreciate the life-enriching potential of such encounters but also the ethical challenges involved. The challenges are often rooted in the particular cultures of the people involved and their willingness to see beyond what is familiar. In social contact, this is a two-way responsibility. The emphasis on the client's needs in counselling places a greater responsibility on the counsellor to be culturally informed and to communicate in culturally appropriate ways. Clients ought to be freed from the burden of educating their counsellors in cultural issues in much the same way as a client would not be expected to educate a counsellor in the basics of depression or the techniques of a particular approach to counselling. This may be easier said than done. The experience of distress is socially constructed and often culturally specific so illnesses, especially mental illness or social problems, may be understood and experienced very differently in other cultures, if they are recognized at all. Counselling requires counsellors to become adept at listening beyond their own personal experience but it takes on new dimensions when listening across cultural differences.

Bill presents a case in supervision about his work with an Asian young woman Aneeta, who is increasingly concerned that her family want her to marry a cousin as part of their plans for strengthening the family cohesion and business. She is the first generation of her family to be educated in Britain and feels caught between her loyalty to her parents and her respect for their wishes against her desire to have a more independent life, like her British friends. Bill is familiar with counselling about tensions between young adult children and their parents but is unsure of the significance of cultural differences and whether there are culturally appropriate ways of responding. His gender does not appear to be an issue for this client, but he is aware that it would be an issue for her parents, who seem to want to protect their daughter from male company. Rachel, his supervisor, like Bill, has limited experience of this particular community originating from a northern region in India. They discuss how best to acquire this knowledge and how far is it appropriate to rely on the client to educate her counsellor?

The cultural differences take on different dynamics depending on whether the counsellor is a member of a cultural minority or majority. This example is fairly typical for most parts of the UK, with the counsellor being part of an indigenous majority recognizing a responsibility to be culturally better informed. There is growing literature on both sides of the Atlantic for all professions working across cultures and some very useful books specifically for counsellors (Grant, 1999; Tuckwell, 2002; Lago, 2008). In this case, it may be appropriate to seek some supplementary mentoring or supervision from someone familiar with the culture. However, caution may be required. If the cultural group is small and well known to each other, it may be impossible to seek mentoring from within this group without risking the anonymity of the client. In most cases, it would be desirable for the client to be consulted about what issues it would be helpful for the counsellor to understand better and whether any of the possible ways of acquiring the knowledge are acceptable to the client. Great care and sensitivity may be required when working with refugees as the client's concern to protect family members in another country may be a much greater priority than receiving help through counselling. Services that routinely work across cultures may wish to build cultural awareness into their training and staff development processes.

The strong association between culture, identity and ethics is so intermeshed that ethical assumptions behind most approaches to counselling may not translate well between cultures (Bond, 2007). Being trustworthy may be a better starting point than prioritizing respect for autonomy. This is particularly so where someone's identity is strongly associated with a family group or clan rather than themselves as an individual. (For further discussion, see Chapter 16 and Bond, 2007.)

How Ethical is the Current Requirement for Regular and Ongoing Supervision?

This might seem to be an absurd question when counselling-supervision has been adopted internationally as one of the ethical safeguards of counselling. However, there are some legitimate questions to be posed from an ethical perspective.

1. Are the resources and time consumed by supervision justified or could these resources be better invested to the benefit of clients and counselling?

This is a question about justice and fairness in the distribution of finite and often limited resources. Counselling-supervision is resource-intensive because it requires the attention of two professionals simultaneously, the supervisor and counsellor, in circumstances where one or both may need to be paid. There is also a substantial opportunity cost as both could be providing frontline counselling services in the time devoted to supervision. It requires some substantial and well-evidenced benefits in order to justify such a recurrent and long-term use of resources as a strict obligation.

2. What is the evidence for the benefits of counselling-supervision?

Frankly, the evidence is not as convincing as one might hope. Perhaps this should not be surprising because it is only relatively recently that the evidence for the effectiveness of counselling based on credible research has accumulated (Cooper, 2008). Researching the impact of counselling-supervision is more complex. The activity is between supervisor and counsellor and in turn mediated to the client. (In the absence of tape- or video-recorded supervision sessions, or even comprehensive supervision records held by counsellor and supervisor, it is difficult to evaluate the interaction and content of supervision sessions with any accuracy. The supervisor/supervisee themselves may find it difficult to recall their interaction, and therefore the information about supervision which is available for research is limited and also potentially subject to criticism for bias, subjectivity or lack of accuracy in its reporting.)

What happens in supervision is often not known to the client and thus they are not able to evaluate it directly. Even if clients were able to provide informed comments, it would be difficult to establish a causal relationship of the type required by this sort of research to demonstrate that what happens in supervision improves the effectiveness of counselling from the client's perspective. Nevertheless, anecdotal evidence and personal experience, including my own, is generally positive about the effects of supervision on the counsellor and, through the counsellor, on the client. A recent systematic review of the available research evidence concluded that although the quality of the research evidence is variable, supervision is consistently demonstrated to have positive effects on the supervisee. The research evidence of beneficial effects on counsellors is strongest for trainee counsellors and less certain for experienced or qualified counsellors. Little is reliably known about the impact on client outcome (Wheeler and Richards, 2007).

3. Does supervision involve some inherent violation of being respectful of clients' rights to privacy and confidentiality that are increasingly recognized in the moral and legal frameworks of contemporary society?

Unless managed ethically, it is possible for supervision to violate client rights and particularly their privacy. Counsellors do not know every aspect of their clients' lives. In particular, they are unlikely to know to whom the client is an identifiable person. Even if the name of a client is not disclosed in supervision, it is possible that a supervisor may identify them from incidental details. Only the client is well placed to make these judgements and decide the level of risk that is acceptable. On balance, I consider that clients ought to be informed about the counsellor's supervision arrangements, including the name of the supervisor. This enables the client to consider whether they are willing to be discussed on an anonymized basis, first name only or as an identifiable person and to give consent. It also gives the client the ability to consider whether they might know the supervisor in some way, and to evaluate for themselves any possible difficulty or conflict of interest if they should be identified or become identifiable within supervision. This is particularly important in situations where the counsellor, supervisor and client all live or work within a small community.

4. What is the impact of compulsory, ongoing supervision on the ethical performance of counselling?

Again, I suspect we do not really know. As counselling takes place mostly in private under conditions of confidentiality, widening the visibility of the work to the constructive scrutiny of a supervisor is probably a useful ethical safeguard. It is probably most effective as a safeguard against unethical practice by counsellors who are well intentioned but drift into poor practice through ignorance or mistake. Where supervision is provided to high standards, it provides a constant pressure towards higher standards and enhancement of ethical and professional standards. However, there may be a price to pay for creating a collective culture that infantilizes the counsellor by fostering dependence on the supervisor. The term 'supervision' is so strongly associated with accountability to a superior and a managerial relationship that it is hard to escape these associations, especially in the eyes of the professions outside counselling. Perhaps it is time to review the term 'supervision' and explore whether some other term would be better for this type of professional consultancy, once the counsellor is adequately trained and experienced to undertake independent practice. It may be that there are no wholly adequate alternatives, but there is value in questioning practices that developed much earlier in the history of a profession in very different circumstances with a less sophisticated ethical infrastructure, fewer formal opportunities for continuing professional development, and only embryonic theory and practice in comparison to current knowledge and experience. If nothing else, it is worth considering the implications of these developments for the functions of and investment in supervision.

I write these questions about supervision from a position of being personally convinced of the value of some form of ongoing professional development and having greatly benefited from a series of very constructive supervisory relationships. I can also think of many instances where my clients have benefited considerably from discussions in supervision. Ongoing, regular and good quality supervision has helped to keep me, and many other counsellors, receptive to my clients issues, supported me when I have felt stuck, challenged my assumptions, helped my self-awareness and kept counselling alive to me.

I am the author of the original proposals for ongoing and regular supervision throughout the working life of the counsellor (Bond, 1990) and I participated in the struggle to establish supervision as the professional norm within BAC, the forerunner of BACP. Counselling requires self-knowledge and the use of self in relationship is an important component in all approaches to counselling and talking therapy. As we develop, we change as people and so there remains a case for regularly reviewing ourselves and how changes in self-awareness impacts on our practice as well how we incorporate new developments within counselling. Regardless of the name, I think it is hard to envisage counselling without some form of regular activity involving facilitated consultations about current practice. Supervision, as a practice, has been adopted in other professional roles, including social work, some forms of education, personnel management, and coaching, which suggests that others, too, have found it to have a valuable contribution that ought to continue.

13

Record-keeping

There are a number of issues around record-keeping which continue to grow in importance. The most fundamental of these concerns is whether there is an obligation to keep records. As there is no consensus among counsellors in Britain on this issue, it is one that has to be decided according to the particular circumstances in which the counselling is being provided. The key factors to be taken into consideration in reaching a personal decision are considered in this chapter, before exploring subsidiary issues about security of records, access to records by clients, colleagues and the authorities, their content and the question of how long records should be retained after the completion of counselling.

Is it Desirable to Keep Records?

The arguments in favour of record-keeping include the following:

(a) The process of writing records involves the counsellor in organizing her own thoughts and feelings. This is in itself helpful to the counselling because it enables the counsellor to reflect systematically on what has occurred and plan for future sessions. In other words, the process of making records enhances the quality of the counselling.

(b) Records provide counsellors with an *aide-mémoire* for incidental details such as the names of the people mentioned by the client and this frees the counsellor to concentrate on issues raised by the client rather than recalling the detail from one session to another.

(c) Systematic record-keeping makes any changes in the client's material over a series of sessions more apparent. The process of recall by memory inevitably involves a degree of 'rewriting' the past in terms of a perspective rooted in the present. Written records produced contemporaneously with the counselling make any changes that have occurred during the counselling more visible. This provides valuable information to the counsellor, who may choose to share this knowledge with the client when it is appropriate.

(d) Systematic record-keeping provides evidence of the degree of care taken by the counsellor in her work, which may be useful if the client makes a complaint against the counsellor to a professional body or starts any legal action against the counsellor. They also protect against differences in memory between the client and counsellor.

(e) As counsellors seek to be professional and credible with other professional services, they need to develop record-keeping practices that support them in performing their role and meet the public expectations of any professional for quality of service and accountability. This is regarded as an increasingly significant reason, which probably explains why most of the counsellors that I meet at workshops around the country have chosen to keep records.

The balance of practice appears to have shifted towards an assumption that counsellors do keep records of their work unless there are good reasons for not doing so. Nonetheless there are a minority of counsellors who prefer not to keep records at all or only keep records for some clients, usually when seeing clients in settings that require records. The arguments most frequently offered against record–keeping are:

(a) The problems of ensuring records are both secure and really confidential. For example, some counsellors may work in settings where burglaries are so frequent that it is difficult to maintain secure records. Community-based services operating out of converted buses or other forms of mobile premises have to consider the possibility of the theft of the entire counselling premises, including the records.

(b) Record-keeping may complicate trust-building with clients. For example, counsellors working with clients who are vulnerable to legal prosecution, e.g. prostitutes, illicit drug users and others, may have to take account of their clients' fear that the police or other authorities could seize any records.

(c) Record-keeping is time-consuming.

(d) Some counsellors are opposed to the possibility of clients acquiring a legal right to see records kept about them. Some counsellors, therefore, prefer not to keep records in order to prevent this eventuality.

(e) Some counsellors have reservations about creating records which may be demanded by clients for use outside the counselling relationship in legal actions against others. They hope that an absence of records will enable them to concentrate on the therapeutic relationship without having to consider how that work would be viewed in a court of law. If they hope that the absence of records will prevent them from being required to provide evidence in court cases involving a client, they will be disappointed. An absence of records means that the counsellor is more likely to be called in person as a witness because as there is no other way of obtaining evidence. Where records exist, the counsellor may be permitted to provide a report of the relevant information based on the records or they may be required to submit all the records as an alternative to appearing in person.

It is clear from this summary of the case for and against the keeping of records that the arguments are, on balance, in favour of record-keeping by counsellors as a general standard of good practice. However, the argument in favour of keeping records can be countermanded by circumstances in which records cannot be kept securely or circumstances where the existence of records would deter clients and work against the public benefit of ensuring the availability of counselling on terms acceptable to clients. A client's attitude to record-keeping would also be relevant in individual cases.

Both the law and professional ethics require that clients have consented to records being kept. Ethically, this forms part of the client's full and informed consent. Legally, it is about citizens' rights to know about and exercise control over personally sensitive information that is being kept about them and to know the purpose for which it is being kept. When a client refuses to permit the counsellor to keep records, the counsellor is faced with a choice between continuing to see the client on this basis or refusing to see them unless some form of record can be kept. In my experience, most counsellors will attempt to establish why the client is so concerned about whether records are kept or not and attempt to adapt their practice to meet the client's needs. Some agencies will not see clients who totally refuse to permit any records at all.

Security of Records

Once it has been decided to keep records, knowledge of their existence and the level of security with which they are kept becomes an aspect of the client's informed consent. There is a strong ethical argument that clients need to know these facts in order to be in control of the information that they decide to disclose to the counsellor. This represents an optimal standard. The minimum standard suggests that if clients are not informed about the security of records, they should be entitled to assume that records are kept with sufficient security to prevent them becoming known to people other than those authorized by the client. Counsellors who have taken this into account have adopted different kinds of procedures according to their circumstances.

The first line of defence against unauthorized disclosure is the physical security of the records. This would normally match the anticipated risks to the records. Locking records in a desk or filing cabinet will prevent casual inspection by anyone with access to the room in which they are kept but this is inadequate against someone willing to force an entry, as most desks and filing cabinets are easily broken into. Where forced entry is reasonably foreseeable, it may be more appropriate to keep the records in a safe.

In addition to the physical security of the records, or sometimes as an alternative to it, some counsellors have adopted systems that ensure the anonymity of records. Four methods are frequently used:

1   The counsellor uses codes to identify records known exclusively by herself. The code might be in the form of numbers, fictitious initials or fictitious names (taking care not to implicate a real person). No information is included within the records that could identify clients. This may be practical with small numbers of records but is usually impractical with larger quantities.

2   An alternative method is a split system of record-keeping. For example, the personally identifiable information (e.g. name, address, contact numbers, names of significant others mentioned by the client) are kept on small file cards which can be readily removed from the premises by the counsellor, especially overnight, from where the lengthier records of sessions may be kept. As each of these cards is numbered or coded and this is the only identification on the records, someone needs access to both the card and the record to obtain significant information about the counselling. The cards on their own only indicate who is receiving counselling but not the issues raised in the counselling. The records on their own merely contain the contents of the sessions but cannot easily be linked to identifiable people. This system works well for some counsellors because they do not usually receive written referral, correspondence and reports that identify clients. The split record system works less well where these types of document are a regular part of the counselling record unless they can be summarized in the counselling notes without including the client's identity and the original destroyed or kept securely elsewhere.

3   Some counsellors work in settings where they are expected to make entries on agency records which are available to all authorized personnel within the agency and may even be passed on to another agency if the client seeks their services subsequently. For example, counsellors in medical settings may be expected to make an entry on the patient's health record or, in social services, on the client's case file. The best practice in these circumstances usually involves the counsellor in negotiating an agreement with both the agency and their clients. Ideally, the agreement permits the counsellor to make brief entries on the agency files and to keep separately more detailed records of the counselling process and any information which is personally sensitive to the client. These latter records would usually be treated as highly confidential and therefore access to them may be restricted to the counsellor and/or the client in routine situations. There is a legal precedent for this arrangement under the Code of Practice issued by the Human Fertilization and Embryology Authority (HFEA, 2008) as required by the Human Fertilization and Embryology Act 1990. In this setting, it is usual for the offer of counselling to be recorded in the central records and the client's response to the offer. However, the counselling notes of individual sessions are stored separately and treated as confidential. Information obtained in counselling may be disclosed in certain circumstances, for example if it 'gives a team member cause for concern about the suitability of a person' to participate in fertility treatment. It is good practice to be clear with clients about how records are kept and the circumstances in which information might be communicated to other team members.

4   Some counsellors may keep records on computer. Such records can be protected by passwords which control different levels of access. Although the technology of computer records is different, the principles are much the same as for paper-based records and are set out in recent data protection legislation and government guidelines. However, there is an additional obligation to register the use of computerized records with the Information Commissioner's Office. For further guidance see www.ico.gov.uk

Access to Records

The question of who ought to have access to records is frequently raised with regard to three situations. The first relates to situations where the counsellor is working in an agency in which the manager or employer is seeking access to client records; the second relates to the client's access to their own records; and the third to police access to files. It is useful to consider each of these separately because the ethical issues and legal considerations are different.

Access by employers

The demand for access to records by an employer is only possible when there is an employer of the counsellor. Counsellors working on their own in private practice are free from this particular concern. In some circumstances this may be an important factor in the client's choice of counsellor.

Counsellors who have not clarified their employers' access to records in advance of counselling and are working without a corresponding agreement with their clients about access are likely to find themselves in a difficult situation. The employer's and client's rights may be in conflict and both may hold the counsellor accountable. The usual principle is that records made on materials provided by an employer or in the employer's time belong to that employer. However, the principles and law of confidentiality (see Chapter 10) suggest that there are restrictions on how the employer exercises that ownership. Ownership is not necessarily the same as unfettered control and access. Breaking a confidence without justification could create legal liabilities for the counsellor, even if the breach is to the counsellor's employer. A prudent counsellor will have established clear guidelines which are known to both the employer and the client about who will have access to records of counselling and for what purposes in order to avoid conflicting responsibilities to the client and employer.

Access by clients

There is a strong ethical case for clients to be granted access to any personally sensitive information recorded about them in order for them to be reassured of its accuracy and to check that the information is consistent with the purpose for which it has been disclosed. In practice, most clients take records on trust, especially if their experience of the counselling is satisfactory. In some instances a counsellor's respect for a client's autonomy over their records may be countermanded by a concern that granting access could destabilize the therapy and that access might be better delayed until therapy is further advanced or completed. Such concerns can often be managed by negotiation. (Counsellors working in health settings may be able to enlist a doctor's authorization for restricting a client's access where the doctor considers such access would be seriously detrimental to the client's physical or mental health or condition, or indeed to any other person (see Data Protection (Subject Access Modification) (Health) Order 2000 5(1) implementing Data Protection

Act 1998 s. 30(1). This is probably the only exemption to a client's right of access likely to arise in counselling provided in a statutory service.)

Generally, data protection law lacks subtlety. It prioritizes a citizen's rights to know personally sensitive information held about them so that they can challenge any inaccuracies and know for what purpose it is being kept and how it is being used. All the client has to do is make the request for access in writing, provide proof of identity if this is in doubt and pay the required fee. However, the data holder should withhold from disclosure parts of the information from which another person could be identified, unless that person's consent has been given.

There is a rather odd legal exception to a client's right to see their counselling records which is mostly restricted to non-statutory services. It is odd because there is no obvious ethical justification for this exemption. Indeed, it removes the right to see records in the very circumstances in which clients might be most concerned to see what is recorded and how the information is being used and protected. The exception arises where the counselling records are held in an unstructured manual file. Such a file might be notes kept on paper and added to a cardboard envelope file in no particular order so that finding a specific piece of information would require sorting and sifting through the file. Similarly, a file to which things are added in chronological order, for example the most recent item is added to the front or back of a ring binder, would be regarded as an unstructured file. The exact point at which a manual file turns from structured to unstructured is not precisely defined in law. It is determined by what is known as the 'temp test', which determines whether someone unfamiliar with the records, such as a temporary secretary, can easily find information they are looking for by the way the record is structured (Bond and Mitchels, 2008: 61). It follows that a file which is divided into sections is more likely to be a structured manual file to which the client has a legal right to see their own notes. In other words, the client's right to see records ceases in just those situations where the client might be most concerned because the counsellor seems disorganized and unsystematic. A client has less rights of access to a jumble of barely sorted papers than they have to a structured file, for example if the sections divide identification and contact details, session notes, discussions in supervision, correspondence, etc., so that someone could easily find a home address, notes of session 3 or discover when this client was last discussed in supervision.

From the clients' perspective, they are best advised to see a well-organized counsellor because not only will they have the benefits of that level of organization, but also the additional protection of access to the counsellor's records should it be desired under the data protection law. A client who sees a less well-organized counsellor may or may not suffer from the lack of organizational skills but will forego their rights of access to their counselling notes.

If a client obtains access to their notes and disagrees with what has been recorded because it is considered misleading or incomplete, the counsellor has a number of options. She may agree some changes. Alternatively, she can record that there is a disagreement and record the client's version as an alternative version of events so that there are now two records of the same event.

Some counsellors have legitimate concerns about granting clients access to their notes. Some counsellors include personal notes about themselves and their own reactions as part of their process observations. The counsellor may be concerned that these are too personally revealing to be shown to a client. Where such notes are integral to the counselling approach or methods, then the counsellor needs to ask why a client should not be entitled to see them? If they are too personal, could they be recorded in another way or held separately in a personal journal without any identifiable reference to the client? Clients are only entitled to access to records which refer to them as identifiable persons because they are named, or their identity can be inferred from the information recorded. A client's notes are arguably not the place for a counsellor to be working through personal processes in depth, especially if they go beyond what is directly relevant to the client or if the counsellor wants to preserve her privacy.

Some psychodynamic counsellors have expressed concern to me about clients seeing records prematurely before transferences have been worked through and how this might disrupt the therapeutic process. There would be nothing to stop a counsellor asking a client to delay access, but the client would be entitled to insist on prompt access in the case of computerized and structured manual records.

It is illegal to keep two sets of records relating to an identifiable client in order to grant access to one and keep the other away from the client. It should also be noted that data protection law does not permit withholding records from a client because they are damaging to the professional. A government department has been ordered to disclose records that described the subject as a 'prat' and 'out-and-out nutter'.

The use of counsellors' records in court

What if one of your clients asks you to supply a report to help him in a legal action against someone else? For example:

Michelle has given birth to a severely handicapped child and is bringing an action for medical negligence. You, as the counsellor, are asked to provide a report about your client's feelings towards the child. The lawyers acting for the medical staff seek access to the therapy notes on which you based your report.

This, in broad terms, was the situation which Stephen Jakobi and Duncan Pratt (1992), as lawyers acting for the Psychologists' Protection Society, were asked to consider. In my experience, counsellors are also asked to provide reports following motor accidents, industrial accidents and in marital disputes.

Many counsellors are understandably reluctant to provide reports, appear as witnesses or to supply case records on behalf of clients. To do so could be seen as a confusion of roles, with the counsellor being drawn into a public arena in ways that may compromise the client's autonomy or privacy. Counsellors may also feel that writing reports for courts is not part of their role and that they have not been trained in how to write them, in comparison to doctors and social workers, who are usually more experienced in court work. So far as I can tell, there is no way a client can compel a counsellor to produce a report on his or her behalf. The choice is the counsellor's. However, refusal to provide a report may result in the client (or more likely the client's solicitor), requesting the court to issue a witness summons for the counsellor to appear in person at court to give evidence and that any records are disclosed to the court. Often preparing a report that answers the solicitor's questions and protects the rest of the information is the better option and, in many cases, makes appearing as a witness unnecessary.

If you are asked to write a report on behalf of a client, Jakobi and Pratt (1992) recommend that a number of precautions are taken:

1   The request for a report is likely to be made by the solicitors acting for the client. Technically, this can be treated as the client's consent to disclosure provided that the request comes from the client's own solicitors and not from solicitors acting for another party in the proceedings. However, it is sensible to see the client to ensure that he or she realizes that the production of the

report could lead to a requirement for disclosure of case records to the other party; that you may need to include sensitive information in the report; and, that the client really is consenting to the production of the report (or client records) in full knowledge of what is entailed.

2   If a counsellor is asked to disclose records in addition to the report, this request should be refused unless either the client consents or a court order is made.

3   If disclosure could cause serious harm to the client, then you should inform his or her solicitor so that an adequate explanation can be given for requiring disclosure. Again, through the client's solicitor, it may be possible to limit disclosure to matters which are highly relevant to the case or to restrict who sees the counselling records, such as to a relevant expert. Alternatively, there may be other ways of obtaining the same information, perhaps by an expert examining the client independently.

4   Sometimes it is possible to request that an expert be appointed to examine the documents rather than have them considered in full in open court.

5   If limitations on the disclosure of documents have been agreed, no reference should be made to the excluded material in court. Any limitations on disclosure cease to have effect once the excluded material is referred to or read out in open court. You will need to bear this in mind if you are called to give evidence.

Once a client is engaged in litigation, a counsellor's notes are vulnerable to disclosure and use in proceedings. It is only in the most exceptional circumstances that you will be able to prevent disclosure. For a fuller account of the issues, see *Therapists in Court: Providing Evidence and Supporting Witnesses* (Bond and Sandhu, 2005) or seek legal advice. Whatever you do, do not delay in seeking advice until the last moment. This makes the situation very hard to resolve by using any alternatives that might have been available even a few weeks earlier.

Access by the police

The law places counsellors' records in a special category, which excludes them from the usual search warrant and substitutes a more demanding procedure before the police can obtain access to them. The legislation that established these procedures is historically significant as being the first to recognize formally the personal sensitivity of counselling records and to grant them legal protection. The Police and Criminal Evidence Act 1984 requires a search warrant, which must be signed by a circuit judge instead of requiring only the more usual magistrate's signature, a less demanding procedure, to access files. The legislation is particularly interesting because it makes several specific references to counselling in its definition of 'personal records'. Personal records are defined in section 12 as:

> documentary and other records concerning an individual (whether living or dead) who can be identified from them and relating:
>
> (a)   to his physical or mental health;
> (b)   to spiritual counselling or assistance given or to be given to him; or
> (c)   to counselling or assistance given or to be given to him for his personal welfare, by any voluntary organization or by any individual who –
>
> > (i)   by reason of his office or occupation has responsibilities for his personal welfare;
> > or
> > (ii) by reason of an order of a court has responsibilities for his supervision.

Counsellors' records therefore belong in the same category as those of doctors, vicars, social workers and probation officers, regardless of whether the counselling is paid or voluntary. Even if a circuit judge has signed a warrant, it is possible to go to the High Court to reverse this decision. In one case, the High Court ruled that an Old Bailey judge acted outside his powers when he ordered the Royal London Hospital to disclose someone's medical records to help in a murder investigation. The case demonstrates that counsellors can resist disclosing records to the police. An exception to the requirement for a warrant may arise if the police are searching for documents in order to detect or prevent terrorism under the current Terrorism Act 2000. However, despite the sweeping power seemingly given to the police under this legislation, they are required to exercise their powers 'reasonably'. It is wise to seek a lawyer's advice whenever counsellors are aware that they are holding information which relates to serious crime.

The Contents of Counselling Records

There are no fixed rules about what ought to be included in counselling records or how they ought to be written. Counselling records that I have seen vary considerably in style from brief factual accounts which focus on what the client reported to ones that include more of the counsellor's thoughts and responses. The guiding principle is that the type of record should be one that supports the therapy and enables it to be delivered to a reasonable standard of care. A good record is written as close as possible in time to the events it records. Some counsellors set a aside 10 minutes between clients for this purpose. If there is any reason to think that a record might need to be produced for legal purposes, it is good to distinguish between what was directly observed, what the client said and the counsellor's own responses or thoughts. For example:

20 January 2010   Session 3

Bob arrived 10 minutes late, out of breath and looking rather flustered. He was more smartly dressed than for previous sessions and explained that a meeting with his boss at work had overrun and delayed him. He said that it had been his annual review. He had been dreading it – see previous session – but had decided to go in positively and make suggestions about how the administrative system that had been troubling him could be improved to everyone's advantage. He thought his boss was not interested initially but warmed to his ideas as he talked them through. This was not what he had expected. He said that he had expected his boss to dismiss his ideas out of hand. He had found the work on the similarities and differences between his boss and his father last week helped him to see them as different people who might react in different ways. He was pleased to be breaking a pattern of feeling silenced and deskilled. However, he is anxious about having to prepare a business plan for two weeks' time and has agreed to the next session being before this. I will monitor his anxiety, which he reports as 'half what it was when I first came to see you'. Noted that he did not mention his girlfriend or difficulties with her this time. As he left, I noticed that I was feeling uncertain about his motivation – between being liked or being successful? Explore further next time?

This would be a reasonably full record and appropriate if the counselling benefits from this level of detail and the counsellor has time to make the record. A shorter record of the same session might be:

20/1/10   Bob arrived late due to 'meeting with boss overrunning'. Bob thought meeting had gone better than expected. He said previous work on distinguishing his father and the boss had helped. Affirmed growing confidence. Consider exploring Bob's motivation at work next time.

There is no single correct way of writing case notes. It still appears to be a neglected topic in basic training. Each counsellor has to develop a style that is sufficient to support the counselling but without being excessive in what is recorded. Other items to be included in the record are:

- any written and signed consents to all treatment;
- any written and signed consents to all passing of confidential information;
- all appointments, including non-attendance by client;
- treatment contracts (if used);
- up-to-date record of counsellor's reasoning behind decisions about significant interventions and general strategies;
- consultations with anyone else about the client;
- copies of any correspondence from the client or relating to work with the client;
- any instructions given to the client and whether or not the client acted on these.

Matters Not To Be Included in Records

Records ought not to include anything that could disrupt the therapy if seen by a client. Prejudice and abusive comments are to be avoided. Negative evaluations should only be included if they serve a therapeutic purpose, for example a negative countertransference would be justified if it is integral to the therapy and a statement about the counsellor's internal processes rather than directly ascribed to the client. For instance: 'I experience uncharacteristic boredom when Sue talks about her relationship with ...', rather than 'Sue is boring about ...'. Information about illegal behaviour, sexual practices or other sensitive information which may embarrass or harm the client or others are rarely appropriate for the record.

   Giving careful consideration to what to include and exclude is good advice. What is included should be written with the possibility of the client seeing the record at a later date and the possibility that the records may be required for use in legal dispute. However, the overall principle should be to write only what is useful for the therapy unless the record is known to be needed for other purposes and these purposes have been consented to by the client.

The Format of Counselling Records

Very little has been written about how best to structure counselling records. Gaie Houston (1995) recommends keeping the records in two sections. The first section contains useful background information about the client and the contractual terms that you have agreed between you. She suggests these headings:

1 NAME [probably coded] AND MEANS OF REFERRAL.
2 PRESENT CIRCUMSTANCES [Mrs A is 28, living since she was 18 with Claud. Works at Boots.]
3 HISTORY [Leave plenty of room to put in facts about her life and her ways of dealing with its events. You can add as the weeks go by. Noting the date can be informative here.]
4 REASON FOR SEEING ME [Has changed jobs three times in the last few months, and thinks she is unreasonably difficult with everyone at work, though she gets on perfectly, her word, with family and Claud.]
5 MY HUNCHES [She said strongly out of the blue that she was not thinking of leaving work and having a baby. I guess she is. Longer-term work probably needs to be about her daring to acknowledge her own needs, and admit the humanness of close family, and therefore self.]
6 TIMES AND PAYMENTS [Tuesdays at 11 am, with 3-week break at Easter when she will be abroad. One month paid in advance, next payment due.]

One way of establishing the contractual relationship with a client is to send her a letter after the first session that includes what you have agreed between you. This letter could be attached to this section, as could copies of any subsequent correspondence.

The second part of the records would be the record of the actual counselling sessions. Houston suggests separating the factual account of what happened from your own personal responses and evaluations by using several vertical columns. The factual account of whether your client arrived on time, what was said, etc., can be put down in the left-hand column. The commentary can be written in a column to the right. There is a lot to commend this approach. My own system is slightly different but has evolved out of a need to separate the background information from the session notes and within those notes to separate factual reporting from my observations and speculations. The system I have used is shown in Figures 13.1 and 13.2.

Name ....

Address ....

Contact tel. nos: ....

Summary of counselling contract (e.g. frequency, duration, review periods, confidentiality, fees, etc.): ....

....

....

Significant names, relationships and places mentioned by client: ....

....

....

Correspondence (attached) Code no* ....

....

* for split records only

FIGURE 13.1   *Counselling records: client background information*

Date: .... Time/duration: .... Code no* ....

Content: Summary of client's narrative, behaviour, feelings and counsellor's interventions: ....

....

Process: any comments made by client about process, counsellor's observations and/or speculations about the process: ....

....

Notes for next session: e.g. any agreement about what client or counsellor would do between sessions, issues to be raised during the session or for the counsellor to be aware of: ....

....

Issues for counselling supervision: ....

....

Notes about any correspondence or telephone conversations: ....

* for split records only

FIGURE 13.2   *Counselling records: record of each session*

At times when I have been seeing lots of clients, or when time is at a premium, I have used pre-printed forms. The code numbers are only required if the two parts of the records are being kept separately. However, if split records are being kept, it is advisable to store any correspondence away from the second part of the record as it usually contains information that would identify clients and defeat the purpose of creating the split records. Recent legal judgments indicate the advisability of systematically recording each time you consider issues of client consent or their capacity to give consent, especially with regard to young people in general and adults over referrals for assistance for serious medical conditions, suicidal intent or serious harm to others. In my system these would be factual notes and included within the content.

Use of Records in Counselling-supervision

Some supervisors insist on counsellors keeping records and using these in counselling-supervision. The process of writing notes helps the counsellor to sort his or her various responses to the counselling session and therefore helps the counsellor to focus attention on important issues. It is agreed that this makes for a much better supervision session. This view is not universal but it is gaining ground. Client consent should be sought for using records in supervision.

How Long Should Records be Retained?

This is a difficult question to answer. Records may be relevant to present or future court proceedings, or to complaints, and so the time limits for legal proceedings or complaints procedures may be relevant. The time limits are different for children and young people than for adults (see Bond and Mitchels, 2008: 72–8).

The important thing is that the client should be aware of the time that records are usually retained by the counsellor, and the client should agree to it. If the client wants the records retained for a longer period, this should be negotiated and agreed with the counsellor, or an alternative solution sought, perhaps that the records may be handed over to the client. In straightforward circumstances, where there are no other legal or professional considerations, the records could be destroyed any time after the end of the counselling relationship. One of the principles that informs good practice in record-keeping is that sensitive information should be destroyed when its usefulness has expired. A retention of one year might be appropriate where there is the possibility of the client returning.

However, where there are unresolved issues which might result in a complaint against a counsellor to a professional body or legal proceedings in which the records might need to be produced, a much longer period is required before the records should be destroyed. In the absence of any better guideline, seven to ten years would be appropriate, if this is both practical and the records can be kept securely. If any legal action involving a client is a possibility, it is prudent to obtain legal advice about how long the records should be kept, as the expiry time for initiating legal action varies according to the type of case. For further consideration of how long to keep records see Bond and Mitchels (2008: 72–8).

Conclusion

Although it is not regarded as essential to good practice to keep records of counselling, the arguments are weighted on the side of keeping them. They are part of a systematic and professional approach to counselling. In my opinion, clients deserve this amount of care.

If counselling were to become regulated under the Health Professions Council, it will become an obligation to keep accurate records. The current obligation following public consultation is:

> Making and keeping records is an essential part of care and you must keep records for everyone you treat or who asks for your advice or services. (Health Professions Council, 2008: section 10)

This obligation is written in such unambiguous terms that ethical dilemmas may arise when it is considered inappropriate to keep records for sound ethical reasons.

14

Monitoring Counselling

Counsellors appear to be divided in their experience of monitoring their own delivery of services. Counsellors working on their own in private practice have not caught up in the new management strategies that have had so much impact on counsellors working in all kinds of organizations. In private practice, a combination of counselling-supervision, ongoing professional development through attending courses and/or involvement in professional associations and watching for fluctuations in numbers of people wanting counselling has often proved adequate as a package of strategies for ongoing monitoring. When I first started counselling in public sector organizations in the 1970s, these were considered adequate methods for monitoring counselling services in organizational settings, with the additional requirement of some form of accountability to management. If mutual respect and trust existed between an individual counsellor and the management, then the requirements of accountability could be nominal or virtually non-existent. Sometimes I look back to those days with fond memories, but times have moved on. Just as counselling has developed over the past three decades, so have management techniques. Counsellors working for private sector organizations, in the public sector and in voluntary organizations are all under pressure to find better strategies to show that resources allocated to counselling are being well used. Some counsellors who have not been willing to participate in greater accountability through the active monitoring of their services have found that they have lost funding.

Most counsellors in organizations now accept the reality of higher expectations about how they monitor their services. Some even welcome greater accountability as a way of enhancing recognition of the contributions a good counselling service can make. This is now my view. However, the problem of how to monitor a counselling service and to communicate the results to other people in the organization without compromising confidentiality and privacy is a major challenge to the ingenuity of counsellors. I think most people involved in developing strategies for monitoring counselling feel there is still more to learn and further new strategies will emerge. Nonetheless, within the current state of the art, it is possible to identify strategies that are consistent with counselling standards and ethics, particularly when the monitoring is carried out by the counsellor and then reported to others. It has been much more problematic to find ways of co-operating with monitoring and inspections conducted by someone from outside the counselling service. It is clear that independent assessments of a counselling service are useful to both the counsellors and the organization. They have additional credibility because they are independent of the service provider and therefore less influenced by vested interests. However, independent inspections pose the greatest problems over confidentiality and privacy, particularly if as part of an inspection someone wants to sit in and observe a client and counsellor working together or to have access to files. This has proved to be an ethical and legal minefield but it is one where it is becoming possible to see a way forward after several years of what has felt like an uneasy stand-off between irreconcilable forces. In this chapter I shall deal with the issues associated with counsellors conducting their own evaluations first. I shall then outline the issues arising from assessments conducted by people from outside the counselling service and the current understanding of how these issues may be resolved.

Self-monitoring by Counsellors

There are two major strategies currently being used to monitor all kinds of services. These are service audit and quality assurance. I will look at each of these because they provide methods of monitoring which counsellors can operate themselves and therefore minimize some of the ethical difficulties of monitoring being conducted by someone else. In my experience, counsellors who have been proactive and taken the initiative by establishing these monitoring procedures adapted to their own circumstances have been much less likely to experience the imposition of external inspections.

Service audit

Service audits aim to identify the users of a service and how resources are allocated within that service. The method used is systematic data collection and analysis. Much of this information is statistical and therefore can usually be provided by methods which protect the anonymity of clients, particularly if the counsellor (or receptionist) maintains a running numerical log of service use according to predetermined categories. Two broad categories of information are usually collected. The first is socio-demographic and categorizes service users according to variables such as age, gender, marital/relationship status, educational attainment, occupation, ethnic origin or geographical location. The choice of variables is important and will be determined by the setting of the service. A counselling service used by the general public might want to use the categories just mentioned. On the other hand, a counselling service within an organization might be more interested in which parts of the organization make greatest use of the counselling service. This can raise problems of confidentiality because even from bare statistical data, it can be possible to deduce the identity of a particular individual if the categories relate to small numbers of readily identifiable people. For example, it would be ethically dangerous if an employee assistance programme providing counsellors for a manufacturer included a category 'secretarial' if secretaries constituted a small number of the staff. It would then be too easy to deduce the identity of the client. It would be better ethically (but perhaps less informative statistically) to include categories of small numbers with others, e.g. 'office-based staff' or 'secretarial and management'. An alternative system of categories may be more appropriate to student counselling. For example, it may be highly informative to know the proportions of clients living in residences and those living out, or whether they are full-time or part-time, or the category of course being attended. Information of this kind can be very useful for predicting future demands on the service or for identifying shortfalls in service delivery.

The second broad category of information collected is about the range of problems and issues presented for counselling. Again, this information is valuable because it may reveal significant clustering of problems within particular client groups which may be most appropriately dealt with by a counselling service or perhaps prevented by some other strategy. For example, it would be appropriate for an educational establishment to review the assessment procedures for some groups of students if these procedures were found to be disproportionately stressful for one course in comparison to other courses.

Provided that care is taken over the way these statistics are gathered and disseminated, they can often be used as the basis of an annual report about a counselling service and, as these accumulate, it becomes possible to identify broader trends and issues that help in longer-term planning.

Quality assurance

Quality assurance aims to monitor the quality of the service that is delivered by setting standards and comparing these with actual performance when services are delivered. Again, it is a management strategy that is useful to counsellors. One of the ways quality assurance can be implemented is by creating a 'quality circle', in which counselling practitioners devise their own standards and evaluate how far these are achieved. It is often less costly of time and resources to measure practicalities such as time taken between someone requesting counselling and actually being seen, and whether appointments run to time, etc. Such practicalities matter, but they can easily be overlooked. However, in order to enhance the quality of the counselling being given to clients, I believe it is important to look at what actually happens in sessions. In this respect, counsellors are more fortunately placed than many others of the caring professions, including some psychotherapists who do not have a system of ongoing supervision. The ethical requirement that counsellors receive counselling-supervision provides a readily available resource that can be incorporated into the quality assurance process. For example, it would be possible to undertake a review of work with clients and to agree some target standards with a counselling-supervisor and then to evaluate how far these are met. In terms of establishing what actually happens in sessions, as opposed to what the counsellor subjectively experiences as happening, it can be useful to include listening to tape recordings of sessions, provided the client's identity is protected and the recording is made with the client's full consent.

Quality assurance is primarily concerned with direct services to clients but other factors may also be taken into account, including strategies adopted nationally by counsellors in order to improve the quality of service to clients. These include the use of ongoing training, quality of presentations at counselling-supervision and the counsellor's opportunities for personal development. Personally, when I see quality assurance assessments of counselling services, I like to see these indicators taken into account as they have a strong influence on actual counselling practice. These indicators may only be indirect evidence of what happens between counsellor and client, but they are direct evidence of the counsellor's, and their organization's, commitment to maintaining a quality counselling service.

Monitoring of Counselling by Others

I have already shown that counsellors can do a great deal for themselves to monitor the services they provide in ways that are both systematic and that can show appropriate accountability to managers and funders. However, it is reasonable that from time to time someone with a legitimate interest in the management of a counselling service will want and need some more direct evidence from first-hand experience or by the use of an independent assessor. This can pose substantial ethical problems around confidentiality and privacy, which is a growing concern for counsellors in both the private and public sectors of the economy. It has become a more significant issue with the spread of 'contract culture' across organizations. One of the purposes of contracts is to clarify responsibilities for service delivery and therefore to facilitate the monitoring or auditing of service delivery. It is a strategy to sharpen the focus on accountability for resources used. The increasing use of this management strategy has caused legitimate ethical concerns for counsellors and raised questions about how they should respond to requests from managers, inspectors and external consultants to be able to observe the counsellor at work with their clients. Some counsellors have encountered similar issues when they have received requests or instructions to permit auditors access to case records in order to conduct a service audit. Although issues of this kind affect many areas of counselling, they have a particular history in higher education. It will be useful to explore something of this history as a case study to serve as a pointer to how the issue might be resolved in other settings, such as health services, employee counselling and voluntary organizations. There may be parallel issues raised in effectiveness research conducted by independent researchers.

HMIs' powers to inspect student counsellors

Since the mid-1980s, Her Majesty's Inspectors (HMIs) of education have been in discussion and ultimately in disagreement with the student counselling division of BACP. (This division was founded as the Association for Student Counselling (ASC) and later renamed as the Association for University and College Counselling (AUCC).) The dispute started with ASC about whether HMIs have the power to insist that they should sit in with a counsellor working with a client to observe the quality of the work. This has not been a problem in Scotland, where I am told the inspectorate accepts that direct observation raises serious ethical concerns and prefers to use other methods to inspect counselling services. The experience in England and Wales has been very different. Here HMIs have routinely asked to sit in with counsellors and clients subject to the client's consent. Although the dispute was at its fiercest in 1992–93, it has a tendency to smoulder unnoticed and then to be periodically revived into a full confrontation. For this reason, I will report the original dispute as an ethical case study. The background to the case has changed over time in that the law and ethical guidance has been updated, but the general principles remain as relevant to current practice as they were in the 1990s. I will conclude the case study with some general principles to help any counsellor facing an ethically problematic form of inspection.

The original dispute began when HMIs insisted that they have the power and authority to insist on direct observation of counsellors working with clients even if the counsellor considers it inappropriate and unethical. ASC disagreed and maintained that HMIs ought to respect professional ethics. For many years, both sides maintained an awkward stand-off while negotiations towards an agreed joint policy took place. These negotiations broke down when it was reported that a senior HMI claimed that the inspectors have the power to enforce whatever they think fit. A passage was cited from the applicable *Code of Ethics and Practice for Counsellors* (BAC, 1990) in support of their right to observe counselling directly, subject to the client's consent. The passage referred to stated:

> B.2.2.7   Clients should be offered privacy for counselling sessions.
> The client should not be observed by anyone other than their
> counsellor(s) without having given his/her informed consent.
> This also applies to audio/visual taping of counselling sessions.
> (BAC, 1990)

The HMI interpreted the section as entitling inspectors to insist that
counsellors found clients willing to consent to being observed. The
negotiators on behalf of ASC were understandably dismayed at having all
their hard work seemingly undermined by a section in BAC's code. This
resulted in a formal motion at BAC's AGM in 1991 asking that the
Standards and Ethics Committee review the wording of this section of
the code in order to clarify the rights of an inspector to observe a live
counselling session.

The first task of the Standards and Ethics Committee was to establish
what legal entitlements and constraints operate in this kind of situation.
Legal advice had been consistently clear about the importance of the
client's consent to someone sitting in to observe. It would constitute a
breach of confidence if someone observed the counselling without the
client's consent and the client could seek a court order to prevent it or
sue for damages. It was much less clear how far the counsellor's professional judgement about whether to ask a client to consent could be taken
into account. A view was expressed by experienced senior managers in
education that counsellors could be ordered to seek a client's consent
under the terms of the counsellors' contracts of employment. Failure to
comply could result in disciplinary procedures and perhaps dismissal. It
was also said that this could apply to counsellors working in other
settings. In the negotiations with HMIs, an additional factor had to be
taken into account. There are specific statutory powers given to HMIs
conducting inspections. Section 77 of the Education Act 1944 states that
a person who wilfully obstructs any person authorized to inspect an
educational institution shall be guilty of an offence which could result in
a fine or up to three months' imprisonment or a combination of both.

On the other hand, it was succinctly argued by Roger Casemore, then
a senior manager in an educational authority and former chairperson of
BAC, and by others, that under administrative law the inspectorate were
required to exercise their powers subject to the constraints and the test
of 'reasonableness'. It was argued that it was manifestly unreasonable to

insist on direct observation with all the difficulties that this raises about confidentiality and consent when there are reasonable alternative methods of inspection that would produce more accurate results without compromising confidentiality. Unfortunately, 'reasonableness' in a legal context has a technical meaning, which is not the same as its everyday meaning, and therefore this highly rational argument may not be legally enforceable. Nonetheless, it is worth summarizing the concerns about the usefulness of direct observation as a means of assessing the quality of a counselling service because they would apply wherever this method of assessment is proposed. The objections to direct observation are:

1   The presence of an observer changes the way the client interacts with the counsellor and therefore invalidates what is observed.
2   The act of observation undermines the counsellor's ethic and practice of offering the client privacy and confidentiality.
3   There are real difficulties in determining whether clients are in a position to give or refuse consent due to their dependence on the counsellor or the institution in which the counselling is provided, e.g. a young person at school, a redundant worker on an out-placement counselling service.
4   The observer may not be suitably qualified or experienced to assess what is observed.
5   There are better methods of conducting assessments of quality, which are more reliable.

The Standards and Ethics Committee was unable to find any way of resolving the conflict of views between the inspectorate and the counsellors. Therefore, BAC sought legal opinion from John Friel, barrister, instructed by Messrs Kenneth Cohen Solicitors; the opinion was given in January 1993. The main points made in the legal opinion are:

1   HMIs statutory powers of inspection [were] based on the Further and Higher Education Act 1992, which came into force on 1 April 1993. Sections 55 and 77 provide for the statutory inspection for schools. Section 70 creates a new system for further and higher education, which requires that each council of further and higher education sets in place a system for assessing the quality of education provided.
2   The confidentiality of the counsellor/client relationship is as strong as that between doctor and patient.
3   Subject to exceptions which this opinion was not asked to address (e.g. in respect of the confidentiality of confessions of crime), there is no right to

override such confidentiality without the client's consent unless there is an express statutory power to do so. The Act does not contain such a power.

4   The inspectorate has no legal basis to insist on observing counselling sessions without the client's consent, and any attempt to do so could be prevented by applying to the courts for judicial review. Counsellors who permitted such observation would be in breach of the BAC's rules.

5   The inspectorate has no right to insist that a request for the client's consent be made against the counsellor's professional judgement. It is a misunderstanding of paragraph B.2.2.7 of the *Code of Ethics and Practice for Counsellors* (BAC, 1990) – which is quoted in full at the beginning of this section – that it gives the inspectorate any such right. At most, this section allows a counsellor who agrees that such an observation is appropriate, to request a client to give consent to observation of a session by an HMI.

What does this legal opinion mean to counsellors? First, it is important to realize that it is a legal opinion and is therefore less authoritative than if it was a judgment given in court. Nevertheless, it is an unequivocal legal opinion and is therefore a reasonable basis for further decisions unless or until it is qualified or contradicted by a decision of the courts. This has not happened. More specifically, counsellors in education subject to inspections under the system first established by the Education Act 1944, or the new systems established under the further and higher education legislation, have much better grounds for defending their entitlement to use their judgement about whether or not to ask a client whether he or she consents to being observed.

The legal importance of confidentiality has implications for counsellors working in establishments outside education. I would encourage any counsellor faced with an ethically problematic inspection by a third party, e.g. a manager, auditor, inspector, independent consultant, to do the following:

•   Ask whether the request is based on a statutory power to inspect.

If the answer is 'no', explain that observation of counselling is an intrusion on the client's legal right to confidentiality and is only possible if, in your professional judgement, it is appropriate to ask whether the client is willing to be observed and the client consents to waive their right to confidentiality. Current professional guidelines will provide documentary evidence in support of this ethical requirement and the law stresses the importance of client consent as a protection of client privacy and the protection of personally sensitive information. You may also wish to suggest that there are alternative and more reliable ways of assessing a counselling service, including the methods mentioned below. If an agreement still proves impossible, seek legal advice.

- If the answer is 'yes', ask for details of the statutory power, in particular the name of the Act, its year and the relevant sections or schedules. Seek legal advice about whether the legislation gives powers to override a client's consent to breaches of confidentiality.

The Association for Student Counselling gave careful consideration to finding more reliable alternative methods of inspection for HMIs. These could be equally applicable to other inspectors by providing:

(a) Access to the appointments book in order to assess the flexibility within the service, an ability to deal with urgent cases, the balance between short-term and long-term work (If the appointments books contain initials only, or code for each client, there is little problem with confidentiality).

(b) A diary or log of one month's work for each counsellor (coding or numbering clients) showing the range of work.

(c) Permission for the inspector to attend one or more team meetings.

(d) The opportunity to meet a range of clients who have come to the end of counselling (with counsellor's and client's consent).

(e) Encouraging the inspector to talk to the general student and staff bodies and to senior management to identify perceptions of the service.

(f) Access to a range of case notes (having due regard to confidentiality), including a statement of therapeutic aims for each of these clients and an assessment of how far these are being met; these should also demonstrate the depth and repertoire of the counselling skills. If there are difficulties in presenting certain cases because of the specific nature of confidential issues (e.g. could identify individuals), then this needs to be explicit and reasons given.

(g) Presentation of a written case study with the informed consent of a client. All means of identifying the client would have to be deleted or altered.

(h) Presentation of taped sessions (audio or video) where this is a normal method of working for the counsellor and client and is considered an appropriate method by the counsellor and supported with the client's consent.

(i) Presentation of taped sessions (audio or video) with client's informed consent.

(j) Direct observation of a supervision session. (Adapted from ASC, 1991)

Since the 1990s many counselling services have become much more attentive to collecting data on their client's experiences of receiving counselling. Some agencies create their own systems or adopt a widely distributed system of which CORE is the best known for providing evidence of service quality and effectiveness (www.coreims.co.uk). This type of information, gathered systematically over an extended period of time, provides some of the most reliable evidence available. It can also be used as an alternative to direct observation where this is considered inappropriate or problematic in terms of gaining client consent.

This case study of the disagreement about the powers of HMIs to inspect counselling services in schools and some colleges shows how complex some of these dilemmas can be that require resolution at an organizational level. I doubt if an individual or small organization would have the resources or perhaps the expertise and stamina to resolve the ethical and legal issues. Counsellors need the collective assurance of large organizations and in this case, two organizational units working closely together (ASC/AUCC and BAC/BACP).

Conclusion

There is a strong ethical case for monitoring and evaluating counselling services. It is one of the ways in which counsellors can demonstrate their commitment to providing the best possible service for clients regardless of whether the counsellor works independently, in private practice or within an organizational setting. For counsellors working within agencies, the process of accountability achieved by monitoring and evaluation increases the possibility of the agency being satisfied as a whole that it is working ethically. In previous editions of this book I reported the call for better ways of monitoring from a variety of well-established authorities on counselling. The collective experience of counselling has moved on to the point that it is possible to see patterns in how the experience of monitoring in agencies develops over time (CORE Partnership, 2007). The effort required to produce measured outcomes should not be under-estimated but, once achieved, they provide invaluable information to inform the management of services and to inform others of the value of what is being achieved.

Part IV

The Whole Picture

15

Ethical Problem-solving

Whenever you are confronted with a problem or dilemma about ethical standards, it is useful to approach it in a systematic way. This maximizes the likelihood of reaching a solution which you are confident is the best possible outcome. This chapter contains a six-step process, which is a development of an ethical problem-solving model derived from American sources (Paradise and Siegelwaks, 1982; Austin et al., 1990). It follows the basic principles of many problem-solving models used by counsellors with their clients but adapted to fit ethical problem-solving. It has stood the test of time and I have heard of many counsellors and supervisors using this model either for private reflection or to structure a professional discussion about a current dilemma. It works best when it is taken as a basic framework and used to consider as wide a range of options as possible before making a decision.

Produce a Brief Description of the Problem or Dilemma

Making sure that you can produce a short spoken or written conceptual description of the main elements of your ethical dilemma is useful. Sometimes doing this reduces confusion to the extent that the problem disappears. On the other hand, if the problem still remains, you then have a good starting point from which to seek assistance and to clarify the main issues to be considered. When I find it difficult to define a problem, I know it is something I need to discuss with my counselling-supervisor(s) or another experienced counsellor, because I have to identify the elements of something in order to summarize it. If it cannot be summarized, perhaps that is a clear indication that even the problem itself is not clear to me yet. It is very difficult to make much progress in discussion of the issues until the main issues of the problem can be identified. It may be that some of the later steps will cause me to revise my description of the main points, but a short and clear statement of what these appear to be is a good starting point.

Whose Dilemma Is It Anyway?

This is a basic question that often casts a sharp light on the darkest of ethical problems in counselling. Counselling is an activity that requires careful monitoring of boundaries of responsibility in order to ensure that these are not becoming blurred. In Chapter 6, I suggested that a useful way of approaching boundary issues is to start from the position that the counsellor is responsible for the methods used and the client holds responsibility for the outcome of the counselling. Often this general principle is very helpful, especially where the ethical issue concerns the relationship or work within the counselling. There may be rare excep-tions to this principle where the counsellor considers that she holds some responsibility for protecting the client from self-harm or protecting others. Protecting the client from self-harm is most likely to arise when the client is a young person or child, or a vulnerable adult. Protecting others may arise where the client threatens serious harm to another named person, especially if that person is also your client. It may be that there are good reasons for believing that your client is so deluded or mentally disturbed that he is incapable of taking responsibility for the outcome of the counselling and he poses a threat to others. Fortunately, these situations are rare and some counsellors may never encounter them. Nonetheless, it is a useful starting point to ensure that you have estab-lished the boundaries of responsibilities between yourself and your client.

The following scenarios are examples of issues relating to ethics and standards classified according to boundaries of responsibility.

- Client's own ethical dilemma:

  Sheila decides she cannot face telling her partner that she has stronger feelings of attraction for someone else. She makes the decision to lie to her partner about the time she is spending with her new lover.

  Trevor is feeling guilty about money he has embezzled from his employer. He had intended to pay it back but he has lost the money through gambling. He knows it puts the future of the business at risk. Should he tell his employer? (If the counselling is taking place in the work setting, it is likely that this would become a dilemma shared by counsellor and client.)

- Counsellor's own ethical dilemma:

  Zoe is very wealthy and, having fallen out with all her close family, has decided that she wants to make a will bequeathing all her possessions to you as her counsellor. You suspect that this is a manipulation to win your support for Zoe's side in a family dispute. You also know that if you accept the bequest, it is likely that it will be suggested that you used your position of influence to persuade Zoe to make you a beneficiary. On the other hand, you would welcome being donated a large six-figure sum of money.

  Frances has been talking in counselling sessions about her difficulties with someone who is already well known to you. Do you tell Frances that you know the person she is talking about and risk inhibiting her, or do you stay silent?

  Rachel has sought counselling from the student counselling service about whether to leave a course before its completion. As the counsellor, you know that if one more student leaves this course it will be closed and the remaining students will be transferred to other courses. For one of your other very vulnerable clients, this could be disastrous as she sees this course as a lifeline. It could also have serious consequences for other students and staff.

  The organization that employs you as a counsellor wishes to impose a restriction on the number of sessions you can offer to any one client. You know that the maximum number of permitted sessions is unrealistically low for a majority of clients you see for counselling. What should you say to new clients who might be affected by the proposed policy? What should you do about the proposed policy?

- Ethical dilemma shared by counsellor and client:

  Bill is unbearably stressed by his work but he needs the income to support his partner and children. He decides that he must leave his employment but is feeling guilty about letting his family down. Therefore he decides to lie to his wife and says that you, as his counsellor, have said that he should give up work. To add credibility to his deception and without your knowledge, he tells his wife that you are willing to see her and to explain your recommendation. Bill's wife has arranged an interview with you. When his wife contacts you, you become aware that Bill has woven you into his deception and you will need to decide how far you are willing to share in the deception or distance yourself from it while respecting Bill's rights as a client.

Susan seeks counselling about an eating disorder. She states that she is not receiving counselling or therapy from anyone else. You agree to be her counsellor. Several sessions later, Susan admits to having lied about not having another therapist. She had a prior agreement to work exclusively with someone else. She does not want to stop seeing you or the other therapist and values her work with you. She feels unable to discuss seeing you with the other therapist.

One of the reasons for deciding at this stage who holds responsibility for the dilemma is that it may make all the subsequent steps in this model unnecessary. If the client has the sole responsibility for the dilemma, it is most appropriate to explain the issue to the client and help him make his own decision. Where there is joint responsibility, some clarification and negotiation with the client are usually indicated. The stages that follow are particularly appropriate for the resolution of dilemmas that are primarily the counsellor's responsibility. On the other hand, the model is flexible enough to be shared, wholly or partially, with some clients in order to help them decide issues which are their own responsibility or joint responsibilities with the counsellor.

Consider All Available Ethical Principles and Guidelines

The aim of this stage is to become better informed about possible ways of resolving the ethical dilemma. The main codes of standards and ethics of use to counsellors in Britain are published by the British Association for Counselling and Psychotherapy, the British Psychological Society, the Confederation of Scottish Counselling Agencies, the Irish Association for Counselling and Psychotherapy, and the United Kingdom Council for Psychotherapy. The guidelines produced for specific professional groups by the United Kingdom Central Council for Nursing, Midwifery and Health Visiting, the British Association for Social Workers and the General Medical Council are highly relevant to counsellors working in related roles. They may also offer useful insights to counsellors in similar settings but some caution may be indicated in assuming that they are directly transferable because of the different legal bases of specific professions and organizations. Some counselling services have developed their own codes and guidance, which can be very informative.

Some ethical issues cannot be decided without consideration of the law. Up-to-date publications may be useful but if the matter is complex or there is uncertainty about the law, I strongly recommend seeking legal advice. The general questions you may want answered are:

1   What actions are prohibited by law?
2   What actions are required to be performed by law?
3   What rights and responsibilities does the law protect?

In the absence of any relevant guidelines or definitive legal advice, you may find yourself considering the issue on the basis of the general ethical principles outlined in Chapter 3.

1   Respect for autonomy – what maximizes the opportunities for everyone involved to implement their choices?
2   Beneficence – what will achieve the greatest good?
3   Non-maleficence – what will cause least harm?
4   Justice – what will be fairest?
5   Fidelity – how can the relationship of trust be honoured?
6   Self-respect – how should the counsellor's own need for 1–5 be taken into account?

In counselling, the first principle is especially important and will often prove decisive, particularly if it is possible to act in ways consistent with client autonomy, which also satisfies one or more of the other principles.

At the end of this stage you would hope to be clearer about the goals which are ethically desirable. This will give you an orientation and some criteria for choosing between possible courses of action.

Identify All Possible Courses of Action

This stage is an opportunity to brainstorm all the possible courses of action open to you that will achieve the ethical goals you identified in the earlier stage. Some courses of action will seem highly probable ways of resolving the dilemma. Others may not seem feasible. However, it is better not to discard the less realistic ideas too readily because sometimes they contain the basis for an original approach or new insight.

Select the Best Course of Action

A former chairperson of the American Counselling Association Development (Holly A. Stadler, 1986a, 1986b) proposed three tests for a chosen course of action that have their origins in moral philosophy and have stood the test of time.

- Universality
    - could your chosen course of action be recommended to others?
    - would you condone your proposed course of action if it was done by someone else?

- Publicity
    - could I explain my chosen course of actions to other counsellors?
    - would I be willing to have my actions and rationale exposed to scrutiny in a public forum, e.g. at a workshop, in a professional journal, newspaper or on radio/TV?

- Justice
    - would I do the same for other clients in a similar situation?
    - would I do the same if the client was well known or influential?

If you find yourself answering 'no' to any of these questions, you may need to reconsider your chosen outcome. A final step in identifying the best course of action may be checking whether the resources are available to implement what is proposed.

The aim of this stage is to make an informed choice between all the possible courses of action you have identified. The consideration of guidelines and the law in the previous stage will be useful but may not be decisive. Therefore, asking yourself these questions is usually very informative.

Evaluate the Outcome

After you have implemented your course of action, it is useful to evaluate it in order to learn from the experience and to prepare yourself for any similar situations in the future.

- Was the outcome as you hoped?
- Had you considered all relevant factors with the result that no new factors emerged after you implemented your chosen course of action?
- Would you do the same again in similar circumstances?

Examples of Ethical Problem-Solving

I have chosen two issues as examples of how this model of ethical problem-solving might work in practice. The first raises the issues of dual relationships. The second poses what participants in training workshops often consider to be one of the most difficult ethical dilemmas which could confront a counsellor. I am offering both these as examples of how the model works rather than suggesting that my conclusions are necessarily right. You may use the same model but come to different conclusions.

Example 1

You are approached by Pam, the teenage daughter of a friend, who asks you to offer her counselling. You hardly know Pam but it is apparent that she is emotionally troubled and has dropped hints about not eating properly. Pam is insistent that from her point of view you are ideal as a counsellor. You are neither too much a stranger nor too close. She turns down any suggestion of seeing anyone else. It has taken her months to pluck up the courage to speak to you. You check with her mother, who is your friend. She is supportive of the idea and offers to pay whatever is your usual fee. You feel her friendship matters to you.

The first step is to produce a brief description of the dilemma. The main elements are:

- divided loyalties if you take on Pam as a client between putting her interests as a client first and your friendship with her mother. What if Pam's difficulties involve her relationship with her mother or perhaps abuse within the family?
- as a subsidiary issue, the management of confidentiality in relation to the mother, your friend. You suspect that neither Pam nor her mother understands some of the potential complications of what is proposed.

- a further subsidiary issue: the payment for counselling by someone other than the client when there is uncertainty about that person's role in the client's problems. This could be considered once the other issues are resolved.

The second step is to consider whose dilemma is it anyway? As it is presented, Pam and her mother are in agreement and the onus is on you to accept or reject the role of counselling Pam.

The third step is to consider all the available codes and guidelines. The BACP *Ethical Framework for Good Practice in Counselling and Psychotherapy* places responsibility on the counsellor for determining the potential beneficial or detrimental impact of dual relationships on the client and that they should be readily accountable to clients and colleagues for any dual relationships that occur (BACP, 2007). Some models of counselling are more open to this type of dual relationship than others. For example, it might be more problematic maintaining the professional distance in a psychodynamic approach than in a person-centred or cognitive-behavioural way of working. The situation raises the question of whether the overlapping and pre-existing relationships are avoidable. The possibility of referral has been considered but this is unacceptable to Pam. There is the additional requirement to explain the implications of maintaining boundaries to Pam, and perhaps secondarily her mother. In what ways might the boundaries become blurred? For the client, it is a potential dual relationship with Pam as 'counsellor' and 'mother's friend' simultaneously. A secondary issue is the potential dual relationship with Pam's mother as 'daughter's counsellor' and 'friend'.

Ethical attitudes to dual relationships have relaxed on both sides of the Atlantic from an instinctive prohibition to placing a great deal of responsibility on the counsellor for determining therapeutic impact of such a relationship and ensuring that the benefits outweigh any detriments (Corey et al., 2003; Syme, 2003; Gabriel, 2005; Sommers-Flanagan and Sommers-Flanagan 2007).

There are no apparent legal constraints. Therefore, the next step is to consider all possible courses of action. These include:

- Refuse to take Pam on as client, stating reasons.
- Offer a 'white lie' for not taking Pam on, e.g. too busy, don't work with teenagers, etc.
- Agree to see Pam but only once she understands the potential conflicts of interest and has explored how she wants you to deal with any issues relating to her mother.

- Agree to see Pam, but for as long as you are seeing Pam, minimize contact with her mother and have a clear agreement with both Pam and her mother about confidentiality and what may be communicated.
- Accept risk of losing a friend by seeing Pam.
- See Pam for a fixed period with review at which the possibility of referral or continuation will be considered.

The final stage is to choose a possible course of action. The choice will depend on the exact circumstances of the situation and your assessment of the possibility of maintaining clear boundaries and the likelihood of being able to help Pam. If I were faced with this dilemma, I would prefer to decline this dual relationship on ethical grounds. It is likely that Pamela will have issues relating to her mother, which she will need to explore and resolve for herself in the process of overcoming her eating disorder. My existing friendship with her mother is likely to complicate this process both for Pam and myself. If I took on any role, it would be to assist Pam in finding a source of help which she considers acceptable and perhaps offering to be present to introduce Pam to her counsellor or therapist before they start working together. I would be willing to be quite firm about the ethical undesirability of taking on the role of counsellor in these circumstances, and quite active in giving Pam information that could assist her search for an alternative source of help. I would not usually charge any fees for providing this information, so the subsidiary problem would not arise. However, this is often an issue when seeing young people so I will consider it.

The third-order issue of payment of fees by someone other than the client is often tricky, especially if a client's relationship with the person making the payment might be an issue in the counselling. It is possible that the client will experience a sense of guilt about using counselling to explore difficulties with the benefactor, and therefore may avoid this subject. The counsellor may also experience similar inhibitions. So this arrangement may be contrary to an ethical commitment to respecting the client's autonomy, which implies actively promoting the client's control over her life. Several alternatives exist:

- reducing the fees to a level where the client can afford direct payment;
- the client making a contribution towards the fees paid by someone else;
- suggesting that the money for fees be given as a gift to client, who takes responsibility for managing payment to the counsellor.

Any of these arrangements would be preferable to direct payment by the mother, which might further confuse an already difficult set of dual relationships. My own preference is to reduce fees to a level the client can afford directly. This provides the best way of placing the client in control of the counselling relationship. However, if this is not feasible, I prefer the client to make a contribution to the fees and to take responsibility for managing the payment of fees.

Example 2

Joanne, a 15 year-old client is seeing you for help with friendship difficulties and low self-confidence. After a few sessions, she hints that she is being sexually abused by someone at home but asks for a promise that you will keep what she says confidential before she is willing to tell you more.

This is an increasingly common situation for counsellors. In many ways, it is a welcome development that young people are more likely to seek help when they are being physically or sexually abused and that there is greater public awareness. It is so much better to be able to talk than suffer in silence. A commitment to prevent and detect child abuse has steadily grown in importance in public policy. It is also the case that child protection services have greatly improved over the last ten years but they remain variable from area to area. No matter how local services have improved, a young person who has experience of being abused is likely to be wary because they have direct experience of the harm that humans can inflict on each other. In this example, a young person has taken the first cautious step in putting her trust in another person, a counsellor. In real life, the counsellor will have some sense of how far this is trust based on a developing sense of each other or whether Joanne is seeking help out of desperation to escape an intolerable situation. Where it is the former, the counsellor will want to honour the trust that is being offered. Where Joanne is beginning to talk out of desperation, the counsellor will be aware of her vulnerability and emotional pain. In my experience, communications about being abused are usually prompted by a mixture of hoping to be able to trust someone and the desire to get out of an intolerable and painful situation. Being ethical in such circumstances is not only a matter of professional integrity but also helping someone to begin to trust again.

The dilemma in this case arises from Joanne's request for confidentiality. Increasingly, counsellors feel a moral obligation to act to protect vulnerable young people from abuse in relationships where they are systematically disempowered or counsellors are under actual legal obligations arising from a contract of employment to report allegations of child abuse. How should a counsellor respond to Joanne's request for a promise of confidentiality? The tension is between working in ways which build the client's confidence and trust to counteract the abusive relationship or to intervene and attempt to build the relationship afterwards. So much will depend on:

- the counsellor's sense of the young person and what they will tolerate or, preferably, actively support and the significance of forming a therapeutic relationship;
- an assessment of the overall best interests of the young person concerned;
- the severity of the abuse and the imminence of any repetition;
- any known risks to other young people being abused by the same perpetrator;
- the legal framework in which the counsellor is working, particularly the contract of employment and whether or not the service falls within statutory children's services (see Bond and Mitchels, 2008).

These sorts of situations are difficult to predict and it is unwise to promise total confidentiality. It is generally much better to actively consider how to remain respectful and trustworthy for the young person concerned. In some cases this may require continuing to be actively involved in the referral process and possible case conferences following a disclosure to the authorities. As services and procedures for investigation are developing rapidly in this field, it is sound practice to seek the advice of specialists in child protection. Such discussions can often be opened in ways that protect the anonymity of the client until it is clear that either the client is ready to consent to disclosure or it is considered that the seriousness of the situation requires immediate disclosure.

Conclusion

Ethical dilemmas occur on a daily basis in counselling. Fortunately, most dilemmas are on a manageable scale after careful reflection. Many are more likely to be of the order of considering whether to refer a client, choosing what to discuss in counselling-supervision or deciding whether your client has consented to your proposed course of action. Resolving ethical dilemmas requires thought, knowledge, feeling and you may also need courage to make and sustain decisions. Michael Carroll (1993) has likened resolving ethical dilemmas to general problem-solving and argues that it is a process in which counsellors can become more skilled with training. The model of ethical problem-solving I have offered is not definitive, but it is intended to be useful in everyday counselling. It is sufficiently flexible to incorporate insights from any of the six sources of professional ethics outlined in Chapter 3. Ethical dilemmas are usually a professional and personal challenge, but they can also be a source of new learning for the counsellor (Bond, 1997), when that learning is shared with the profession as a whole.

16

Implications for practice

The ethical context of counselling continues to change in ways that require counsellors to reconsider established ethical practice. Changes tend to be progressive and incremental, moving at the pace of social change, but may in some instances require substantial jumps to keep up. One such jump is imminent.

Statutory Regulation of Counselling

The possibility of statutory regulation seems to have been hanging over the field of counselling for an interminable number of years. It is a possibility that produces very mixed feelings among practitioners, from enthusiastic support to total opposition. Most have mixed feelings. Many of the different positions relate to the person's views about providing counselling as a committed radical (more likely to be resistant) or as a professional (more likely to cautiously accepting or even enthusiastic) (see Table 3.1 on p. 46). When regulation happens, it will be a major step-change that will significantly alter the ethical landscape for practitioners. The best guide to the full impact of regulation will be the developments in counselling psychology as it advances towards statutory regulation in England and Wales under the Health Professions Council.

The implications will be more far-reaching than those in ethics alone, but in this closing section I will concentrate on ethics. The voice of ethics on some issues will change and will be determined by a more authoritative voice on baseline issues identified as essential to fitness to practise. To some extent, this has been happening anyway within professional bodies. As ethics have developed in sophistication, professional bodies have increasingly sought to distinguish between those requirements which carry such ethical significance that they are mandatory, such as prohibitions on sexual relationships between counsellors and their clients, and those which are more appropriately determined by the practitioner, for example other types of dual relationship. The Health Professions Council (HPC) takes its authority from a publicly declared and legally endorsed aim to protect the public as its only purpose. This makes the development of its ethical framework rather different from professional bodies which combine protection of the public with addressing the needs of their members. It encourages a voice that is decisive and cuts incisively between what is considered essential to the protection of the public and what is not. The ethical infrastructure is still evolving. Where the Council has taken a stand, the requirements encompass all the professions within its register, currently 13, rising to 14 when psychologists enter. The language in which requirements are stated tends to simple, straightforward and authoritative. For example:

Your duties as a registrant
The standards of conduct, performance and ethics you must keep to

1   You must act in the best interests of service users.
2   You must respect the confidentiality of service users.
3   You must keep high standards of personal conduct.
4   You must provide (to us and any other relevant regulators) any important information about your conduct and competence.
5   You must keep your professional knowledge and skills up to date.
6   You must act within the limits of your knowledge, skills and experience and, if necessary, refer the matter to another practitioner.
7   You must communicate properly and effectively with service users and other practitioners.
8   You must effectively supervise tasks that you have asked other people to carry out.
9   You must get informed consent to give treatment (except in an emergency).

10   You must keep accurate records.
11   You must deal fairly and safely with the risks of infection.
12   You must limit your work or stop practising if your perform-
     ance or judgement is affected by your health.
13   You must behave with honesty and integrity and make sure
     that your behaviour does not damage the public's confidence
     in you or your profession.
14   You must make sure that any advertising you do is accurate.

This document sets out the standards of conduct, performance and
ethics we expect from the health professionals we register. The
standards also apply to people who are applying to become regis-
tered. (HPC, 2008)

On matters where the Council has taken a view, there is little room for
equivocation. For example, the starting point on record-keeping will be
(unless it changes in the meantime) that all registrants will keep records.
This is very different from the range of positions within counselling at the
moment (see Chapter 13). Although there is an obligation to keep records,
the form of those records will be a matter of professional judgement, for
which the practitioner is accountable. Further guidance emphasizes that
there is some limited room for professional judgement exercised in the
best interests of clients.

We often receive questions from registrants who are concerned that
something they have been asked to do, a policy, or the way in which
they work might mean that they cannot meet our standards. They
are often worried that this might have an effect on their registration.
  If you make informed, reasonable and professional judgements
about your practice, with the best interests of your service users as
your prime concern, and you can justify your decisions if you are
asked to, it is very unlikely that you will not meet our standards.
(HPC, 2008)

I find it difficult to extract parts of this document and give a true
flavour of the whole. It is well worth reading it in full (www.hpc–uk.org).
It has all the hallmarks of having been carefully drafted as an integrated
and carefully considered stance on issues considered essential to the
protection of the public.

One of the issues that is not included is the requirement for ongoing and regular supervision. This does not necessarily mean that this requirement will lapse. The HPC encourages professional bodies in making educational and developmental contributions. It may be it will remain as a requirement of membership of key professional bodies for counsellors. A great deal will become clearer as the admission process to registration advances. As things stand at the moment, post regulation counsellors will be working in a more multi-layered ethical environment, in which they will be expected to take account of:

- the ethics and standards required for regulation;
- the law as it applies to the role of counsellor;
- contracts of employment;
- ethical requirements of professional bodies;
- the counsellor's own informed, reasonable and professional judgements about the best interests of clients.

Ethical Mindfulness

I closed the previous edition of this book with a section on the importance of 'ethical mindfulness'. This caught the imagination of some readers and has been one of the more widely referred to passages. I proposed that ethical mindfulness was an alternative to responding to the difficulty of determining an appropriate ethical position by abandoning the task or by imposing rigidity to create certainty. My thinking has moved on and I have attempted to define what ethical mindfulness might mean.

A commitment to professional and personal integrity by acting in ways that are informed by ethical sensitivity and thoughtfulness in response to the complexity and diversity of contemporary social life.

The case for ethical mindfulness is stronger now than it has ever been. It has much in common with the strand of thinking in the *Standards of Conduct Performance and Ethics* (HPC, 2008) concerning informed, reasonable and professional judgements, although the language is less rooted in scientific logic and perhaps a little more open to the softer and more abstract dimensions of social sciences and even those areas of values and insight linked to human spirituality. In the closing section of this edition I want to leave another ethical thread blowing in the wind to see what emerges over the next few years. It concerns the relational dimension of ethics.

Respect and Trust as the Basis for Creating Ethical Understanding across Cultural and Relational Barriers

When I started work on the first edition of this book in 1992 I was still enthused by the radical potential of the principle of respect for individual autonomy. It provided a radical challenge to the ongoing paternalism of much professional practice. I was somewhat perplexed by the reservations of some of my feminist friends. It is only as I have become more conscientious in listening beyond my own experience in terms of gender and culture that I have started to appreciate the way an ethic of autonomy validates the possibility of difference between people without necessarily addressing the relational dimensions and the links between patches in a quilt as a metaphor for society. Virtues seem much better at capturing the sense of the presence of people interacting with each other and their ethical responsibilities to each other. Respect is the virtue that most closely corresponds to a principle of autonomy but is much more portable across social inequalities (Sennett, 2003) and values relationships across inequalities. 'Being trustworthy' reaches even further in this direction of giving ethical significance to relationships across many different types of personal, social and cultural difference.

In some senses there is nothing new in ethics that has not been thought before. Much of the writing is presenting something afresh to capture and inspire the ethical imagination with glimpses of possibilities of better ways of being with each other. My interest in being trustworthy grew out of working with people from cultures where the primary focus of ethical concern is not the individual but a family group (Bond, 2007), which must be a substantial part of the world's population. I have become intrigued with situations where the counsellor is embedded in a culture in which she works, where clients and counsellors are encountered in both the public spaces of society, such as the school playground, the gym or in restaurants. What if, as in a small rural town in the British Isles, the counsellor is part of networks of family relationships living in a tightly defined and densely populated geographical space where everyone has some form of relationship or knowledge of everyone else? The counsellor has to hold back information revealed in the privacy of counselling even if that information would be beneficial to another client. This is by no means a unique problem of geography. Counsellors working within tightly defined interest groups or social sub-groups often experience similar dilemmas. Being trustworthy may be relevant to grappling with both the incomprehensibility of reaching across some cultural differences but also the density and intensity of relationships in some settings. My working definition, developed by trial and error, is:

> Being trustworthy involves striving to form a relationship of sufficient quality and resilience to withstand the challenges arising from difference, inequality, risk and uncertainty.

I offer this as a way of reflecting about the relational dimension of counselling and what are the challenges facing the client within the relationship and from the surrounding social circumstances of both people? There is another ethical journey to be travelled. I will be interested to see whether other counsellors can see its potential applications to our work.

Appendix: Useful Resources

Professional associations

British Association for Counselling and Psychotherapy – BACP
BACP House
15 St John's Business Park
Lutterworth, Leicestershire, LE17 4HB
Tel: 01455 883300 Fax: 01455 550243
Website: www.bacp.co.uk Email: enquiries@bacp.co.uk

The British Psychological Society – BPS
St Andrews House
48 Princess Road East
Leicester, LE1 7DR
Tel: 0116 254 9568 Fax: 0116 247 0787
Website: www.bps.org.uk Email: mail@bps.org.uk

Counselling and Psychotherapy in Scotland – COSCA
16 Melville Terrace
Stirling, FK8 2NE
Tel: 01786 475140 Fax: 01786 446207
Website: www.cosca.org.uk Email: info@cosca.org.uk

Irish Association for Counselling and Psychotherapy – IACP
21 Dublin Road
Bray
County Wicklow
Eire
Tel: 00 353 1 2723427 Fax: 00353 1 2869933
Website: www. irish-counselling.ie Email: iacp@iacp.ie

United Kingdom Council for Psychotherapy – UKCP
2nd Floor, Edward House, 2 Wakeley Street
London, EC1V 7LT
Tel: 0207 0149955 Fax: 0207 0149977
Wesite: www.psychotherapy.org.uk Email: info@ukcp.org.uk

Professional associations in related roles

British Medical Association
BMA House
Tavistock Square
London, WC1H 9JP
Tel: 020 7387 4499 Fax: 020 7383 6400
Website: www.bma.org.uk Email: use online enquiry form

Sources of specialized information

The Children's Legal Centre
University of Essex
Wivenhoe Park
Colchester
Essex, CO4 3SQ
Tel: 01206 877 910 Fax: 01206 877 963
Website: www.childrens legal centre.com Email: clc@essex.ac.uk

London Office:
38 Great Portland Street
London, W1W 8QY
Tel: 0207 5801664 Fax: 0207 5801341
Email: clclondon@essex.ac.uk

MENCAP
123 Golden Lane
London, EC1Y 0RT
Helpline: 0808 808 1111 Tel: 020 7454 0454 Fax: 020 7608 3254
Website: www.mencap.org.uk Email: information@mencap.org.uk

MIND – Mental Health Charity with over 200 local associations
15–19 Broadway, London, E15 4BQ
Information Line: 0845 766 0165 Tel: 020 8519 2122 Fax: 020 8522 1725
Website: www.mind.org.uk Email: contact@mind.org.uk

WITNESS – Professional Boundaries Charity
32–36 Loman street
London, SE1 OEH
Tel: 020 7922 7802 Support line: 0845 4 500 300
Website: www.professional boundaries. org.uk Email: training@professional
boundaries.org.uk

NHS *The Information Governance Toolkit*
Website: www.igt.connectingforhealth.nhs.uk or nww.igt.connectingfor
health.nhs.uk
The IGT provides guidance on how organizations should satisfy confidentiality, data protection, information security, Freedom of Information Law,
records management and information quality requirements. It includes an
extensive knowledge base of exemplar documents, guidance materials and
useful links.
Email: helpdesk@cfh.nhs.uk (an email helpline for assistance with the
Information Governance Toolkit – content, technical advice and administration
issues)

NICE – National Institute for Clinical Excellence
MidCity Place
71 High Holborn
London, WC1V 6NA
Tel: 0845 003 7780 Fax: 0845 003 7784
Website: www.nice.org.uk www.nice.org.uk/CG026publicinfo www.nice.
org.uk/CG026NICEguideline www.nice.org.uk/CG026quickrefguide
The distribution list for the quick reference guide to this guideline is
available from www.nice.org.uk/CG026distributionlist
Email: nice@nice.org.uk

Patients' Association
PO Box 935
Harrow
Middlesex, HA1 3YJ
Helpline: 0845 608 4455 Tel: 020 8423 9111 Fax: 020 8423 9119
Website: www.patients-association.com Email: mailbox@patients-association.
com   helplines@patients-association.com

Patient Concern
PO Box 23732
London, SW5 9FY
Tel: 020 7373 0794
Website: www.patientconcern.org.uk Email: patientconcern@hotmail.com

Patient Information Advisory Group – PIAG
Website: www.advisorybodies.doh.gov.uk/piag
Provides the minutes of PIAG meetings and guidance on the use of powers provided under section 60 of the Health and Social Care Act 2001, which allow confidentiality requirements to be set aside in limited circumstances for purposes such as research and public health work. PIAG also provides guidance on issues of major significance that are brought to its attention. (Changing to become National Information Governance Board for Health and Adult Social Care (NIGB) www.NIGB.nhs.uk.)

Regulatory body

Health Professions Council – HPC
Park House
184 Kennington Park Road
London, SE11 4BU
Tel: 020 7582 0866 Fax: 020 7820 9684
Website: www.hpc-uk.org Email: see website for contact details

Policy and Standards (for consultations, standards and policy issues)
Tel: 020 7840 9815 Fax: 020 7820 9684
Email: policy@hpc-uk.org

Professional Indemnity Insurance Providers for Counselling and Psychotherapy

Please note that this list is not exhaustive. There are many insurance companies who offer cover for businesses. These are some insurers that indicate a specialism in working with counsellors and psychotherapists.

Holistic Insurance Services
183a Watling Street West
Towcester
Northants, NN12 6BX
Tel: 01327 354 249 or 0845 222 2236 Fax: 01327 353 555 or 0845 222 2237
Website: www.holisticinsurance.co.uk Email: info@holisticinsurance.co.uk

Howden Insurance Brokers
Bevis Marks House
Bevis Marks
London, EC3A 7JB
Tel: 020 7623 3806
Website: www.howdenpro.com Email: enquiries@howdengroup.com

Towergate Partnership Ltd
Towergate House
Eclipse Park
Sittingbourne Road
Maidstone
Kent, ME14 3EN
Tel: 0844 892 1500 Fax: 0844 892 1501
Website: www.towergateprofessionalrisks.co.uk/psychotherapists Email: enquiries@towergate.co.uk

Bibliography

Ali, L. and Graham, B. (1996) *The Counselling Approach to Careers Guidance.* London: Taylor & Francis Ltd.

Allen, R.E. (1990) *The Concise Oxford Dictionary of Current English.* Oxford: Oxford University Press.

American Association for Counseling and Development (AACD) (1988) *Ethical Standards of the American Association for Counseling and Development.* Alexandria, VA: American Association for Counseling and Development.

American Counselling Association (ACA) (2005) *ACA Code of Ethics.* Alexandria, VA: American Counseling Association.

Anthony, K. (2007) *Introduction to Online Counselling and Psychotherapy.* BACP Information sheet P6. Lutterworth: British Association for Counselling and Psychotherapy.

Argyle, M. (ed.) (1981) *Social Skills and Health.* London: Methuen.

Asquith, S. (ed.) (1993) *Protecting Children: Cleveland to Orkney – More Lessons to Learn?* London: HMSO.

Association for Student Counselling (ASC) (1991) *HMI Inspection of Counselling Services.* Rugby: Association for Student Counselling.

Association for Student Counselling (ASC) (1992) *Requirements for Accreditation.* Rugby: Association for Student Counselling.

Austin, K.M., Moline, M.E. and Williams, G.T. (1990) *Confronting Malpractice: Legal and Ethical Dilemmas in Psychotherapy.* Newbury Park, CA: Sage.

Aveline, M., Shapiro, D.A., Parry, G. and Freeman, C. (1995) 'Building research foundations for psychotherapy practice', in Aveline, M. and Shapiro, D.A. (eds), *Research Foundations in Psychotherapy Practice.* Chichester: Wiley.

Bancroft, J. (1989) *Human Sexuality and its Problems.* Edinburgh: Churchill Livingstone.

Banks, S. (2006) *Ethics and Values in Social Work* (Third edition). Basingstoke: Palgrave Macmillan.

Bates, Y. and House, R. (eds) (2003) *Ethically Challenged Professions: Enabling Innovation and Diversity in Psychotherapy and Counselling.* Ross-on-Wye: PCCS Books.

Bauman, Z. (1993) *Post-modern Ethics.* Oxford: Blackwell.

Beauchamp, T.L. and Childress, J.F. (2008) *Principles of Biomedical Ethics* (Sixth edition). New York: Oxford University Press.

Bond, T. (1989) 'Towards defining the role of counselling skills', *Counselling – Journal of the British Association for Counselling*, 69: 3–9.

Bond, T. (1990) 'Counselling supervision – ethical issues', *Counselling – Journal of the British Association for Counselling*, 1 (2): 43–6.

Bond, T. (1991a) 'Sex and suicide in the development of counselling', *Changes: an International Journal of Psychology and Psychotherapy*, 9 (4): 284–93.

Bond, T. (1991b) *HIV Counselling – Report on National Survey and Consultation 1990*. Rugby: British Association for Counselling.

Bond, T. (1994) 'Ethical standards and the exploitation of clients', *Counselling – Journal of the British Association for Counselling*, 4 (3), Stop Press: 2–3.

Bond, T. (1997) 'Therapists' dilemmas as stimuli to new understanding and practice', in Dryden, W. (ed.), *Therapists' Dilemmas*. London: Sage.

Bond, T. (1998) *Confidentiality: Counselling and the Law – Information Guide No. 1*. Rugby: British Association for Counselling.

Bond, T. (1999) 'Guidelines for professional practice', in Bor, R. and Watts, M. (eds), *The Trainee Handbook: A Guide for Counselling and Psychotherapy Trainees*. London: Sage.

Bond, T. (2006) 'Intimacy, risk, and reciprocity in psychotherapy: intricate ethical challenges', *Transactional Analysis Journal*, 36 (2): 77–89.

Bond, T. (2007) 'Ethics and psychotherapy: an issue of trust', in Ashcroft, R.E., Dawson, A., Drapes, H. and McMillan, J.R. (eds), *Principles of Health Care Ethics* (Second edition). Chichester: John Wiley and Sons.

Bond, T. and Cliff, D. (1998) *Trust Matters: The Management of Sensitive Information Held by Drugs Agencies*. Durham: Durham and Darlington Drug Action Team.

Bond, T. and Mitchels, B. (2008) *Confidentiality and Record Keeping in Counselling and Psychotherapy*. London: Sage.

Bond, T. and Sandhu, A. (2005) *Therapists in Court: Providing Evidence and Supporting Witnesses*. London: Sage.

Bowlby, J. (1988) *A Secure Base: Clinical Applications of Attachment Therapy*. London: Tavistock/Routledge.

Brammer, L.M. and Shostrum, E.L. (1982) *Therapeutic Psychology: Fundamentals of Counselling and Psychotherapy*. Englewood Cliffs, NJ: Prentice-Hall.

British Association for Counselling (BAC) (1984) *Code of Ethics and Practice for Counsellors*. Rugby: BAC.

British Association for Counselling (BAC) (1985) *Counselling: Definition of Terms in Use with Expansion and Rationale*. Rugby: BAC.

British Association for Counselling (BAC) (1990) *Code of Ethics and Practice for Counsellors*. Rugby: BAC.

British Association for Counselling (BAC) (1991) *Companies Act 1991: Memorandum of Association of the British Association for Counselling*. Rugby: BAC.

British Association for Counselling (BAC) (1992) *Complaints Procedure*. Rugby: BAC.

British Association for Counselling (BAC) (1993) *Membership Survey 1993 – Individual Members and Organisations: A Short Summary of Results*. Rugby: BAC.

British Association for Counselling (BAC) (1994) *Accreditation Criteria*. Rugby: BAC.

British Association for Counselling (BAC) (1995) *Code of Ethics and Practice for Supervisors of Counsellors*. Rugby: BAC.

British Association for Counselling (BAC) (1996) *Code of Ethics and Practice for Trainers*. Rugby: BAC.

British Association for Counselling (BAC) (1997) *Code of Ethics and Practice for Counsellors*. Rugby: BAC.

British Association for Counselling (BAC) (1998a) *Code of Ethics and Practice for Those Using Counselling Skills at Work*. Rugby: BAC.

British Association for Counselling (BAC) (1998b) *How Much Supervision Should You Have?* Information Sheet 3. Rugby: BAC.

British Association for Counselling and Psychotherapy (BACP) (2007) *Ethical Framework for Good Practice in Counselling and Psychotherapy*. Lutterworth: BACP.

British Association for Counselling and Psychotherapy Information Services (2008a) *What is Counselling?* Lutterworth: BACP.

British Association for Counselling and Psychotherapy Information Services (2008b) *What is Supervison?* Lutterworth: British Association for Counselling and Psychotherapy.

British Medical Association (BMA) (1981) *Handbook on Medical Ethics*. London: BMA.

British Medical Association Foundation for AIDS (1988) *HIV Infection and AIDS: Ethical Considerations for the Medical Profession*. London: BMA.

British Psychological Society (BPS) (1991) *Code of Conduct, Ethical Principles and Guidelines*. Leicester: BPS.

British Psychological Society (BPS) (1993) *Code of Conduct, Ethical Principles and Guidelines*. Leicester: BPS.

British Psychological Society (BPS) (1995a) *Guidelines for the Professional Practice of Counselling Psychology*. Leicester: BPS.

British Psychological Society (BPS) (1995b) *Recovered Memories*. Leicester: BPS.

British Psychological Society (BPS) (1995c) *Regulations and Syllabus for the Diploma in Counselling Psychology*. Leicester: BPS.

British Psychological Society (BPS) (1998) *Regulations and Syllabus for the Diploma in Counselling Psychology*. Leicester: BPS.

British Psychological Society (BPS) (2000) *Guidelines for Psychologists Working with Clients in Contexts in which Issues Related to Recovered Memories May Arise*. Leicester: BPS.

British Psychological Society (BPS) (2005) *Guidelines for the Professional Practice of Counselling Psychology*. Leicester: BPS.

British Psychological Society (BPS) (2006) *Code of Ethics and Conduct*. Leicester: BPS.

British Psychological Society (BPS) (2007) *Professional Practice Guidelines: Division of Counselling Psychology*. Leicester: BPS.

British Psychological Society (BPS) (2008a) *Careers and Qualifications: What is Counselling Psychology?* Leicester: BPS.

British Psychological Society (BPS) (2008b) *Generic Professional Practice Guidelines* (Second edition). Leicester: BPS.

Brooke, R. (1972) *Information and Advice Guidance: The Social Administration Research Trust*. London: G. Bell and Sons.

Burnard, P. (1992) *Perceptions of AIDS Counselling*. Aldershot: Avebury.

Burnard, P. (2006) *Counselling Skills for Health Professionals*. Cheltenham: Nelson Thornes.

Butler–Sloss, E. (1988) *Report of the Inquiry into Child Abuse in Cleveland 1987*. Cmnd 412. London: HMSO.

Butler–Sloss, E. (1993) *Protecting Children: Cleveland to Orkney – More Lessons to Learn?* London: HMSO.

Canadian Guidance and Counselling Association (CGCA) (1995) *Guidelines for Ethical Behaviour*. Ottawa: CGCA.

Carroll, M. (1993) 'Ethical issues in organisational counselling'. Unpublished paper, Roehampton Institute, London.

Carroll, M. (1996) *Counselling Supervision: Theory, Skills and Practice*. London: Cassell.

Carroll, M. and Holloway, E. (1999) 'Introduction', in Carroll, M. and Holloway, E., *Counselling Supervison in Context*. London, Sage. pp. 1–4.

Casement, P. (1985) *On Learning from the Patient*. London: Tavistock/Routledge.

Children's Legal Centre (1989) 'A child's right to confidentiality?' *Childright*, 57: 7–10.

Children's Legal Centre (1992) *Working with Young People – Legal Responsibility and Liability*. London: Children's Legal Centre.

Clarkson, P. (1995) *The Therapeutic Relationship*. London: Whurr.

Cohen, K. (1992) 'Some legal issues in counselling and psychotherapy', *British Journal of Guidance and Counselling*, 20 (1): 10–26.

Confederation of Scottish Counselling Agencies (COSCA) (2009) *Statement of Ethics and Code of Practice*. Stirling: COSCA.

Cooper, M. (2008) *Essential Research Findings in Counselling and Psychotherapy: The Facts are Friendly*. London: Sage.

CORE Partnership (2007) 'Impact of the use of the CORE System on service quality', *CORE Partnership Occasional Paper* No. 3. Rugby: CORE IMS.

Corey, G., Corey, M.S. and Callanan, P. (2003) *Issues and Ethics in the Helping Professions* (Sixth edition). Pacific Grove, CA: Brooks/Cole.

Craig, Yvonne S. (1998) *Advocacy, Counselling and Mediation in Casework*. London: Jessica Kingsley.

Culley, S. and Bond, T. (2004) *Integrative Counselling Skills in Action* (Second edition). London: Sage.

Department for Children, Schools and Families (2007) *Quality Standards for Young People's Information, Advice and Guidance (IAG)*. London: Department for Children, Schools and Families.

Department for Children, Schools and Families (2009) *Every Child Matters*. London: Department for Children, Schools and families.

Department of Health (2003) *Confidentiality: NHS Code of Practice*. London: Department of Health.

Division of Counselling Psychology (2007) *Professional Practice Guidelines*. Leicester: British Psychological Society (BPS).

Dryden, W. (ed.) (1998) *Therapist' Dilemmas* (Second edition). London: Sage.

Dryden, W. (1990, Second edition 1999) *Rational-Emotive Counselling in Action*. London: Sage.

Dryden, W. and Neenan, M. (2004) *Rational Emotive Behavioural Counselling in Action*. London: Sage.

Einzig, H. (1989) *Counselling and Psychotherapy – Is It for Me?* Rugby: British Association for Counselling.

Eldrid, J. (1988) *Caring for the Suicidal.* London: Constable.

Evans, J. (2008) *Online Counselling and Guidance: A Practical Resource for Trainees and Practitioners.* London: Sage.

Every Child Matters (2006a) *What to do if you are worried a child is being abused.* Norwich: TSO.

Every Child Matters (2006b) Working Together to Safeguard Children: A Guide to Inter-Agency Working to Safeguard and Promote the Welfare of Children. Norwich: TSO.

Firestone, R.W. (1997) *Suicide and the Inner Voice.* Thousand Oaks, CA: Sage.

Foskett, J. and Lyall, D. (1988) *Helping the Helpers – Supervision and Pastoral Care.* London: SPCK.

Friel, J. (1993) In the Matter of the Powers of Her Majesty's Inspectorate of Schools to Inspect Counselling in Polytechnics, Colleges of Further Education etc., Legal opinion obtained by British Association for Counselling.

Friel, J. (1998) In the Matter of the British Association for Counselling, the Association for Student Counselling and the Association of Colleges, Legal opinion obtained by British Association for Counselling.

Gabriel, L. (2005) *Speaking the Unspeakable: The Ethics of Dual Relationships in Counselling and Psychotherapy.* London: Routledge.

Gawthop, J.C. and Uhlemann, M.R. (1992) 'Effects of the problem-solving approach to ethics training', *Professional Psychology: Research and Practice*, 23 (1): 38–42.

General Medical Council (1988) *HIV Infection and AIDS: The Ethical Considerations.* London: GMC.

Gibson, W.T. and Pope, K.S. (1993) 'The ethics of counseling: a national survey of certified counsellors', *Journal of Counseling and Development*, 71: 330–6.

Giddens A. (1991) *Modernity and Self Identity: Self and Society in the Late Middle Age.* Cambridge: Polity Press.

Gillon, R. (1985) 'Autonomy and consent', in Lockwood, M. (ed.), *Moral Dilemmas in Modern Medicine.* Oxford: Oxford University Press. pp. 111–25.

Gillon, R. (2003), 'Ethics needs principles – four can encompass the rest – and respect for autonomy should be "first among equals"', *Journal of Medical Ethics*, 29 (5): 307–12.

Gothard, B., Mignot, P., Offer, M. and Ruff, M. (2001) *Careers Guidance in Context.* London: Sage.

Grant, L. (1992) 'Counselling: a solution or a problem?', *Independent on Sunday*, 19 April: 22–3, and 26 April: 20.

Grant, P. (1999) 'Supervison and racial issues', in Carroll, M. and Holloway, E., *Counselling Supervison in Context*. London: Sage. pp. 7–22.

Guardian Law Reports (1992) 'Re J (a minor) (medical treatment)', *The Guardian*, 22 July.

Gummere, R.M. (1988) 'The counselor as prophet: Frank Parsons 1854–1908', *Journal of Counseling and Development*, May, 66: 402–5.

Halmos, P. (1978) *The Faith of Counsellors*. London: Constable.

Hawkins, P. and Shohet, R. (2007) *Supervison in the Helping Professions* (Third edition). Milton Keynes: Open University Press.

Hawton, K. and Catalan, J. (1987) *Attempted Suicide: A Practical Guide to its Nature and Management*. Oxford: Oxford University Press.

Hayman, A. (1965) 'Psychoanalyst subpoenaed', *The Lancet*, 16 October: 785–6.

Health Professions Council (HPC) (2003) *Fitness to Practise*. London: HPC.

Health Professions Council (HPC) (2008) *Standards of Conduct Performance and Ethics*. London: HPC.

Herlihy, B. and Corey, G. (1992) *Dual Relationships*. Alexandria, VA: American Association for Counseling and Development.

Herlihy, B. and Corey, G. (1996) *ACA Ethical Standards Casebook* (Fifth edition). Alexandria, VA: American Counseling Association.

Her Majesty's Inspectorate (1988) *Careers Education and Guidance from 5 to 16*, Department of Education and Science. London: HMSO.

Heron, J. (2001) *Helping the Client: A Creative Practical Guide* (Fifth edition). London: Sage.

Heyd, D. and Bloch, S. (1991) 'The ethics of suicide', in Bloch, S. and Chodoff, P. (eds), *Psychiatric Ethics*. Oxford: Oxford University Press.

Hicks, C. and Wheeler, S. (1994) 'Research: an essential foundation for counselling, training and practice', *Counselling – Journal of the British Association of Counselling*, 5 (1): 38–40.

Hiltner, S. (1949) *Pastoral Counselling*. Nashville, TN: Abingdon.

Holloway, E. and Carroll, M. (1999) 'Introduction', in Holloway, E. and Carroll, M., *Training Counselling Supervisors*. London: Sage. pp. 1–7.

Holmes, J. and Lindley, R. (1998) *The Values of Psychotherapy*. Oxford: Oxford University Press.

Hooper, D. (1988) 'Invited editorial – "York 1988"', *Counselling – Journal of the British Association for Counselling*, November, 66: 1–2.

House, R. and Totton, N. (eds) (1997) *Implausible Professions: Arguments for Pluralism and Autonomy in Psychotherapy and Counselling*. Ross-on-Wye: PCCS.

Houston, G. (1995) *Supervision and Counselling* (Second edition). London: Rochester Foundation.

Howard, A. (1996) *Challenges for Counselling and Psychotherapy*. Basingstoke: Macmillan.

Hoxter, H. (1998) Counselling as a Profession: Status, Organisation and Human Rights. Conference programme. London: International Association for Counselling, and Paris: UNESCO.

Human Fertilization and Embryology Authority (HEFA) (2008) *Code of Practice* (Eighth edition) (Consultation draft). London: HEFA.

Independent Law Report (1992) 'Re T – Court of Appeal', *The Independent*, 31 July.

Inskipp, F. (1986) *Counselling: The Trainer's Handbook*. Cambridge: National Extension College.

Inskipp, F. and Proctor, B. (1994) *Making the Most of Supervision*. Twickenham: Cascade Publications.

Inskipp, F. and Proctor, B. (1995) *Becoming a Counselling Supervisor*. Twickenham: Cascade Publications.

International Association for Counselling (IAC) (1998) Counselling as a Profession: Status, Organisation and Human Rights. Conference report. London: IAC, and Paris: UNESCO.

International Association for Counselling (IAC) (2003) *Who We Are*. London: International Association for Counselling, and Paris: UNESCO.

Irish Association for Counselling and Psychotherapy (IACP) (2005) *Code of Ethics and Practice*. Bray: IACP.

Irish Association for Counselling and Psychotherapy (IACP) (2007) *Code of Ethics for Supervisors*. Bray: IACP.

Jacobs, M. (2004) *Psychodynamic Counselling in Action*. London: Sage.

Jakobi, S. and Pratt, D. (1992) 'Therapy note and the law', *The Psychologist*, May: 219–21.

James, I. and Palmer, S. (eds) (1996) *Professional Therapeutic Titles: Myths and Realities*. Leicester: British Psychological Society.

Jehu, D. (1994) *Patients as Victims: Sexual Abuse in Psychotherapy and Counselling*. Chichester: Wiley and Sons.

Jenkins, P. (1996) *False or Recovered Memories? Legal and Ethical Implications for Therapists*. London: Sage.

Jenkins, P. (2007) *Counselling, Psychotherapy and the Law* (Second edition). London: Sage.

Jones, G. and Stokes, A. (2008) *Online Counselling*. Houndsmills: Palgrave Macmillan.

Khele, S., Symons, C. and Wheeler, S. (2008) 'An analysis of complaints to the British Association for Counselling and Psychotherapy 1996–2006', *Counselling and Psychotherapy Research*, 8 (2): 124–32.

Lago, C. (2008) *Race, Culture and Counselling: The Ongoing Challenge* (Second edition). Milton Keynes: Open University Press.

Laing, R.D. (1967) *The Politics of Experience and the Bird of Paradise*. Harmondsworth: Penguin.

Law Commission (1981) *Breach of Confidence*. Cmnd 8388. London: HMSO.

Leissner, A. (1969) 'Family Advice Service', *British Hospital Journal and Service Review*, 17 January: 120.

Lynch, G. (2002) *Pastoral Care and Counselling*. London: Sage.

Masson, J. (1985) *The Assault on Truth*. Harmondsworth: Penguin.

Mays, J., Forder, A. and Keidan, O. (1975) *Penelope Hall's Social Services of England and Wales*. London: Routledge and Kegan Paul.

McGuire, A. (1998) *False Memory Syndrome*. Rugby: British Association for Counselling.

McLeod, J. (1998) *An Introduction to Counselling* (Second edition). Buckingham: Open University Press.

McLeod, J. (2007) *Counselling Skill*. Maidenhead: Open University Press.

Mearns, D. (1991) 'On being a supervisor', in Dryden, W. and Thorne, B. (eds), *Training and Supervision for Counselling in Action*. London: Sage.

Megranahan, M. (1989) *Counselling: A Practical Guide for Employers*. London: Institute of Personnel Management.

Mellor-Clark, S. and Barkham, M. (1996) 'Evaluating counselling', in Bayne, R., Horton, I. and Bimrose, J. (eds), *New Directions in Counselling*. London: Routledge.

Menlowe, M.A. and McCall Smith, A. (1993) *The Duty to Rescue: The Jurisprudence of Aid*. Aldershot: Dartmouth.

Miller, A. (1998) *Thou Shalt Not Be Aware*. London: Pluto Press.

Mitchels, B. (2006) *Love in Danger. Trauma, Therapy and Conflict Explored through the Life and Work of Adam Curle*. Charlbury: John Carpenter.

Mitchels, B. and Bond, T. (Forthcoming) Essential Law for Counsellors and Psychotherapists. London: Sage.

Mowbray, R. (1995) *The Case against Psychotherapy Registration: A Conservation Issue for the Human Potential Movement*. London: Trans Marginal Press.

Munro, A., Manthei, B. and Small, J. (1988) *Counselling: The Skills of Problem-Solving.* Auckland, New Zealand: Longman Paul, and London: Routledge.

Murgatroyd, S. (1985) *Counselling and Helping.* Leicester: British Psychological Society, and London: Methuen.

Musgrave, A. (1991) *What is Good Advice Work?* NAYPCAS discussion paper. Leicester: Youth Access.

National Association of Citizens Advice Bureaux (NACAB) (1990) 'Quality of advice: NACAB membership scheme requirements', 3 (1), in *National Homelessness Advice Service – Guidance on CAB Minimum Housing Advice Standards.* London: NACAB.

National Association of Citizens' Advice Bureaux (NACAB) (2008) *How CAB Advisers Can Help.* London: NACAB.

New Zealand Association for Counsellors (NZAC) (2003) *Code of Ethics: A Framework for Ethical Practice.* Hamilton, New Zealand: NZAC.

New Zealand Association of Counsellors (NZAC) (1998) 'Code of ethics', in *New Zealand Association of Counsellors Handbook 1998.* Auckland, New Zealand: Association of Counsellors NZAC.

Nickel, J. (1988) 'Philosophy and policy', in Rosenthal, D.M. and Shehad, F. (eds), *Applied Ethics and Ethical Theory.* Salt Lake City, UT: University of Utah Press.

O'Connor, R.C. (Forthcoming) 'Psychological perspectives on suicidal behaviour', in Kumar, U. and Mandal, M.K. (eds), *Suicidal Behaviour: Assessment of People at Risk.* New Delhi: Sage.

Page, S. and Wosket, V. (2001) *Supervising the Counsellor: A Cyclical Model,* (Second edition). London: Routledge.

Palmer Barnes, F. (1998) *Complaints and Grievances in Psychotherapy: A Handbook of Ethical Practice.* London: Routledge.

Paradise, L.V. and Siegelwaks, B. (1982) 'Ethical training for group leaders', *Journal for Specialists in Groupwork,* 7 (3): 162–6.

Pearsall, J. (1998) *New Oxford Dictionary of English.* Oxford: Oxford University Press.

Pope, K.S. (1988) 'How clients are harmed by sexual contact with mental health professionals: the syndrome and its prevalence', *Journal of Counseling and Development,* 67: 222–6.

Pope, K.S. and Bouhoutsos, J.C. (1986) *Sexual Intimacy between Therapists and Patients.* New York: Praeger Press.

Pope, K.S., Sonne, J.L. et al. (2006) *What Therapists Don't Talk about and Why: Understanding Taboos that Hurt Us and Our Clients.* Washington, DC: American Psychological Association.

Pope, K.S. and Vasquez, M.J.T. (1991) *Ethics in Psychotherapy and Counseling: A Practical Guide for Psychologists*. San Francisco, CA: Jossey-Bass.

Prevention of Professional Abuse Network (POPAN) (1998) 'Who is abused and who abuses?', *Annual Report 1997–8*. London: POPAN.

Pritchard, C. (1995) *Suicide – the Ultimate Rejection? A Psycho-social Study*. Buckingham: Open University Press.

Proctor, B. (1988) 'Supervision: a co-operative exercise in accountability', in Marken, M. and Payne, M. (eds), *Enabling and Ensuring Supervision in Practice*. Leichester: National Youth Bureau.

Reason, P. and Rowan, J. (1981) *Human Inquiry: A Sourcebook of New Paradigm Research*. Chichester: Wiley.

Reeves, A. and Seber, P. (2007) *Working with the Suicidal Client*, BACP Information sheet P7. Lutterworth: British Association for Counselling and Psychotherapy.

Reiter-Theil, S., Eich, H. and Reiter, L. (1991) 'Informed consent in family therapy – necessary discourse and practice', *Changes: an International Journal of Psychology and Psychotherapy*, 9 (2): 91–100.

Rogers, C. (1980) *A Way of Being*. Boston, MA: Houghton Mifflin.

Rogers, W.V.H. (1998) *Winfield and Jolowicz on Tort* (Fifteenth edition). London: Sweet and Maxwell.

Rogers, W.V.H. (2006) *Winfield and Jolowicz on Tort* (Seventeenth edition). London: Sweet and Maxwell.

Rose, N. (1990) *Governing the Soul: The Shaping of the Private Self*. London: Routledge.

Rowan, J. (1983) *The Reality Game: A Guide to Humanistic Counselling and Therapy*. London: Routledge and Kegan Paul.

Rowan, J. (1988) 'Counselling and the psychology of furniture', *Counselling – Journal of the British Association for Counselling*, 64: 21–45.

Russell, J. (1993) *Out of Bounds: Sexual Exploitation in Counselling and Therapy*. London: Sage.

Russell, J. (1996) 'Sexual exploitation in counselling in future developments in counselling', in Bayne, R., Horton, I. and Bimrose, J. (eds), *New Directions in Counselling*. London: Routledge. pp. 65–78.

Russell, J., Dexter, G. and Bond, T. (1992) *A Report on Differentiation between Advice, Guidance, Befriending, Counselling Skills and Counselling*. Rugby: British Association for Counselling, and London: Department of Employment.

Rutter, P. (1989) *Sex in the Forbidden Zone*. London: Mandala.

Schutz, B.M. (1982) *Legal Liability to Psychotherapy*. San Francisco, CA: Jossey-Bass.

Scoggins, M., Litton, R. and Palmer, S. (1997) 'Confidentiality and the law', *Counselling – Journal of the British Association for Counselling*, 8 (4): 258–62.

Segal, J. (1985) *Phantasy in Everyday Life*. Harmondsworth: Penguin.

Sennett, R. (2003) *Respect: the Formation of Character in an Age of Inequality*. London: Penguin.

Shohet, R. and Wilmot, J. (1991) 'The key issue in the supervision of counsellors: the supervisory relationship', in Dryden, W. and Thorne, B. (eds), *Training and Supervision for Counselling in Action*. London: Sage.

Silverman, D. (1996) *Discourses of Counselling: HIV Counselling as Social Interaction*. London: Sage.

Soisson, E., Vandecreek, L. and Knapp, S. (1987) 'Thorough record keeping: a good defense', *Professional Psychology: Research and Practice*, 18 (5): 498–502.

Sommers-Flanagan, R. and Sommers-Flanagan, J. (2007) *Becoming an Ethical Helping Professional: Cultural and Philosophical Foundations*. Hoboken, NJ: Wiley.

Southern Derbyshire Health Authority (SDHA) (1996) *Report of the Inquiry into the Care of Anthony Smith*. Derby: Southern Derbyshire Health Authority and Derbyshire County Council.

Stadler, H.A. (1986a) *Confidentiality: The Professional's Dilemma – Participant Manual*. Alexandria, VA: American Association for Counseling and Development.

Stadler, H.A. (1986b) 'Making hard choices: clarifying controversial ethical issues', *Counseling and Human Development*. 19 (1): 1–10.

Standing Conference on Drug Abuse (SCODA) (1994) *Building Confidence: Advice for Alcohol and Drug Services on Confidentiality Practices*. London: SCODA/Alcohol Concern.

Stoltenberg, C.D. and Delworth, U. (1987) *Supervising Counselors and Therapists: A Developmental Approach*. San Francisco, CA: Jossey-Bass.

Sugarman, L. (1992) 'Ethical issues in counselling at work', *British Journal of Guidance and Counselling*, 20 (1): 64–74.

Sykes, J.B. (ed.) (1982) *The Concise Oxford Dictionary of Current English*. Oxford: Oxford University Press.

Syme, G. (1994) *Counselling in Independent Practice*. Buckingham: Open University Press.

Syme, G. (1997) 'Ethical issues concern us', *Voice of Counselling*, August.

Syme, G. (2003) *Dual Relationships in Counselling and Psychotherapy: Exploring the Limits*. London: Sage.

Szasz, T. (1986) 'The case against suicide prevention', *American Psychologist*, 41: 806–12.

Thistle, R. (1998) *Counselling and Psychotherapy in Private Practice*. London: Sage.

Thompson, A. (1990) *A Guide to Ethical Practice in Psychotherapy*. New York: John Wiley and Sons.

Thorne, B. (1984) 'Person-centred therapy', in Dryden, W. (ed.), *Individual Therapy in Britain*. London: Harper & Row.

Thorne, B. (1992) 'Psychotherapy and counselling: the quest for differences', *Counselling – Journal of the British Association for Counselling*, 3 (4): 244–8.

Thorne, B. and Mearns, D. (2007) *Person-centred counselling in Action* (Third edition). London: Sage.

Times Law Reports (1992) 'Nichols v. Rushton', *The Times*, 19 June.

Trower, P., Casey, A. and Dryden, W. (1988) *Cognitive-Behavioural Counselling in Action*. London: Sage.

Trumble, W.R. and Stevenson, A. (eds) (2002) *The Shorter Oxford English Dictionary on Historical Principles* (Fifth edition). Oxford: Oxford University Press.

Tuckwell, G. (2002) *Racial Identity, White Counsellors and Therapists*. Milton Keynes: Open University Press.

United Kingdom Central Council for Nursing, Midwifery and Health Visitors (UKCC) (1996) *Code of Professional Conduct*. London: UKCC.

United Kingdom Council for Psychotherapy (UKCP) (1993) *Training Requirements*. London: UKCP.

United Kingdom Council for Psychotherapy (UKCP) (1996) *Recovered Memories of Abuse*. London: UKCP.

United Kingdom Council for Psychotherapy (UKCP) (1998) *Ethical Requirements of Member Organisations*. London: UKCP.

United Kingdom Council for Psychotherapy (UKCP) (2005) *Code of Ethics*. London: UKCP.

Wacks, R. (1989) *Personal Information: Privacy and the Law*. Oxford: Clarendon Press.

Wheeler, S. and Richards, K. (2007) *The Impact of Clinical Supervision on Counsellors and Therapists, Their Practice and Their Clients: A Systematic Review of the Literature*. Lutterworth: British Association for Counselling and Psychotherapy.

Wise, C. (1951) *Pastoral Counseling: Its Theory and Practice.* New York: Harper & Bros.

Woolfe, R., Murgatroyd, S. and Rhys, S. (1987) *Guidance and Counselling in Adult and Continuing Education: A Developmental Perspective.* Milton Keynes: Open University Press.

Zytowski, D. (1985) 'Frank, Frank! Where are you now that we need you?', *Counseling Psychologist*, 13: 129–35.

Index

Page numbers in *italics* are tables or figures